Discover!
Social Studies

5A

Discover! Social Studies 5

Published in Catasauqua, Pennsylvania by Discover Press, a division of Edovate Learning Corp.

334 2nd Street

Catasauqua, PA 18032

edovate.com

ISBN: 978-1-956330-13-7

Printed in United States of America

1st Edition

Table of Contents

Worktexts & Instructor Guides

Worktexts

- Your Discover! course integrates all reading, writing, practice, ideas to extend learning, and opportunities for students to capture their ideas and connect learning to what matters to them.

- By providing both direct instruction and assessment opportunities, students are able to gain knowledge, reflect on what they learned, and apply it in both academic and real-world environments.

- To meet the needs of all learners, each worktext includes activities, instruction, and extensions that appeal to all learning styles.

- Each chapter is made up of lessons that connect to a central theme. Students have the opportunity to demonstrate understanding and think critically as they move through each lesson, and each chapter culminates with a student review, assessment, and opportunities for students to show what they know.

Instructor Guides

- Each instructor guide is specifically constructed to complement the worktext, provide helpful suggestions for a home-based instructor, offer support, and broaden a student's knowledge base.

- Instruction and curriculum are differentiated with remediation, enrichment, assessment, and supporting activities suitable for a variety of learning styles.

- Answer keys for all activities are included in your instructor guide.

Planning Your Day & School Year

- Each lesson takes approximately two to three days to complete, for a total of around 150 days of instruction through the school year. NOTE: Your worktext and instructor guide provide enrichment activities and discussion questions to take learning further and may add extra days to the school year. These are designed to inspire the instructor to customize the learning experience even further and encourage students to dive deeper into the topic.

- As you begin each lesson, we recommend completing three pages on the first day and two pages, including Show What You Know, on the second day.

- In the chapter reviews and assessment lessons, we recommend completing three pages on the first day and the remaining pages on the second day.

Parts of a Lesson

Lesson Overview (PAGE 1):

Each lesson opens with a list of goals or objectives designed to set the student up for success. Your instructor guide provides additional resources to reinforce concepts and add creativity to the lesson.

Explore (PAGE 2):

This page is key, as it is designed to engage students and encourage the discovery of new concepts.

Direct Instruction (PAGES 3–5):

In this section, the student gets to work by reading the content, capturing their own thoughts and ideas, and then practicing the concepts:

- **Read**: Students read informational text to gain knowledge about the lesson topic.
- **Write**: Students reflect on what they have read by creating a written response.
- **Practice**: Students practice what they have learned through various engaging activities, such as graphic organizers, matching, drawing, experiments, and hands-on learning.

Show What You Know (PAGE 6):

This is where students demonstrate what they've learned by completing a carefully crafted assessment aligned with the lesson's objectives.

To reinforce learning, additional extension activities are included throughout each lesson:

- **Create**: Students are tasked with constructing a piece of art, such as a drawing, song, poem, model, etc., to demonstrate learning.
- **Take a Closer Look**: With these activities, students make observations about the world around them. In doing so, students are able to generate predictions, inferences, or conclusions based on those observations. In science, these are scientific investigations or STEM-based activities.
- **In the Real World**: These activities connect the lesson to real-world situations. Students get the opportunity to investigate or interact with real-world examples.
- **Online Connection**: Students use technology-based solutions to research and investigate concepts related to the lesson or create artifacts demonstrating their understanding.
- **Play**: In these activities, students create or play games related to the lesson, such as board games, card games, role-playing, etc.

Cultural Features of Asia

By the end of this lesson, you will be able to:

- identify cultural features found in Asia
- describe how cultural features in a region of Asia influence factors of daily life, such as the economy, government, or transportation

Lesson Review

If you need to review exploration, please go to the lesson titled "New World."

Academic Vocabulary

Read the following vocabulary words and definitions. Look through the lesson. Can you find each vocabulary word? Underline the vocabulary word in your lesson. Write the page number of where you found each word in the blanks.

- **culture:** the characteristics of a particular group of people or regions such as art, language, religion, food, music, architecture, clothing, shared beliefs, and values (page _____)
- **economy:** the way goods are made, bought, and sold in a country or area (page _____)
- **government:** the exercise of control or authority over a group of people, country, land area, or organization to make and/or enforce laws (page _____)
- **metallurgy:** the science of heating metals to give them certain desired shapes or properties, of tin and copper (page _____)
- **population:** a particular section, group, or type of people or animals living in an area or country (page _____)
- **transportation:** the way something or someone moves from place to place (page _____)

Culture

Have you ever traveled to a new city or country and noticed the differences in food, language, and way of life? The characteristics of a particular group of people such as art, language, religion, food, music, and architecture, clothing, shared beliefs, and values are examples of culture. As you complete the lesson, select a region in Asia that is discussed. Investigate the cultural features of that particular region and think about what makes them unique. Compare these cultural features to the ones from your own life. Are there any similarities or differences? Share your findings by creating a collage or picture book.

EXPLORE

If you take a trip to the Asian Art Museum in San Francisco, you'll find exhibits that showcase the key cultural features of Asia, including religion and art. Cultural features are an important way to represent people's values, social interactions, challenges, and way of life. Famous Asian art such as the jade bracelets of China, religious sculptures in India, and Mughal paintings of West Asia showcase how cultural features influence people's beliefs. Take a look at these three images of famous Asian art. Why do you think jade jewelry was so important to Chinese culture? Why do you think the Chinese valued jade more than gold? Write your ideas on the lines below.

Beaded Jade Necklace (China)

Religious Sculptures (India)

Mughal Painting (West Asia)

....

....

....

....

....

TAKE A CLOSER LOOK

Regions in Asia
What is the largest continent in the world? If you guessed Asia, you are correct! Asia covers 9% of the total surface on Earth and includes 48 countries, such as China, Japan, Turkey, Lebanon, Iran, Israel, Pakistan, and India. Using an online search engine, select a country in Asia and research some of their famous ancient or modern art. Identify the region in Asia where the country is located. Then, compare the types of art that you found with the images in Explore. How are they similar or different?

READ

Religions

Did you know that Asia is the birthplace of all the world's major religions? Major religions in Asia include Hinduism and Islam. These religions are an important part of Asian cultures. These religions have greatly influenced the way people live and think.

HINDUISM

Hinduism is a polytheistic religion, which means the belief in many gods. It is the oldest religion in the world and dates back several thousand years, even before the beginnings of ancient Egypt! Hinduism has no single founder, but the religion was believed to have originated in South Asia, near the borders of India and Pakistan. One of the features of Hinduism is a rigid caste system, which determines the status of people in society from birth until death. The system has four classes: the Brahmins, the Kshatriyas, the Vaishyas, and the Shudras. There are also people who fall outside the system, such as the Dalits, who perform unpopular jobs such as cleaning sewers or digging graves. People who practice Hinduism, or Hindus, believe that all life goes through a cycle of birth, life, death, and rebirth, or reincarnation. They believe that the ultimate goal in life is to achieve moksha, which is the unity of people and their Supreme God, known as Brahmin, as one being. To achieve moksha, people need to have good karma and dharma throughout many lifetimes. Karma refers to the belief that a person's actions in life will determine their fate in the next life. For example, if people commit crimes throughout their lives, they can be punished and be reincarnated as pests, such as rodents or mosquitoes! Dharma refers to the specific set of rules that people should live by such as honesty, patience, and forgiveness, which are similar to the Ten Commandments in Christianity and the Five Pillars in Islam.

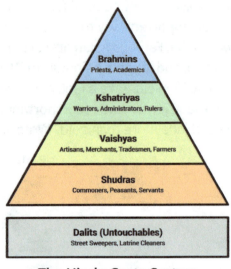

The Hindu Caste System

ISLAM

Unlike Hinduism, Islam is a monotheistic religion, which means the belief in only one god. Today, Islam is the second largest religion in the world after Christianity. It started in present-day Saudi Arabia in West Asia by the prophet Muhammed during the 7th century. Throughout his life, Muhammed received messages that he believed were from God, or Allah, and recorded them in a holy book called the Quran. According to the Quran, Muslims, or the people who practice Islam, are expected to follow specific rules. These rules are known as the Five Pillars, which include:

- The shahada (to declare one's faith to God and the prophet Muhammed)
- The salat (to pray five times a day)
- The zakat (to give to those in need)
- The sawm (to fast, or stop eating and drinking)
- The hajj (to make a pilgrimage to the holy city of Mecca at least once in a lifetime)

The *Quran*

TAOISM

Taoism started as a philosophy, or a set of ideas and beliefs, and later became a minor religion in East Asia. It is practiced in Taiwan, parts of China, and Hong Kong. As a philosophy, it was created by the philosopher Lao Tzu in the 6th century BC, who believed that humans and animals should live in balance, harmony, and "go with the flow." Over time, it became a polythestic religion with the worshipping of many gods, including ancestors. An important feature of Taoism is the belief in balancing forces known as the yin and yang to show that everything in the world exists as opposites in creating one universe. These include light and dark, hot and cold, and the North Pole and the South Pole. People who practice Taoism, or Taoists, also believe in the idea of reincarnation and believe that living an honest and righteous life prevents people from being reincarnated as undesired animals or insects.

The Yin and Yang Symbol

WRITE

What are some similarities and differences between Hinduism, Islam, and Taoism?

Art

Like the religions you just read, Asia is also the birthplace of many types of art, including the sculptures and paintings of South Asia and bronze and jade of East Asia.

SCULPTURES AND PAINTINGS

In ancient India and Cambodia, sculptures of the most famous Hindu gods known as Brahma (creator), Vishnu (preserver), and Shiva (destroyer) were carved into the exterior walls of many religious temples to honor them. Paintings of Hindu gods were also decorated in many ancient palaces. Mughal paintings, which were simple illustrations from India and influenced by Persia, were also developed. These paintings illustrated plants, animals, and people to record people's way of life. Over time, more sophisticated forms of painting were developed, known as Deccan paintings. Unlike Mughal art, these paintings were more colorful and detailed, featuring faces of people instead of their profiles. Deccan paintings have also been used in Islamic art to portray idealized versions of important kings known as sultans.

Mughal Painting, 1635

Jahangir Receives Prince Khurram at Ajmer on His Return from the Mewar Campaign.jpg by Balchand is in the public domain.

A yogini in her own right, Deccan, 18th c..jpg by unknown is in the public domain.

BRONZE AND JADE

In ancient China, natural resources like bronze and jade were frequently used or worn by emperors and palace leaders to symbolize power and status. You may have seen bronze in medals and instruments. Bronze was created from advanced **metallurgy** of tin and copper, and was strong and durable. Objects made from bronze included bowls, axes, money, and bells. Jade, which is a green translucent stone, was worn as necklaces, bracelets, or rings during important events, including banquets, feasting, and music performances. The ancient Chinese believed that the subtle color of jade gave it magical powers, such as immortality. Jade remains a precious stone to the Chinese and is even more valuable than gold!

WRITE

Name two unique features of the different types of art in Asia.

....

....

....

....

READ

Economy, Government, and Transportation

For centuries, religion has greatly influenced the **economy** of Asia. The Vedas of Hinduism, which include a collection of sacred texts, says that people should see everything in the world as the energy of the gods, especially the Supreme God. The Vedas teach people that if they can find meaning in all things, then they will conduct business in an honest way to respect Brahman. To do this, the rules of dharma should be used. For example, if farmers sell crops to people, they shouldn't cheat, steal, or lie to earn money. Instead, they should be honest and righteous to avoid becoming greedy or being punished. This is because when people engage in business with other people, they are also engaging in business with the Supreme God. Similarly, Taoists encourage honesty and charity in all business practices. The Quran also required Islamic merchants to deal fairly with others, including not charging interest on loans.

GOVERNMENT

Since ancient times, the Hindu caste system was strictly enforced. The **government** could only be run by people born into the upper castes, like the Brahmins and Kshatriyas. People were also forbidden to take jobs or marry people from different classes. Over time, the lower castes and Dalits protested the inequality and injustice of the Hindu caste system. After India became independent from British rule, laws were introduced to make the discrimination of the lower castes and Dalits illegal. This improved their status in society by allowing them to attend colleges and get jobs, some even in the government.

Islam has also influenced the government. Today, countries like Iran, Pakistan, and Afghanistan are Islamic Republics, which means they are governed by the rules written in the Quran. These rules tend to be strict and conservative, such as limiting people's freedom of speech and self-expression. In fact, women in these countries are expected to be modest and are required to cover themselves in clothing from head to toe.

TRANSPORTATION

China, India, and Indonesia have some of the largest **populations** in the world. To accommodate the people who live in these countries, a variety of **transportation** systems are available. In some countries, the population is so large that people often fill up the streets, which makes it hard for large vehicles to navigate. To solve this problem, small vehicles called rickshaws in India and tuk tuks are used to transport people, as they can easily pass through crowded streets. In Japan and China, which have high-speed trains called bullet trains can transport people from region to region at speeds greater than 300 mph (473 kph)! By contrast, countries in Western Asia, such as Saudi Arabia and Afghanistan, have limited transportation.

WRITE

Name two ways cultural features have influenced the economy, government, and transportation in Asia.

....

....

PRACTICE

Use your knowledge of Asia's cultural features to fill in the chart below.

How Cultural Features Influence...

TRANSPORTATION	ECONOMY	GOVERNMENT

REVIEW

In this lesson, you learned that:

- Major religions such as Hinduism and Islam and minor religions such as Taoism originated from different regions in Asia.

- Mughal and Deccan paintings were important types of art in South Asia. Mughal paintings were simpler and featured plants, animals, and human profiles while Deccan paintings were more colorful and featured facial details in humans.

- Objects made with bronze and jade were frequently used or worn by kings and leaders to symbolize power and status.

- Religions have influenced the economy by encouraging people to be honest and righteous.

- The Hindu caste system has influenced the government by limiting the type of people that can receive an education or find jobs in the government.

- Islam has influenced the creation of Islamic Republics to govern people in countries like Iran, Pakistan, and Afghanistan. Islamic Republics enforce strict rules from the Quran and usually limit people's freedom of speech and self-expression.

- Higher populations of people increase the demand for vehicles that can navigate through crowded roads.

Think About It

How can cultural features influence the economy, government, or transportation of a region in Asia?

SHOW WHAT YOU KNOW

1. Which of the following is NOT a correct feature of its religion? Circle all correct answers.

   A. moksha - Taoism

   B. yin and Yang - Hinduism

   C. the Five Pillars - Islam

   D. the caste system - Islam

   E. "Go with the flow" - Taoism

   F. the Vedas - Hinduism

2. What are the Five Pillars of Islam? Describe each rule.

   ....

   ....

   ....

   ....

3. What is the difference between Mughal and Deccan paintings?

   A. Mughal paintings were developed after Deccan paintings.

   B. Mughal paintings came from East Asia while Deccan paintings came from South Asia.

   C. Mughal paintings were simpler than Deccan paintings, which were more colorful and detailed.

   D. Mughal paintings focused more on the facial features of people while Deccan paintings focused more on their profiles.

4. What did bronze and jade symbolize in ancient China?

   A. good health

   B. power and status

   C. intelligence

   D. longevity

   E. talent and wealth

ONLINE CONNECTION

Select a region or country in Asia that is discussed in the worktext. Using an online search engine, investigate other types of cultural features, such as food, architecture, or music, that have influenced that region's economy, government, and transportation. Discuss your findings with your instructor.

5. Which of the following sentences correctly describes how cultural features can influence the economy, government, and transportation?

   A. The Vedas encourage people to engage in fair and honest business practices.

   B. While the Hindu caste system is weakened, it has prevented people, like the Dalits, from getting jobs in the government until only recently.

   C. Religions like Islam have influenced some countries to become Islamic Republics where they follow strict rules written in the Quran.

   D. Countries with large populations of people have developed several types of transportation, including small vehicles and railway systems.

   E. All of the above.

Lesson 21

Asian Cultures Influence the World

By the end of this lesson, you will be able to:

- investigate the cultural geography of Asia
- explore influences of Asian culture on individuals and civilizations around the world
- discover the lasting impact of Asian culture on everyday aspects of life

Lesson Review

If you need to review exploration, please go to the lesson titled "New World."

Academic Vocabulary

Read the following vocabulary words and definitions. Look through the lesson. Can you find each vocabulary word? Underline the vocabulary word in your lesson. Write the page number of where you found each word in the blanks.

- **cultural geography:** the study of human connection to natural resources, the economy, religion, government, and many other ways that humans interact with their world (page _____)

Famous Asian Dishes

Have you ever walked through the international aisle of a local grocery store and noticed that the types of spices, herbs, and sauces vary by geographic region? Perhaps you've noticed that the Asian section features spices like cumin and turmeric from South Asia; herbs like asafoetida, which tastes like garlic, from West Asia; and sauces like Shoyu that are used in ramen noodles in East Asia. Use an online search engine and research famous dishes in Asia that use these herbs, spices, or sauces. Then, compare them with your own favorite dishes. How are they the same or different? Create a poster to share your findings.

When you think of the word bamboo, what image comes to mind? You may visualize that it's the favorite food of pandas or that it has a rough texture. You may even think about China, the country where it originated from, or that it is tall and grown in tropical climates. But did you know that there are edible parts of the bamboo plant that can be eaten by humans? These parts are called bamboo shoots, and they are found on the top part of the plant. Bamboo shoots are an important feature used in many dishes in Taiwan, China, Japan, Indonesia, and India. As you read about the **cultural geography** of Asia, think about where these cultural features are located and how they influence societies around the world.

Unpeeled Bamboo Shoots

Peeled Bamboo Shoots

Take a look at these images of bamboo shoots above. What do you think they feel like or taste like?

....

....

....

....

....

....

IN THE REAL WORLD

Think about the types of food that you like to eat. It may be a hearty pepperoni pizza, a bowl of macaroni and cheese, or a tasty peanut butter sandwich with chocolates and bananas. Using a separate piece of paper, sketch your favorite food and list as many of its ingredients as you can in the space below. Which part of the world do these ingredients come from? Then share your findings by discussing them with your instructor.

....

....

....

....

....

....

....

....

....

....

....

....

READ

Food

CORIANDER

If you've ever tried guacamole, you may have tasted cilantro, which is a green leafy plant used to flavor dishes. The small, round seeds on the plant are called coriander. These dried seeds are typically used as whole seeds or are ground up to use in popular dishes in West Asia, South Asia, and Southeast Asia. Unlike the cilantro, which has a stronger aroma and a more citrus taste, coriander has a subtler aroma and a spicier taste.

CASSIA

If you are a fan of cinnamon, you may want to try cassia, which is a cousin of cinnamon. Cassia, or Chinese cinnamon, is a spice that is often used in East Asian and South Asian food, such as teas, desserts, and meats. Unlike the warm and sweet taste of cinnamon that you may have sampled in pies or cookies, cassia has a reddish brown color, is coarser, and has a more bitter taste. The bark of cassia plants is also used in traditional Chinese medicine to control blood sugar. Cassia is traditionally used in popular Indian dishes, such as chicken curry and chicken masala, and to flavor popular Chinese, Japanese, and Korean teas, such as the cassia seed tea.

INFLUENCE

The influence of coriander is seen worldwide, as it is used to flavor many dishes in different parts of the world such as North Africa, Central America, Latin America, and Southern Europe. Some of these dishes include African couscous, Mexican guacamole and salads, and Italian pastas. Coriander is also used in traditional medicine to relieve stomach aches and boost the immune system. The influence of cassia, which is one of the oldest plants in the world, was also well-known in Biblical times. The book of Exodus describes the oil of the cassia plant as one of the ingredients of anointing oil, which was a holy oil used to smear a person or object, as a way to purify the soul or get rid of an illness. Today, cassia is also added to some dark chocolates to create a bitter taste. These dark chocolates, known as cassia truffles, are sold in some chocolate stores around the world.

Coriander Seeds

Cassia Cinnamon Sticks

WRITE

What are two cultural influences of the coriander and cassia plants?

....

....

....

....

....

READ

Architecture

Most Asian architecture was influenced by religions, such as Buddhism and Hinduism. In East Asia, tall, multi-tiered buildings called pagodas were built to honor Buddha, the founder of Buddhism, and to spread his teachings. These pagodas, also known as Chinese pagodas, were designed to resemble the tall, sacred mountains of China and were commonly used as a place of meditation. Pagodas were typically made from wood, although they could sometimes be made out of stone. In addition, pagodas were derived from earlier buildings, called stupas, which were shorter and had dome-shaped roofs. These stupas were typically made from stone and brick and were popular in South Asia and Southeast Asia, in the countries of India and Cambodia. Stupas were used as a place of meditation, as a temple, and to store important Buddhist art. Unlike Buddhist temples, Hindu temples in South and Southeast Asia were usually dedicated to their gods. Hindu temples were frequently decorated with sculptures and carvings of different gods and goddesses along the exterior walls.

INFLUENCE

Today, Buddhism and Hinduism are among the top five religions in the world. As a result, many Buddhist and Hindu temples have been built around the world, including for organizations that help spread the teachings of both religions. The influence of Chinese pagodas have also spread to other East Asian countries, including Japan, Korea, and Taiwan, each having distinct uses. For example, unlike Chinese pagodas, Japanese pagodas are not used as a place of meditation. Instead, they are used for tea ceremonies and other important events, to represent the importance of harmony and respect for people and nature.

Pagoda of Nachi Falls (Japan)

Great Sanchi Stupa (India)

WRITE

How do Buddhist and Hindu temples differ in their architecture?

....
....
....
....
....

READ

Technology

PAPERMAKING AND PRINTING

Did you know that the smooth white paper that you write on got its start in the Han Dynasty of China in the 7th century AD? Before the invention of paper, ancient civilizations like the Egyptians wrote on papyrus paper that they made from the papyrus plant. However, papyrus paper was very expensive and hard to make. The Chinese made their first paper from the bark of mulberry trees. The bark fibers were broken and pounded into a sheet. Later, the Chinese discovered that they could make higher quality paper by adding hemp rags, a type of cloth used to wash clothes, and old fishing nets. Over time, early papermaking technology in ancient China led to the development of the first machine used to print paper, which had previously been made by hand.

FLYING MACHINES

In West Asia during the 9th century AD, Muslim astronomer and inventor Abbas ibn Firnas was the first person to develop a flying machine and attempt to fly. His first design used a winged structure that resembled a bird costume. Although he was able to fly briefly after jumping off a building, he eventually fell to the ground and suffered broken bones. Years later, he created a glider made of wood, silk, and decorated feathers. This was his second attempt at flying and it was more successful, as he was able to stay in the air for two to ten minutes. The wood glider that Firnas made was the first type of parachute that was invented, because it was able to slow his descent. It was also the first time that any inventor discovered the importance of wind currents, or the movement of air, in flying. For example, tailwinds speed you up by blowing in the direction the flying object, like a plane, is moving. On the other hand, headwinds slow you down by blowing opposite to the direction the plane is moving.

INFLUENCE

Firnas's flying inventions influenced the flying designs of Leonardo da Vinci and the flying machines of the Wright Brothers hundreds of years later. Today, airplane wings are designed from the knowledge of wind currents. Early papermaking technology by the Chinese led to the invention of the Gutenberg printing press in Europe during the 15th century. The Gutenberg printing press, which was a mechanical device that transferred ink to paper without applying pressure by hand, influenced the first news network and the printing of many famous books from the Renaissance, such as William Shakespeare's Hamlet, and religious texts, such as the Gutenberg Bible and the Quran. The development of the Gutenberg printing press also encouraged more people to become more literate, or to learn how to read and write.

PRACTICE

Fill in the chart below by providing one or two examples of cultural features of food, architecture, and technology in Asia.

Cultural Features of Asia

FOOD	ARCHITECTURE	TECHNOLOGY

REVIEW

In this lesson, you learned:

- Coriander is used to flavor popular dishes in different parts of the world.

- Coriander is also used in traditional medicine to relieve stomach aches and boost the immune system.

- The influence of cassia, one of the oldest plants in the world, was an ingredient of anointing oil during Biblical times.

- Most Asian architecture was influenced by religions, such as Buddhism and Hinduism. In East Asia, tall, multi-tiered buildings called the pagodas were built to honor Buddha.

- Earlier pagodas in South and Southeast Asia were called stupas, which were shorter and had dome-shaped roofs.

- The ancient Chinese were the first to invent the technology of papermaking in the 7th century AD.

- Early Muslim inventor Abbas ibn Firnas, was the first person to develop a flying machine and attempted to fly.

Think About It
What other cultural features in Asia have influenced the world?

SHOW WHAT YOU KNOW

1. Describe the differences between coriander and cassia plants. What are some of their notable influences in the world?

....

....

....

....

....

2. Which of the following statements about pagodas and stupas are correct? Circle all correct answers.

   A. Pagodas are shorter and have dome-shaped roofs while stupas are tall, multi-tiered buildings.

   B. Pagodas are younger while stupas are older.

   C. Pagodas are a feature of East Asia while stupas are a feature of South and Southeast Asia.

   D. Pagodas were developed to honor the Hindu gods while stupas were created to honor Buddha, the founder of Buddhism.

   E. Pagodas were typically made from wood and stone while stupas were commonly made from brick and stone.

3. Which of the following is not a likely influence of pagodas and stupas on Asian societies and societies around the world? Circle all correct answers.

   A. They allowed more people to follow Hinduism.

   B. They increased the development of sculptures and carvings of gods and goddesses on the exterior walls of their buildings.

   C. They inspired the development of Buddhist temples around the world.

   D. They featured a place for people to meditate.

   E. They inspired more people to follow Buddhism.

ONLINE CONNECTION

Paper
Using an online search engine, research how ancient civilizations created paper. Compare the papermaking process in ancient times to the papermaking process in modern times. How are they similar or different? Showcase your findings by creating a timeline.

4. Which of the following is not an influence of Chinese papermaking and printing?

   A. They allowed the invention of the Gutenberg printing press hundreds of years later.

   B. They inspired the flying designs of Leonardo da Vinci.

   C. They created the first news network in history.

   D. They produced copies of famous texts, such as William Shakespeare's Hamlet.

   E. They helped people become more literate over time, especially after the development of the Gutenberg printing press.

5. What were some of the influences of flying machines?

....

....

....

....

Lesson 22

Chapter 2 Review

By the end of this lesson, you will:

- review the information from the lessons in Chapter 2, "Asia."

Lesson Review

Throughout the chapter, we have learned the following big ideas:

- The continent of Asia has diverse physical features, but most Asian cities with large populations are located near bodies of water and river deltas where resources such as fresh water and fertile soil can be found. (Lesson 13)

- Smaller wandering populations called nomads live on the steppes, or harsh grasslands. (Lesson 13)

- Countries with an abundance of natural resources, such as coal, oil, water, and forests, can use them for trade. (Lesson 17)

- A variety of resources on small islands like Japan are scarce, so Japan trades its abundant supply of fish for supplies it needs. (Lesson 18)

- Rare luxury resources, such as silk, brilliant diamonds and gems, and delicious teas, can help nations build wealth through trade. (Lesson 18)

- Migrants contribute to new communities when they move due to job opportunities, environmental changes, political unrest, or natural disasters. (Lesson 19)

- The importance of religion in Asian cultures can be seen in art, architecture, economy, and government. (Lesson 20)

- Asian spices, architecture, and invention have influenced the world. (Lesson 21)

Go back and review the lessons as needed while you complete the activities.

Asia is the source of many luxury resources such as diamonds, spices, tea, and silk. For centuries Chinese silk has been traded with other nations. This luxury resource helped bring wealth to China. This cultural feature has impacted fashion and design around the world. Think about what you have learned about the continent of Asia. Create your own silk pattern on a piece of white paper inspired by what you have learned. Share your pattern with your instructor.

REVIEW

The Importance of Resources

As the largest continent, it's not surprising that Asia's regions have so many different physical features. The Himalayan Mountains in China and Nepal lure tourists to explore their harsh beauty and perhaps even climb Mount Everest, the tallest mountain in the world. The steppes, large areas of dry grassland in northern China and Mongolia, are home to nomads who roam the plains without making permanent homes for themselves. Large rivers in China, such as the Huang He and Yangtze, overflow onto river deltas. Large populations in Asia first grew along these rivers, taking advantage of the fresh water and soil ideal for planting crops.

Today Asia's plentiful fresh water and soil, along with rich deposits of coal, iron, and oil, are key natural resources, or materials found in nature that can be used. With an abundant supply, both Russia and China export large quantities of iron and oil. They have more than they need, so they are able to sell what they have left over to other countries. Timber, or wood, cut in the forests of Indonesia is also a valuable export, bringing wealth to the country.

Some regions have limited or scarce resources, as can be seen on the island of Japan. Japan's islands may not have plentiful land for planting crops, but being surrounded by the sea allows them to use fish to trade for resources they need. They import, or buy goods from other nations, so they are available for the population.

Regions of Asia

Six regions in Asia are each composed of different countries with unique geographical features. These features, along with unique climates, result in the natural resources available to the regions' populations.

How does trade help the nations of Asia?

REVIEW

Migration and Cultural Features

Individuals and groups in Asia migrate, or move to new places, for many reasons. Some relocate for better, new opportunities. Some migrate because they must. Natural disasters, such as the 2011 earthquake in Fukushima, Japan, cause populations to migrate. Political unrest can also cause migration. In 1949, violence became commonplace when China embraced communism, the idea that land and property belong to everyone rather than individuals. Many people fled. As populations have migrated, they have brought their culture to new places.

Many of Asia's cultural features have influenced populations on other continents. Asia is the birthplace of the world's most popular religions: Christianity, Judaism, Islam, Buddhism, and Hinduism. These religions have inspired art, jewelry, and architecture. Pagodas were originally built in Asia as temples. Today buildings inspired by pagodas can be seen around the world.

First traded on the Silk Road hundreds of years ago, luxury resources, such as silk, tea, and spices, have become part of other cultures' traditions as well. Wearing embroidered silk clothing and cooking with Asian spices such as coriander and cassia are common.

Asian advancements and inventions are also global influences. Paper and algebra were invented in Asia approximately 2,000 years ago. Few schools today can teach students without paper or algebra! Asian cultural features have made many contributions to societies around the world.

Displacement

Some populations do not want to migrate but become displaced due to human development projects. Human development projects are often government-funded projects designed and constructed for the greater good of a community. The Three Gorges Dam on the Yangtze River is an example of the displacement these projects can cause. One and a half million people migrated to new homes in China when this dam was built. This may seem unjust, but some projects are necessary to improve lives and safety.

How has Asian culture been shared globally?

PRACTICE

Vocabulary

Fill in the missing vocabulary word in each sentence.

Word Bank: abundant steppes migrate scarce river delta cultural feature
communism displaced luxury resources

1. Nomads wander the grasslands called _____ in northern Asia.

2. A _____ provides natural resources such as fresh water and fertile soil to crops.

3. Countries can export resources if they are _____.

4. If a resource is _____, a country will need to import it.

5. The polytheistic religion Hinduism is an example of a _____ of Asia because it is a part of many populations' way of life.

6. _____ such as silk are not needed to live, but they are special products made by people that are traded between nations.

7. Some individuals and groups are forced to _____ during times of political unrest.

8. Some Chinese citizens decided to move when the country decided property should belong to everyone rather than individuals. This idea is called _____.

9. Human development projects have _____ citizens from their homes to complete a project that will help or save lives.

As you grow up, you learn about your own culture. Your family, friends, teachers, and community teach you about your culture. A culture is a way of life. There are many aspects or components of each culture. These can include religion, government, transportation, language, history, food, symbols, and traditions. Each of these components of a culture is called a cultural feature. If we learn about cultural features from around the world, we can learn to appreciate and honor the differences between groups of people and the similarities too!

PRACTICE

Cause and Effect

How did populations react to the causes below? Fill in the effect side of the cause and effect chart below.

Cause	Effect
China has an abundant supply of iron.	
Japan has a scarce supply of agricultural resources.	
China found that other nations wanted luxury resources such as silk.	
Natural disasters such as earthquakes destroyed communities.	
Human development projects such as dam-building need land.	
Communism causes political unrest in China.	
River deltas such as those next to the Yangtze River have plentiful resources.	

REVIEW

The Yangtze River provides freshwater and deposits fertile soil on its riverbanks. As populations settled in China, they took advantage of these resources. Large communities developed in these areas where there were enough natural resources for growing populations.

Today many cities line the Yangtze River. The Three Gorges Dam can also be found on the Yangtze. It is the largest hydroelectric power producer in the world. It uses the water from this river to produce electricity.

PRACTICE

Asian Culture

What are some cultural features of Asia? Draw a picture of each feature in the circles on the graphic organizer. Label the features you draw.

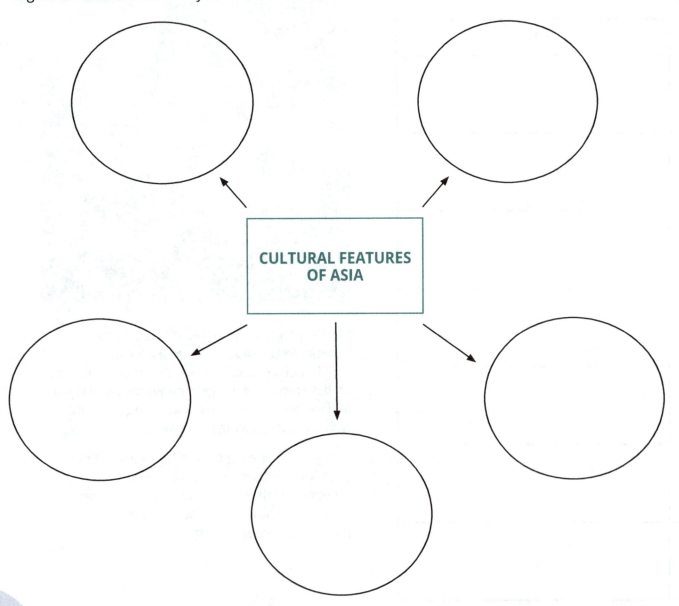

CULTURAL FEATURES OF ASIA

WRITE

Think about your learning. What stands out to you in the lessons? What questions do you have? What do you wonder about? You can use this page to take notes, write out your responses, and then discuss them with your instructor.

Chapter 3
Central America and the Caribbean

Bonjour, mon amie! Hello, my friend! Pierre here!

I have been trying to help my friend Chang find a new home. We traveled to the Philippines for that reason.

But no luck! There are deadly snakes there. We met one who was a Philippine Cobra, and we did not like him. He tried to eat us!

Want to hear what we did next? Viens avec moi! Come with me!

Chang, Monsieur Jean, and I were panting heavily. We had outrun the deadly cobra. "I am not living here," Chang said. "Yes, that is out of the question. That is the scariest snake I have ever seen," said Monsieur Jean.

I asked them where we should go next. Monsieur Jean straightened his elegant suit, wiped the sweat off his brow, and said, "I am going to the Mayan Mountains in Belize to look for ruins. I am writing a book about the great Mayan civilization. There is a big wildlife sanctuary there. Maybe that will be a good place for Chang to live."

We arrived in Belize a week later. My friend Marley, the glass frog, came to meet us at the airport. We were so excited to see each other that we hopped around the airport.

Once we had made our introductions, Monsieur Jean rented a jeep. We were going to drive out into the jungle. Our quest was to find Mayan ruins and maybe a new home for Chang.

Want to hear what happened next? Fantastique!

What Will I Learn?

This chapter focuses on the Central American and Caribbean regions. It examines the geography and resources of the area as well as its cultural and human history.

Lessons at a Glance

Lesson 23

How Maps of Central America Tell Stories

By the end of this lesson, you will be able to:

- examine different maps of Central America
- determine the story a map of Central America can tell
- compare and contrast the location of cities and geographic features in Central America and your community

Academic Vocabulary

Read the following vocabulary words and definitions. Look through the lesson. Can you find each vocabulary word? Underline the vocabulary word in your lesson. Write the page number of where you found each word in the blanks.

- **elevation:** the distance of the land from sea level (page ____)
- **geopolitical maps:** maps that show boundaries of countries, states, cities, and counties (page ____)
- **topographic maps:** maps that show the elevation and the shape of Earth's surface (page ____)
- **tourist:** a person who is visiting or traveling to a place for enjoyment (page ____)
- **tourist maps:** maps that shows destinations that are popular for tourists, help tourists determine various destinations to visit, and assist with planning daily activities in a particular place (page ____)

Maps

Search for different maps of where you live! Look at the geographic features (like mountains, rivers, volcanoes, and lakes). Also, look for important locations in the community, like churches, schools, and hospitals.

After looking at the different maps, describe one that you liked the most. What made that map most attractive? What did the map show?

....

....

....

....

EXPLRE

When you think about maps, what comes to mind? Do you imagine all of the places you want to go? Do you think of figuring out how to get from place to place? Maps can tell us much more than where a location can be found.

After looking up different maps of where you live, think about how the maps were similar and different. Look at these maps of Central America. What information do these maps give you?

....

....

....

....

....

....

READ

How Maps of Central America Tell Stories

Maps change over time. They show what countries or continents used to look like and how they look now. Maps show us exciting locations to visit in a country. They also tell us where countries begin and end. Each map tells a different story.

Topographic Maps of Central America

Topographic maps show physical features of the land. These maps take a long time to change. They describe the landforms and how the elevation changes from one place to another. Colors on topographic maps show **elevation**, or height above sea level. Brown shows higher locations, and green shows lower locations. The darker brown a location is, the higher it is in elevation. The darker green a location is, the lower it is in elevation. This map shows that Central America is very mountainous with many volcanoes.

The Cordillera Isabelia and the Cordillera de Talamanca are the longest mountain ranges in Central America. The tallest volcanoes in Central America are the Volcán Tajumulco and the Volcán Tacana. Topographic maps show us where mountains and volcanoes are located. Can you find the mountains and volcanoes on the map?

This topographic map of Central America is a great storyteller! Central America has seven countries: Belize, Costa Rica, Panama, Guatemala, Honduras, Nicaragua, and El Salvador.

READ

Geopolitical and Tourist Maps

Geopolitical maps define the borders of states, cities, and countries. Each country is marked by a different color. This is different from a topographic map, which changes colors only when elevation changes. Central America is not one country, and it is not a continent. It is a land bridge that connects the continents of North America and South America. When Central America was first recognized in 1821, it began with only five countries. Panama did not join Central America until its independence from Columbia and the former country of Yucatán in 1903. This geopolitical map of Central America tells us that places change over time by adding or splitting up countries.

TOURIST MAPS OF CENTRAL AMERICA

Tourist maps also tell a story about Central America. A **tourist** is a person who travels to different places for enjoyment. **Tourist maps** help guide tourists to places to visit during their travels. These maps help visitors decide what to see while they visit a specific destination. Central America has wildlife, towering mountains and volcanoes, and beautiful coastlines for people to explore. Tourist maps not only tell a story of where to visit, but they also help tourists choose what to see and explore!

This is a geopolitical map of Central America.

WRITE

How do tourist maps help tourists?

....

....

....

....

....

....

....

....

....

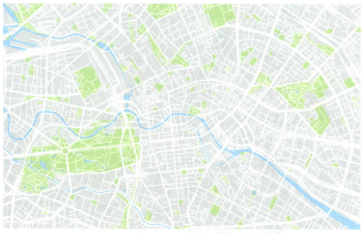
A tourist map may look similar to this, with road names and locations labeled.

READ

Cities in Central America

Let's examine some cities in Central America. Find the location of each city on the map. Read about the city. As you read, think about how these cities relate to the city or town that you live in.

GUATEMALA CITY, GUATEMALA

- Known as the Land of Trees
- Has volcanoes, mountains, and beaches nearby
- 25 languages spoken
- Created chocolate and instant coffee
- Population of more than 15 million people

SAN SALVADOR, EL SALVADOR

- Small but highly populated city
- Capital of El Salvador
- Mountainous
- Close to the coast and a large lake
- Has many earthquakes
- Population of more than 2 million people
- Surrounded by volcanoes

SAN JOSE, COSTA RICA

- Has world-class museums, parks, and historic buildings
- Has volcanoes and green hills nearby
- Has many forests
- Has many earthquakes
- Population of more than 4 million people
- Was the previous capital city

PRACTICE

Complete a Venn diagram by explaining at least one similarity and one difference between two of the following cities: Guatemala City, Guatemala; San Salvador, El Salvador; and San Jose, Costa Rica.

_____   _____

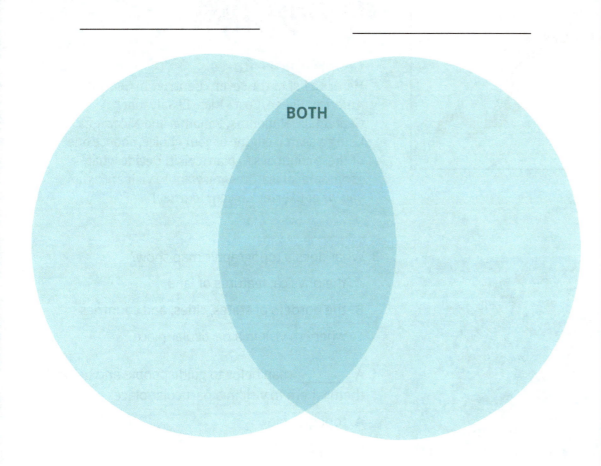

BOTH

1. Which map is a geopolitical map showing the location of different countries and their boundaries throughout Central America?

A.

B.

2. Which of these maps is a geopolitical map?

A.

B.

ONLINE CONNECTION

Geographic Features
Here is a list of the seven countries in Central America: Belize, Costa Rica, El Salvador, Guatemala, Honduras, Panama, and Nicaragua. Using a search engine of your choice, choose one of these countries to plan a visit! Decide what geographical features you want to visit and who you want to bring on your journey!

3. What does a topographic map show?

A. the physical features of land

B. the borders of states, cities, and countries

C. where to visit in a particular place

4. A _____ map helps to guide people and help tell them where to visit in a particular place.

A. topographic

B. geopolitical

C. tourist

Lesson 24

Examining Geographic Features in Central America

By the end of this lesson, you will be able to:

- analyze geographic factors that influence where people live in Central America
- identify the significance of key physical geographic features in Central America
- compare and contrast patterns of human settlements of different regions in Central America
- analyze how the environment influenced these settlements

Lesson Review

If you need to review geographic features in Central America, please go to the lesson titled "How Maps of Central America Tell Stories."

Academic Vocabulary

Read the following vocabulary words and definitions. Look through the lesson. Can you find each vocabulary word? Underline the vocabulary word in your lesson. Write the page number of where you found each word in the blanks.

- **agriculture:** the practice of farming (page ____)
- **diverse:** different types (page ____)
- **equator:** an imaginary line around the center of Earth where the sun shines the most directly, causing areas close to the equator to be very warm (page ____)
- **geographic features:** naturally created or man-made features of Earth's surface (page ____)
- **isthmus:** a land bridge with two bodies of water on either side (page ____)
- **proximity:** closeness to something (page ____)
- **tropical climate:** a location near the equator with high levels of humidity and year-round warm temperatures (page ____)

Think about the neighborhood, city, or town that you live in. What makes it fun and attractive to newcomers? Why did your family choose to live in this area? What kind of geographical features, such as mountains, rivers, oceans, or deserts are in or near your city or town? Maybe you live near a beach, where people would love to go fishing and take long walks. If you had to convince someone to move to your town, how would you promote it? Interview someone in your family to find out why they choose to live where they do. Then, on a separate sheet of paper, draw a picture that shows the best features of your neighborhood, city, or town.

Geographic features are naturally created or human-made features of Earth's surface. Examples of geographic features include hills, rivers, valleys, and bodies of water. Take a look at each of the pictures below. As you examine each picture, think about the similarities and differences you notice. Do any of the pictures compare to areas you live in or near? Which types of geographic features do you see in each of the pictures below? Write your answers on the lines.

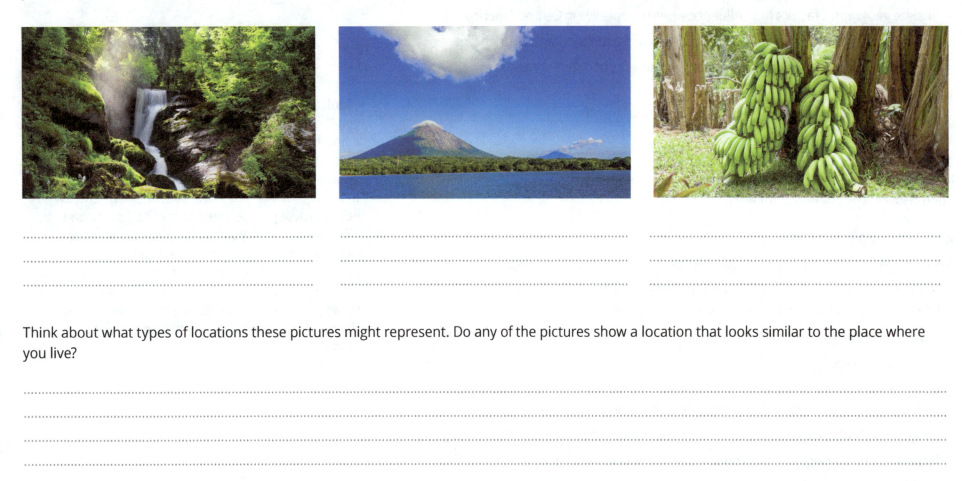

....
....
....

Think about what types of locations these pictures might represent. Do any of the pictures show a location that looks similar to the place where you live?

....
....
....
....

The Countries of Central America

Why do people live where they live? Geographic features influence why people live in certain areas. **Geographic features** are naturally created or human-made features of Earth's surface. Central America has seven countries: Belize, Guatemala, Honduras, El Salvador, Costa Rica, Panama, and Nicaragua. Each country in Central America has many **diverse**, or different types of, geographic features, allowing people to settle in these areas.

Geographic Features of Central America

Central America is an **isthmus**, or land bridge, connecting North and South America. The Pacific Ocean is west of Central America, and the Gulf of Mexico is east of it. A chain of mountains named the Sierra Madres is in the center of Central America.

The **equator**, the imaginary line around the center of Earth, runs right through Central America. The sun is the closest to this part of Earth, which causes this area to be warm. Due to Central America's **proximity**, or location in relation, to the equator, it has a **tropical climate,** high levels of humidity, and warm temperatures year-round. This is good for **agriculture**, or growing crops. Central America's main crops are bananas, coffee, and cacao, which makes chocolate!

When people settled in Central America, they chose to live in drier, less humid areas. These less-humid regions allow for crops to grow. Central America also has rainforests, which are good for plants and animals but are more challenging for humans to live in! Rainforests have many venomous snakes and insects, thick forests, and uneven land, making it hard for people to navigate.

Central America has approximately 40 volcanic cones. Some are active and have been known to erupt! Volcanoes are not all bad, though. Lava from volcanic eruptions creates fertile soil and allows for agriculture, turning these areas into lush farmlands.

READ

Human Settlement Patterns in Central America

Think about the geographic features in Central America. People in Central America settled in different areas for different reasons. As you read about each region below, think about some similarities and differences in the human settlement patterns.

CENTRAL AMERICA REGION	GEOGRAPHIC FEATURES	LOCATION	HUMAN SETTLEMENT PATTERN
Atlantic Lowlands (also called Caribbean Lowlands)	Dense forests Tropical rainforests Borders the Caribbean Sea Plains between mountain ranges and coast	Much of Nicaragua, Honduras, and Belize	Last region in Central America to be settled by humans Shorter dry seasons Highest amounts of precipitation Transportation was more difficult than humid zones Road construction and control of disease difficult More difficult for agricultural success Settlement occurs near ports and banana-producing areas
Central Highlands	Mountains Pine tree forests 40 volcanoes Called the Pacific Ring of Fire Many islands	Middle of Central America	Human settlement more popular here Heavily populated near isthmus Moderate amounts of rain Has a short dry season Agriculture strong here
Pacific Lowlands	Narrow plains Borders the Pacific Ocean	From Guatemala to Nicaragua	Human settlement more popular here Heavily populated Extended dry season of about eight months High temperatures Agriculture is strong here

WRITE

Choose a region that you think would be the best area to live in. Provide at least two reasons why you chose this area.

....

....

....

....

Discover! SOCIAL STUDIES • GRADE 5 • LESSON 24

Exploring Central America Environment Through Maps

Look at the map below. It shows different climate zones in Central America. Arid areas are areas that lack water. They are excessively dry areas that cannot support agriculture. Humans need agriculture to survive. Arid areas are not the best for human settlement. We have already learned that rainforests are also difficult areas for humans to settle in. Rivers were good places for people to settle near because they provide water for humans. They also provide access to larger bodies of water such as the Pacific Ocean or Caribbean Sea for trade routes.

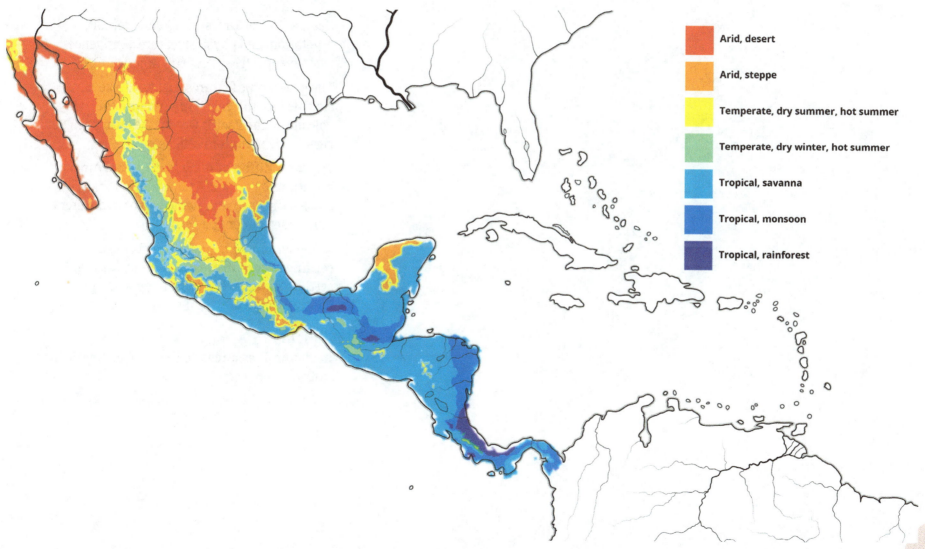

Legend:
- Arid, desert
- Arid, steppe
- Temperate, dry summer, hot summer
- Temperate, dry winter, hot summer
- Tropical, savanna
- Tropical, monsoon
- Tropical, rainforest

PRACTICE

Choose two regions in Central America. Compare and contrast those regions using the Venn diagram below. Make sure to include the differences or similarities in human settlement.

_____   _____

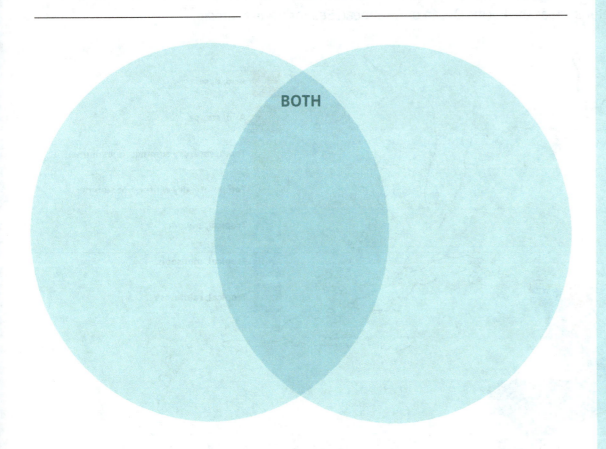

BOTH

SHOW WHAT YOU KNOW

Circle the correct answer for each question.

1. What are geographic features?

   A. museums, hotels, movie theatres, in a given location

   B. naturally created or human-made features of Earth's surface

   C. the study of locations on Earth and where people settle

2. True or False   Tropical rainforests were easy places for humans to settle in Central America.

3. Which two statements are true when comparing and contrasting human settlement in the regions of Central America?

   A. Atlantic Lowlands were a much harder area for humans to settle in than the Central Highlands and the Pacific Lowlands.

   B. Atlantic Lowlands were a much easier area for humans to settle in than the Central Highlands and the Pacific Lowlands.

   C. Central Highlands and Pacific Lowlands were easier for human settlement.

   D. Central Highlands were harder for human settlement than Atlantic Lowlands.

4. Which geographic feature is not found in Central America?

   A. mountains

   B. rainforests

   C. glaciers

   D. volcanoes

TAKE A CLOSER LOOK

Look back at your maps of Africa and Asia. Refer to the maps with geographic features on these continents. Identify the locations of the geographic features in Central America and how they are similar and different to the ones in Africa and Asia. Answer the following questions.

• What is similar and different about the geographic features in Central America to those in Africa and Asia?

• What is similar and different about human settlement and the locations of these geographic features?

• What is similar and different in the cultures of Africa, Asia, and Central America?

5. How do the environment and geographic features of Central America influence where people live?

....

....

....

....

....

....

Physical Geography of Central America

By the end of this lesson, you will be able to:

- describe the physical geography of Central America
- analyze the influence of people's relationship to natural resources in Central America

Lesson Review

If you need to review some of the features of Central America, please go to the lesson titled "Geographic Features of Central America."

Academic Vocabulary

Read the following vocabulary words and definitions. Look through the lesson. Can you find each vocabulary word? Underline the vocabulary word in your lesson. Write the page number of where you found each word in the blanks.

- **economy:** the way goods are made, bought, and sold in a country or area (page _____)
- **fertile:** land that is great for growing crops (page _____)
- **isthmus:** a land bridge with two bodies of water on either side (page _____)
- **natural resources:** any usable substance that can be found in nature (page _____)
- **physical features:** a part of the landscape that you can touch or see (page _____)
- **tropical rainforest:** an area with large amounts of rainfall that is close to the equator (page _____)

IN THE REAL WORLD

Research a Country

Decide on a Central American or Caribbean country of interest to study more closely. The countries in Central America are: Belize, Costa Rica, Nicaragua, Honduras, Panama, El Salvador, and Guatemala. The Caribbean has 26 countries to choose from as well. Choose one of these countries, and identify three of its geographic features. Look at three types of maps of this country (topographic, tourist, or geopolitical) in a book or online, and identify one industry in this country. For example, tourism and agriculture are important industries to Costa Rica. Share your findings with your instructor.

EXPLRE

Humans need many things to survive. We have many needs that have to be met in different ways for our survival and for us to thrive. Make a list of three things humans need to survive on the lines below.

....

....

....

Now that you have thought of things humans need for survival, make a list of three items you could get outside your house in your yard or in a park to help you survive. Write your answers on the lines below.

....

....

....

Compare the two lists. Were you able to fulfill all of your needs just from the items outside? Where do you get most of the things that you need to survive? Write a list of three places some of your needs come from.

....

....

IN THE REAL WORLD

Human-Made Vs. Natural

Take a look outside. Name three things you see that are human-made and three things you see that are natural. Was it easier to identify human-made objects, or was it easier to identify the naturally occurring items? Make a list of the three human-made objects and the three naturally occurring items below.

Human-Made Things	Natural Things

Some people pick up their food from the supermarket

Some people pick their food from outside

Physical Features in Central America

Physical features are the parts of the landscape that you can touch or see. A great example of an area with a lot of unique physical features is Central America. For example, one of the first things you notice when looking at a map of Central America is its location and shape. Central America is a land bridge, also known as an **isthmus**, connecting North America and South America. It also separates the Gulf of Mexico and the Caribbean Sea from the Pacific Ocean. In addition to being an isthmus, Central America is home to tropical rainforests, volcanoes, mountains, and more.

Central American Rainforests

All seven Central American countries and all but one of the Caribbean Islands have rainforests. These rainforests are **tropical rainforests**, which means they are hot and humid much of the year. The rainforest is home to two-thirds of all plant and animal species on Earth. Rainforests only cover about two percent of Earth's surface, but they have the highest number of unique plants and animals than any other place on Earth! Avocado trees, banana trees, venus fly traps, rubber trees, and brazil nut trees are all examples of plants found in the rainforest. Rainforest plants are not just unique. They also account for 25 percent of all medicines we use today! In addition to the wide variety of rainforest plants, the animals that call the rainforest home are also unique. Sloths, jaguars, spider monkeys, lemurs, toucans, and tigers are just a few of the colorful and exciting animals found in the rainforest. Most of these animals can blend well into their surroundings.

Jaguar in the Rainforest

Venus Fly Trap

Central American Volcanoes and Mountains

When people hear the word volcano, they often think of boiling hot lava and destruction. That can be the case, and Central America has seen its fair share of volcanic eruptions. In the last 300 years, there have been around 200 volcanic eruptions in Central America. In fact, Central America is home to over 70 volcanoes! But volcanoes can also bring **fertile** soil, or land that is great for growing crops. This allows for plenty of farming in Central America.

The Caribbean Islands also have 19 active volcanoes. Volcanoes built the Caribbean Islands. The rock from the volcanoes forms the base of the islands. The most active and studied of the volcanoes is Soufriere Hills on Montserrat. Volcanic activity there has been going on since 1995. As a result, people cannot live on two-thirds of the island.

In addition to the many volcanoes found in Central America, there are also 25 mountain peaks. The mountain range called the Sierra Madres runs from north to south. These mountains are connected to the Rocky Mountains, which travel through a large portion of the western United States. Mountains allow for the climate to be less humid and more comfortable. Many of the mountain peaks are volcanic.

ONLINE CONNECTION

Natural Disasters

Due to Central America's many physical features, this region experiences many natural disasters. One of these natural disasters is volcanoes. Hurricanes are also common in Central America and the Caribbean Islands. They often cause large amounts of flooding. Earthquakes can also occur and have had devastating consequences for the people of Central America. Choose one of these natural disasters to learn more about by researching it online.

Natural Resources in Central America

Central America and the Caribbean Islands have a large amount of natural resources. **Natural resources** are usable substances found in nature. Natural resources found in Central America are iron, copper, coffee, sugar, silver, rubber, and lumber. These natural resources play a large role in the **economy**, or the way goods are made, bought, and sold in a country or area. The many natural resources have allowed people in Central America and the Caribbean to make money farming, mining, and searching for these resources.

Due to these natural resources being unique, they are needed throughout the world. This has taken a toll on the people and the land in Central America. Overmining has caused the loss of land for many people, animals, and plants. People native to Central America and the Caribbean Islands are asking for a change to help protect their countries and their natural resources.

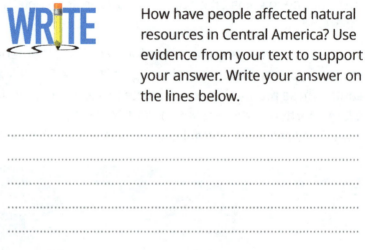

How have people affected natural resources in Central America? Use evidence from your text to support your answer. Write your answer on the lines below.

....

....

....

....

....

....

PRACTICE

Look at the pictures. Identify the physical feature and the natural resource shown. Then identify one thing this natural resource is used for.

PHYSICAL FEATURE AND NATURAL RESOURCE	WHAT IT'S USED FOR

REVIEW

In this lesson, you learned:

- The physical geography of Central America is full of many types of landforms, including rainforests, mountains, and volcanoes.

- Natural resources influence people's relationship to the land in Central America and the Caribbean, including allowing people to mine to make money, but also causing people to overmine and lose valuable land and natural resources.

Think About It
How are the physical features of Central America the same or different from where you live?

1. What is a natural resource?

....

....

....

2. Name three natural resources found in Central America.

....

....

....

3. Natural resources can affect a country's _____ because people buy and sell these resources for money.

Match the physical feature to the picture.

4. Volcano _____

5. Mountain Range _____

6. Rainforest _____

Country Study
Let's dig in and get to know the country you selected in the last lesson a little better. For this lesson, do the following activity about your country:

- Identify the geographic features of your chosen country.

- Identify the population and population density of your chosen country.

- Identify the agricultural goods that your chosen country is known for.

- Identify the climate and typical temperatures for your chosen country.

Once you answer these questions, create a pamphlet or brochure to help others learn about your chosen country.

A.

B.

C.

Changes in the Central American and Caribbean Environment

By the end of this lesson, you will be able to:

- identify how people make changes to and respond to changes in their environment
- describe the significance of the Panama Canal and the amazing capabilities of those who envisioned and built it
- examine ways people in Central America made changes to their environment
- illustrate examples of how they responded to changes in the environment

Lesson Review

If you need to review Central American physical features and geography, please go to the lesson titled "Physical Geography of Central America."

Academic Vocabulary

Read the following vocabulary words and definitions. Look through the lesson. Can you find each vocabulary word? Underline the vocabulary word in your lesson. Write the page number of where you found each word in the blanks.

- **agriculture:** the practice of farming (page ____)
- **dam:** a structure that is built to hold back water (page ____)
- **deforestation:** the cutting down of large groups of trees or forests (page ____)
- **locks:** strong gates that block off portions of the canal (page ____)
- **mining:** the process of digging underground to retrieve valuable resources (page ____)
- **urbanization:** the process of making an area into a city (page ____)

Country Study

Since the beginning of this chapter, you have been working on a country study for one of the following Central American countries: Belize, Honduras, Guatemala, Costa Rica, Panama, El Salvador, or Nicaragua, or one of the many Caribbean islands. To further this project, examine changes to the environment made by people in this country. These could include farming, mining, adding dams, or anything human-made that alters the natural environment. Then, compare and contrast this with changes from previous chapters.

EXPLORE

Have you ever seen changes made to your environment? Maybe you helped an adult plant a vegetable or flower garden. You might have helped an adult build a treehouse or a playhouse in your yard. Humans make changes to their environments in different ways.

Look at the images below. They show changes humans made to the environment. These images show a change in the land. How do you feel when you look at these pictures? Do you feel positively or negatively about these changes to land? Discuss the answers to these questions with your instructor.

READ

Changes to the Central American and Caribbean Environment

Earth has experienced a lot of changes. Some changes happen naturally, like seasons changing. Many changes that take place on Earth's surface are human-made. Central America has experienced many human-made changes throughout the years. One change to the land is **agriculture**, the practice of farming. Due to Central America's climate, it has many crops that are exported around the world. Corn, bananas, coffee, and chocolate are grown in Central America. The farming of these crops has changed the land from forests to farms. This creates food for people and jobs for farmers, but it is also bad for the plants and animals that grow or live in these countries.

Another human-made change to the Central American environment is **deforestation**, the cutting down of trees or forests. This land is used for creating farms, houses, or cities. Central America has lost much of its rainforest to deforestation. This means some of its plant and animal life have lost their homes in the rainforest. Many native people in Central America are impacted by the loss of the forests. Like the animals, they too have lost large portions of their home. Many native people have had to move elsewhere to find new homes. Although many people suffer due to deforestation, other people may gain from this loss by making large amounts of money off of the newly cleared land.

Mango Tree Farm in Costa Rica

Deforestation in Central America

Urbanizing Central America

Urbanization, the process of making an area into a city, is another human-made change taking place. Approximately 80 percent of Central America's people live in cities. Much of the country's vast forest and coastal regions have been turned into cities to make room for its booming population. Urbanization has positive and negative impacts. The positives are more jobs and places to live for the people of Central America. The negatives are the loss of the environment, to make room for cities, the loss of natural resources, and the loss of homes for plants and animals.

Dam Building

A **dam** is a structure that is built to hold back water. This human-made change to the land benefits people by preventing flooding and by generating electricity. The Monción Dam is the largest dam in the Caribbean and is located in the Dominican Republic. It is made to generate power and store water for crops. Although people typically benefit from dams, ecosystems that live in the water or near the water can be harmed.

Mining

Mining is the process of digging underground to retrieve valuable resources. Gold, copper, nickel, and ore are commonly mined in this region of the world. Mining allows precious metals to be sold and can benefit the economy, but it negatively impacts the land. Digging underneath the land for resources can disrupt the ecosystems above the ground.

People's Response to Changes

Earth has changed a lot over time, and humans have had to find ways to manage these changes. Like we've read above, most of the changes in recent years are due to human use. Deforestation and overuse of land have led to less rainfall, which is bad for growing crops. Farmers and other residents of Central America are leaving the area to find more fertile land and money for their families. Hundreds of thousands of families flee Central America each year to find safer places to live, homes that can provide them with food to feed their families, and jobs that pay them a living wage.

Walkway in Panama City

Dam in the Dominican Republic

Underground Gold Mine

The Panama Canal

Not all human-made changes are negative. The Panama Canal is a great example of a positive impact. The Panama Canal is a human-made waterway that connects the Atlantic Ocean to the Pacific Ocean. It uses **locks**, strong gates that block off portions of the canal, to lower ships for a safe passage. This canal cuts down on time for ships to travel from the Atlantic Ocean to the Pacific Ocean. This route used to be very dangerous and lengthy before the Panama Canal was created and completed in 1914. It helped shorten trade routes and allowed for more trade between countries from all over the world. The Panama Canal was one of the largest and most challenging projects to build at that time in history. At certain times, about 45,000 men were working on the canal at once. Workers battled disease, poisonous snakes, mudslides, and poor living conditions. The Panama Canal benefited many people by providing more jobs and allowing goods to travel faster. It also helped Panama's economy and the economy of many other countries. It also had a positive impact on the environment by creating a faster route for ships and cutting down on their use of resources.

Bridge over the Panama Canal

Ship Lowering into the Panama Canal

Think about the Panama Canal and its many successes. Write three ways this positively about impacted the world. Use the text to support your answer.

....

....

PRACTICE

Now that you learned about changes in Central America, think about why these changes happened and what the consequences are. In the table, define the type of environmental change, state a reason why this change takes place, and state an impact on the environment due to these changes.

THE ENVIRONMENTAL CHANGE	WHY THE CHANGE TOOK PLACE	IMPACT ON THE ENVIRONMENT
Agriculture is		
Deforestation is		
Urbanization is		
Dam building is		
Mining is		

REVIEW

In this lesson, you learned:

- People change their environments through agriculture, deforestation, urbanization, dam building, and mining.

- The Panama Canal was an amazing feat of engineering and had a positive impact on the economy of Panama and the world because ships no longer had to go around South America to travel from the Atlantic Ocean to the Pacific Ocean.

- People in Central America made changes to their environment to the point where a great portion of the rainforest has been cleared to allow for farms and cities to be built.

- People responded to changes in the environment, with 80 percent of Central Americans and Caribbean Islanders living in cities.

1. Name the five types of man-made changes to the environment you learned about in this lesson.

....
....
....
....

2. True or False   The Panama Canal was not helpful and negatively impacted trade.

3. Explain three ways Central American and the Caribbean people react to environmental changes.

....
....
....

4. How did the Panama Canal impact the world?

....
....
....
....
....
....
....
....

More Information on Deforestation

Deforestation is impacting Central America in many negative ways. One of these is its loss of plant and animal species. Some of the most well-known animal species may be lost due to deforestation. Jaguars, tapirs, and scarlet macaws could lose their homes in the tropical rainforest. A large portion of deforestation is to allow for livestock. Cattle ranching is the number one reason for deforestation in the rainforest. Although it is a negative change, there are ways to help! You can plant trees, eat less meat, buy recycled products, recycle, and raise awareness in your community!

Physical Processes in Central America and the Caribbean

By the end of this lesson, you will be able to:

- identify the physical processes that contribute to the availability and abundance of natural resources
- compare and contrast the availability and distribution of natural resources in Central America

Lesson Review

If you need to review natural resources in Central America and the Caribbean, please go to the lesson titled "Changes in the Central American and Caribbean Environment."

Academic Vocabulary

Read the following vocabulary words and definitions. Look through the lesson. Can you find each vocabulary word? Underline the vocabulary word in your lesson. Write the page number of where you found each word in the blanks.

- **erosion:** the wearing away of the land by forces such as water, wind, and ice (page ____)
- **geothermal energy:** heat that comes from Earth (page ____)
- **physical process:** the natural force that changes Earth's physical features (page ____)
- **tectonic plates:** pieces of land that connect together and make up Earth's surface (page ____)

IN THE REAL WORLD

Earth is full of important natural resources to allow us to survive and thrive. But based on where you live, your access to natural resources may be different from someone else's. For example, imagine you have a banana tree growing in your backyard. It would be much easier for you to access these bananas than someone who lives in another area. Can you name natural resources you may have more access to based on your location? Discuss with your instructor and list below.

....

....

....

EXPLRE

Imagine you are lost on a deserted island. The first thing that comes to mind is survival. You have to find substances to keep you alive. What would these be? Think about all of the things you would need to help you survive. Create a list of three things.

....

....

....

What did you notice about your list of three things you needed to survive? Most likely, all of the things you chose were natural resources, such as water, food, and shelter. Water is the most important natural resource, and all living things must have it. Food is probably also very high on the list and is also a natural resource. The shelter you need is most likely made with natural resources, like timber or boulders. Maybe you even thought of mud for sunscreen! Discuss your list with your instructor and identify which of the items are natural resources.

Now imagine you are an explorer on a quest to search for natural resources. Search for natural resources outside, like in a yard or park. Make a list of what you discover. Draw pictures to show what each natural resource looks like.

Natural Resource	Drawing

READ

Physical Processes

A **physical process** is the natural force that changes Earth's physical features. Just like people change and grow over time, Earth's surface is no different. Many of these changes take a very long time to occur, but they can greatly alter the way our planet looks and what natural resources we are able to use!

Volcanoes are a large part of the physical geography of Central America. They make up a large part of the landscape, and many of these volcanoes are still active today! The volcanoes in Central America were formed by two tectonic plates. **Tectonic plates** are pieces of land that connect together and make up Earth's surface. One of these plates, the Cocos Plate, went beneath the Caribbean Plate. Over time, magma rose to the surface and created a volcano! Don't be fooled, though. This process takes a very long time. Most of the volcanoes in Central America are formed this way. Central America is a part of the Pacific Ring of Fire, which is a series of volcanoes that surround the Pacific Ocean. The Pacific Ring of Fire has 450 volcanoes. That is around 75 percent of Earth's volcanoes!

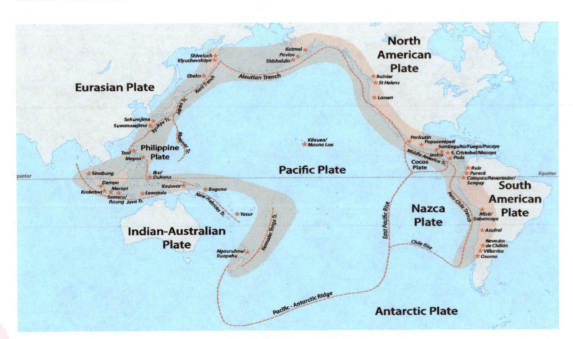

Pacific Ring of Fire

IN THE REAL WORLD

Earthquake Measurements

Earthquakes are measured on something known as the Richter Scale. The Richter Scale is a number scale that tells the size and strength of an earthquake. The scale ranges from 1 to 10, with 1 being the smallest and almost impossible to feel and 10 being very intense. A 10 has never been recorded. Earthquakes can topple buildings, break apart roads, and cause deaths and injuries.

Destruction After Earthquake in Haiti, 2010

Volcanoes, Earthquakes, and Erosion

Volcanoes can cause severe damage, but their eruptions also help many people. The fertile ash after eruptions are used by farmers to help crops grow. Volcanic eruptions also form new islands. Volcanoes push formations to the surface with large amounts of pressure. This process formed the Caribbean Islands. Volcanoes also create **geothermal energy**, or heat, from Earth. This energy can be used to heat homes, stoves, and water. This energy source is much better for the planet and causes less pollution than other sources.

Plant Growing in Volcanic Ash

Destruction After Earthquake

Central America and the Caribbean average about 16 earthquakes a day! Some earthquakes are very violent and cause destruction. Others are more gentle and may go unnoticed. Earthquakes have shaped Central America and the Caribbean by changing the land over time and after strong quakes. Earthquakes can cause soil to mix with groundwater. This makes the soil more like mud and can harm agriculture.

Erosion also impacts the land in Central America and the Caribbean. **Erosion** is the wearing away of the land by forces such as water, wind, and ice. Since Central America and the Caribbean are surrounded by water, erosion is common. The main types of erosion are physical, chemical, soil, water, and wind erosion. Soil erosion is a major problem in Central America. Agriculture is very important to this area, and soil erosion removes the top layer of soil. This prevents crops from growing. Since these areas ship crops all over the world, this could cause a lack of resources throughout the world.

Sand Stone Erosion

READ

How Physical Processes Affect Natural Resources

Central America and the Caribbean have many rainforests full of natural resources like trees, gold, copper, diamonds, medicine, and oil. Unfortunately, even though these natural resources are abundant, accessing them means harming plants and animals. Many rainforests have been cut down to remove timber, gold, and diamonds and to make space for human needs.

Both Central America and the Caribbean are very close to the equator, have volcanoes and beaches, and are rich in natural resources. Some Central American natural resources include gold, silver, lead, copper, oil, ore, natural gas, nickel, timber, and fish. Due to its resources, most people work in these industries. Many people are farmers, fishermen, foresters, and miners. Caribbean natural resources include gold, silver, copper, oil, fishing, limestone, clay, bauxite (used to make aluminum), manganese (a mineral used to make clear glass and steel), and cobalt (a mineral used in batteries). Unfortunately, many of these resources are sent out to other countries and are not kept within the borders of Central America or the Caribbean. Many people in this region struggle to access natural resources even though they live near them.

REVIEW

In this lesson, you learned:

- Volcanoes, earthquakes and erosion contribute to the availability and abundance of natural resources, like gold, silver, fish, forests, and more.

- The availability and distribution of natural resources in Central America across regions can be similar and different.

Fishing is one of the leading industries of Central America and the Caribbean.

Rainforest of Central America

PRACTICE

Use the Venn diagram to compare and contrast the similarities and differences between the natural resources in Central America and the natural resources in the Caribbean. List at least three similarities and three differences. What do you notice about the similarities and differences?

....
....
....

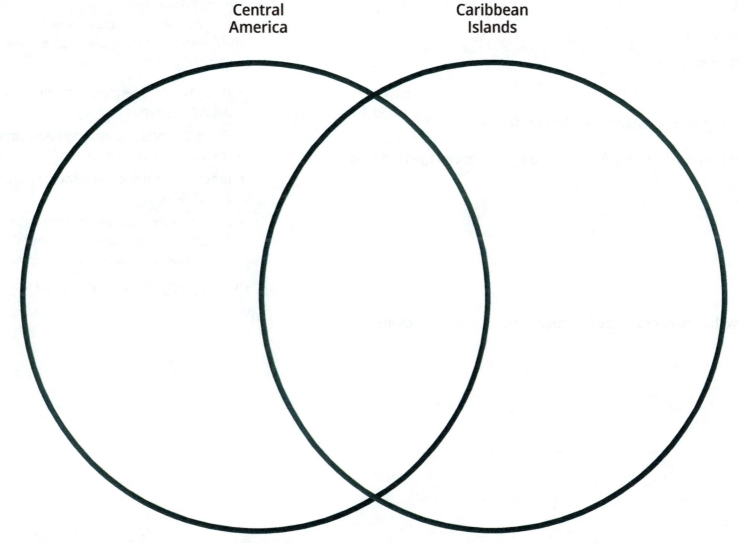

Central
America

Caribbean
Islands

SHOW WHAT YOU KNOW

Circle the correct answer.

1. True or False   Islands are made by erosion.

2. How are the volcanoes in Central America formed? Circle all that apply.

   A. tectonic plates

   B. earthquakes

   C. Pacific Ring of Fire

   D. underwater volcanoes

Answer the following questions with complete sentences.

3. List natural resources in Central America and the Caribbean mentioned in this lesson.

   ....

   ....

   ....

4. Describe how the resources in the Caribbean and Central America are similar and why.

   ....

   ....

   ....

   ....

   ....

ONLINE CONNECTION

Country Study

Let's go back to your country of study! Focus on the natural resources that can be found in your country and trade.

- Using the internet, identify your country's natural resources.

- Using the internet, identify how your country trades this natural resource.

- Research what natural resource your community has access to.

- Does your community have any of the same natural resources as this country? What different natural resources does your community have?

Record the information you found in your notes.

Using Natural Resources in Central America

By the end of this lesson, you will be able to:

- identify key natural resources found in Central America
- describe how the use, distribution, and importance of natural resources can affect different groups
- identify the impact of trade on the availability of natural resources
- examine the significance of ecotourism in Costa Rica

Lesson Review

If you need to review natural resources in Central America, please go to the lesson titled "Physical Processes in Central America and the Caribbean."

Academic Vocabulary

Read the following vocabulary words and definitions. Look through the lesson. Can you find each vocabulary word? Underline the vocabulary word in your lesson. Write the page number of where you found each word in the blanks.

- **abundance:** a large amount of something (page ____)
- **distribution:** the act of dividing, spreading, or supplying something (usually goods) among people or areas (page ____)
- **ecotourism:** tourism that is more natural and focuses on protecting and conserving the environment (page ____)
- **trade:** the action of exchanging something for something else (page ____)

Look at the picture below. What do you see? Do you see natural resources? Do you see human-made resources? Write what you see and also what you think the image is showing.

I see ....
....
....

I think ....
....
....

EXPLORE

Stop what you are doing! Now think about all kinds of food—chocolate, bananas, pineapples, oranges, cupcakes, loaves of bread, pizza—any food that makes your mouth water. Now, list the last three food items that you ate on the lines below.

....

....

....

Now think about where you got this food from. Write where you think these places got their food from below.

....

....

Countries all over the world work together to get natural resources from one area of the world to another. Below are some modes of transportation used to make this happen.

Cargo Ship

Train

Plane

The Importance of Natural Resources

Have you ever thought about how much humans need to survive, including food, shelter, clothing, and more? All of these items come from natural resources that Earth provides. The natural resources available to you will differ depending upon where you live. For example, people who live in the Appalachian Mountains in the United States have easier access to coal, while people who live in Central America may have easier access to gold or copper. Living in an area with an **abundance**, or large amount, of natural resources can be beneficial to the residents of a country. Sometimes countries have many natural resources, and other countries with more power take these resources.

Central America and the Caribbean have many unique natural resources due to their physical geography. Some resources they have include gold, copper, silver, fish, timber, limestone, oil, lead, aluminum, and many others that are used all over the world. The volcanoes and other plate tectonic activity have allowed for landforms to develop that produce these resources. These resources are incredibly important to the world and its economy.

Haiti, one of the poorest countries in the Caribbean

Dominican Republic, one of the richest countries in the Caribbean

Nicaragua, one of the poorest countries in Central America

Panama, one of the richest countries in Central America

Distribution of Natural Resources

Unfortunately, not all natural resources are distributed equally. **Distribution** is the act of dividing, spreading, or supplying something (usually goods) among people or areas. Some countries, especially in Central America and the Caribbean, do not distribute these natural resources evenly among groups. If you look closely at two neighboring countries in the Caribbean, this poor distribution is easy to see.

Haiti and the Dominican Republic share an island. Haiti is the poorest country in the Caribbean and the Western Hemisphere. The Dominican Republic is the richest country in the Caribbean. How can next-door neighbors have such different access to resources? When France colonized and ruled Haiti, its people were not treated well. They were forced to overuse Haiti's natural resources to produce sugar. Planting sugar over and over ruined the soil over time. Years of deforestation have taken away many natural resources. Haiti's mountains also cut off the country's rainfall, which means crops do not grow well in Haiti. The rain blows into the Dominican Republic, helping the crops in the Dominican Republic. When Spain colonized the Dominican Republic, they worked with the native residents and developed a political system and economy. The people of the Dominican Republic were not treated poorly. The Dominican Republic also has fewer residents than Haiti, which allows for more access to resources for Dominicans. Deforestation, a large issue in Haiti, is not as problematic in the Dominican Republic.

Using a search engine of your choice, research ecotourism in different areas of the world. Identify what other countries offer ecotourism and identify what these countries have in common with Costa Rica and what is different.

WRITE Explain three differences in Haiti and the Dominican Republic.

....

....

....

....

....

....

READ

Trade in Central America and the Caribbean

Trade is the action of exchanging something for something else. Trade helps the economy, helps people get jobs, and allows for people to share natural resources with other parts of the world. Central America's trade has relied heavily on bananas and coffee. Both of these goods are an important part of many people's daily diet. Trade is a helpful part of our world, but it does come with its consequences. Some countries have such an abundance of natural resources, but do not have enough money to hold onto their products. This means almost all of their natural resources are exported out of the country. Other countries have very few natural resources and depend on trade to import their necessities. The availability of natural resources can cause unequal distribution.

Ecotourism in Costa Rica

As you have learned, tourism is traveling for enjoyment. Tourism can be fun and exciting, but it does take a toll on the environment. Costa Rica's solution is **ecotourism**, or tourism that is more natural and focuses on protecting and conserving the environment. Costa Rica has inspired many travelers from around the world to take in its natural beauty. This form of tourism educates people to take care of the environment and maintain the natural land. Visitors are supposed to protect the land. They need to stay on the paths provided and not start fires. They also need to protect resources and not waste fresh water or take anything from nature. Costa Rica is leading the world in ecotourism. Tourists just have to make sure they leave nature just as they found it.

REVIEW

In this lesson, you learned:

- Gold, copper, and fish are natural resources found in Central America.

- The use, distribution, and importance of natural resources can affect different groups.

- Trade has an impact on the availability of natural resources.

- Ecotourism is significant to Costa Rica.

SHOW WHAT YOU KNOW

Choose the correct answer for each question.

1. Identify natural resources found in Central America and the Caribbean. Circle all that apply.

   A. gold

   B. silver

   C. timber

   D. fish

2. True or False.   All countries have resources distributed evenly.

3. How does trade impact Central America and the Caribbean?

   ....

   ....

   ....

   ....

   ....

4. Costa Rica is the leader of _____ across the world.

PLAY

Pretend you are a tour guide for ecotourism in your community. Create a map of your yard, a local park, or building of your choice. Ask a friend or family member to go on a tour with you. Introduce them to what ecotourism is and explain why it is important! Have fun!

The Columbian Exchange and Migration

By the end of this lesson, you will be able to:

- research the global impact of the Columbian Exchange on the distribution of people and resources across Central America
- describe the reasons that humans migrate
- identify the factors that led to the migration of people from one region in Central America
- examine the influences and contributions of the migrants to the new region

Lesson Review

If you need to review natural resources in Central America, please go to the lesson titled "Using Natural Resources in Central America."

Academic Vocabulary

Read the following vocabulary words and definitions. Look through the lesson. Can you find each vocabulary word? Underline the vocabulary word in your lesson. Write the page number of where you found each word in the blanks.

- **Columbian Exchange:** the process by which animals, plants, people, ideas, and diseases have been introduced by the Americas, Europe, Asia, and Africa to one another (page _____)

- **domesticated:** a change that happens in animals if owned by humans over a long period of time (page _____)

- **migrate:** to move from one area to another, sometimes in search of resources (page _____)

Pretend you are a news reporter or writer for a magazine. Find a person in your family, a friend, or your instructor and ask about their ancestors. Interview them and find out where they are originally from. For example, they may have relatives that moved from England to the United States. Come up with four questions to ask your person of choice.

1. ....
....
2. ....
....
3. ....
....
4. ....
....

EXPLORE

Did you know that people have moved all over the world? Most of the people you know have ancestors who left where they were. Look at the questions below. Which questions can you answer on your own, and which questions do you need help answering? First, try to answer each question on your own. Then, discuss your answers with your instructor. Which questions did you have right? Which questions did you have wrong?

1. Where is your family from?

....

....

....

2. Where does your family live now?

....

....

....

3. Are these places close to each other or far away?

....

....

....

4. Why do you think they originally left the area?

....

....

....

Melting Pot

Did you know that around 260 million people live in another country than where they are from? That sounds like a lot, but it is actually only around 3.4 percent of the total world population! The continents of Asia and Europe have the most transfers from other countries. The United States has the largest population of newcomers and is often described as a melting pot of different nations and cultures!

Example of Melting Pot of Different Cultures

READ

The Columbian Exchange

Did you know that before the 1400s, Native Americans had never seen a horse? Or that Europeans had never seen a tomato? All of that changed due to something called the Columbian Exchange. The **Columbian Exchange** is the process by which animals, plants, people, ideas, and diseases have been introduced by the Americas, Europe, Asia, and Africa to one another. This exchange began to develop when ships became more common for shipping goods and connected the different continents and parts of the world together. The Columbian Exchange changed the course of history for Central America and the world forever.

One of the consequences of the Columbian Exchange was the transfer of diseases. Before the shipping interaction of different continents, some parts of the world had not been exposed to a large portion of diseases. These diseases included measles, smallpox, influenza, mumps, whooping cough, and more. Once continents began interacting together and exchanging goods, these diseases spread wildly. For example, in the 1600s the Caribbean lost 99 percent of its native population due to the new diseases brought to the islands.

Bananas, onions, grapes, and rice were introduced to the Americas during the Columbian Exchange.

Poverty in Honduras

Over 48 percent of people in Honduras live in poverty or are very poor. There are not enough jobs for people or the jobs do not pay enough, which causes people to leave. Honduras also has a large amount of violence, and people flee this area for safety.

Kids play in a boat in a poor area in Honduras.

READ

The Columbian Exchange (cont.)

Another exchange happened between plants and animals. The only **domesticated** animals, a change that happens in animals if owned by humans over a long period of time, in Central America were llamas. This was before the Columbian Exchange. Europeans brought different animals to this side of the world. They brought cattle, pigs, sheep, and horses. The different animals meant the land was used differently to support these new species. Native Americans were also able to have more protein sources, hides, and more help in the fields. This then helped to improve the economy of the Americas. The plants native to Central America were maize (a type of corn), potatoes, beans, tomatoes, pineapples, cacao, peanuts, avocados, and more! Other countries introduced onions, lettuce, rice, oats, turnips, pears, peaches, sugarcane, and more! These crops helped farming to expand in Central America.

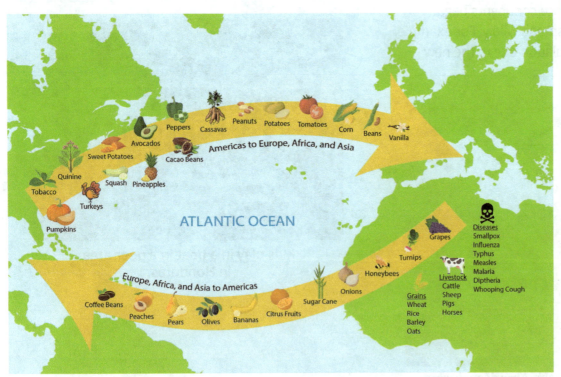

Examples of Goods in the Columbian Exchange

Using a search engine of your choice, research one country in Central America or the Caribbean and identify whether more people are migrating to or away from this country and find out why.

List one positive result and one negative result of the Columbian Exchange in Central America and the Caribbean.

READ

Migration Reasons

Humans also **migrate**, or move from one area to another, sometimes in search of resources. People migrate to try to improve their lives. People migrate for economic, political, safety, environmental, or social reasons. Migrating for economic reasons means people look elsewhere for work or to follow a certain career path. Political reasons cause people to flee based on how they are treated by the government. People migrate because they do not feel safe in their current country or area. They migrate to an area where they feel much safer. Environmental reasons can cause people to migrate due to natural disasters, like flooding or earthquakes.

Migration is very noticeable in Central America. Many people flee Central America due to safety and environmental concerns. The countries of Guatemala, Honduras, and El Salvador are three of the most dangerous countries on Earth. Hundreds to thousands of people leave these areas to find a safer place for themselves and their families. Another reason for migration out of Central America is due to environmental reasons. Central America experiences many natural disasters. This can cause hardships for the people who live there, like lack of food and shelter.

REVIEW

In this lesson, you learned:

- The Columbian Exchange impacted the distribution of people and resources across Central America.
- Humans migrate for different reasons.
- Factors led to the migration of people from one region in Central America.

People migrate to get away from dangerous countries.

Damage after an earthquake in Ecuador.

PRACTICE

Identify a possible reason for migration stated in the text. Draw a picture to represent this reason.

Reasons	Example	Picture
Economic		
Political		
Safety		
Enviromental		
Social		

Choose the correct answer for each question.

1. What is the Columbian Exchange?

   A. an exchange of goods with the country Colombia

   B. Christopher Columbus's journey across the sea in 1492

   C. where animals, plants, people, ideas, and diseases have been introduced to different countries

   D. an interaction between North America and South America

2. True or False   Guatemala, Honduras, and El Salvador are considered three of the safest countries on Earth.

3. Which of the following is not a reason for people to migrate mentioned in the text?

   A. social

   B. environmental

   C. educational

   D. economic

Country Study
Throughout this chapter, you've been working on a country study for one of the countries in Central America or the Caribbean. This study will continue, and you will compare and contrast the effects of migration with your country of choice and the worktext. Answer the following questions.

- Why have people migrated to your country?
- Why have people migrated away from your country?

Answer the following question with complete sentences.

4. Why are people migrating from some Central American countries?

   ....
   ....
   ....
   ....
   ....
   ....

Cultural Features of Central America and the Caribbean

By the end of this lesson, you will be able to:

- identify the location of key cultural features in Central America and the Caribbean
- relate how cultural features in a region of Central America and the Caribbean influence population, the economy, government, and transportation

Lesson Review

If you need to review the natural resources found in Central America and the Caribbean, please go to the lesson titled "Using Natural Resources in Central America."

Academic Vocabulary

Read the following vocabulary words and definitions. Look through the lesson. Can you find each vocabulary word? Underline the vocabulary word in your lesson. Write the page number of where you found each word in the blanks.

- **culture:** the characteristics of a particular group of people or regions such as art, language, religion, food, music, architecture, clothing, shared beliefs, and values (page ____)
- **economy:** the way goods are made, bought, and sold in a country or area (page ____)
- **government:** the exercise of control or authority over a group of people, country, land area, or organization to make and/or enforce laws (page ____)
- **population:** a particular section, group, or type of people or animals living in an area or country (page ____)
- **transportation:** the way something or someone moves from place to place (page ____)

TAKE A CLOSER LOOK

Cultural Features

Have you ever traveled to a new city or country and noticed the differences in food, language, and way of life? The characteristics of a particular group of people such as art, language, religion, food, music, architecture, clothing, shared beliefs, and values are examples of culture. As you complete the lesson, select a region in Central America or the Caribbean that is discussed. Investigate the cultural features of that particular region and think about what makes them unique. Compare these cultural features to the ones from your own life. Which cultural features from your own life do you value and are unique to you? Share your findings by creating a collage or scrapbook.

EXPLORE

If you take a trip to the Art Museum of the Americas in Washington, DC, you'll find exhibits that showcase the key cultural features of Central America and the Caribbean, including art, language, religion, and shared beliefs. Cultural features are an important way to represent people's values, social interactions, challenges, and hopes for the future. Famous Central American art such as the frog pendant of Costa Rica and Panama and Caribbean art such as the pendant mask of the Taíno showcase how cultural features can influence their way of life. Take a look at these three images of famous Central American and Caribbean art. What do they have in common? Write your ideas on the lines below.

....

....

....

....

....

....

....

Frog Pendant by The Met is in the public domain.

Pendant Mask by The Met is in the public domain.

Masked Figure Pendant by The Met is in the public domain.

Art, Language, and Religion

Before Europeans arrived in the Americas in the 15th century, ancient civilizations in Central America and the Caribbean created Pre-Columbian art from both scarce and common materials. Scarce materials included gold and obsidian. Common materials included rock and clay. The Mayans of South Mexico and Central America used picture symbols called hieroglyphs to write. They created art that showed mythical creatures. They believed mythical creatures caused disasters like floods and disease. For example, many Mayan sculptures featured the mythical creature alux. Mayans believed alux was a tiny elf who took care of crops. If the alux was not given gifts in return, it would harm people and plants through disease.

Some ancient Caribbean civilizations, such as the Taíno, did not have a written language. They used art to express their religion, astronomy, and way of life. They created petroglyphs, which were carvings on rock surfaces. The Taíno left petroglyphs on cave walls, large rocks in riverbeds, and stone monuments called monoliths. These petroglyphs represented gods and goddesses, natural disasters, and astronomy.

Thousands of indigenous languages were spoken in the Americas before the Europeans arrived. These languages are either no longer spoken or at risk of disappearing for good. Major languages of Central America and the Caribbean, like Spanish, Portuguese, English, and French Creole, have replaced older languages.

Today, the major religion of Central America and the Caribbean is Roman Catholicism, which is a monotheistic religion. Monotheism is the belief in one god. The Mayan civilization worshiped over 200 gods they believed to control things like weather, disease, and crop growth. They even sacrificed humans and animals to show their devotion to their many gods! The Taíno also worshiped many gods. These gods, called the Zemi, controlled the weather and disease by transforming into animals that you would find on Earth such as toads, alligators, and snakes.

Petroglyph (Rock Cave), Taíno

What examples of art, languages, and religions can be found in Central America and the Caribbean?

....

....

....

....

....

....

READ

Population and Economy

Central America and the Caribbean have some of the highest birth rates in the world and account for seven percent of the global **population**. Population is the particular section, group, or type of people or animals living in an area or country. Cultural features that influence population growth in these regions include improvements in technology and medicine. For example, better technology has allowed vaccines and medicines to be created. Vaccinations prevent people from getting sick with diseases like polio and influenza. Medicines help people recover from illness. These developments have allowed people to live longer in Central American countries like Costa Rica and Panama and Caribbean countries like Cuba.

Improvements in technology and medicine can also affect the economy. An **economy** is the way goods are made, bought, and sold in a country or area. In Costa Rica, advances in technology have helped the Costa Rican people build more schools and have increased job opportunities. If you ever visit the Bahamas, which is one of the largest island groups in the Caribbean, you'll probably notice some of the largest hospitals in the region. The creation of these hospitals has resulted in better medical care, which has attracted more tourists from around the world. Tourism is an important part of the Caribbean economy, and some countries there, like Antigua and Barbuda, depend almost entirely on tourism for people to make a living!

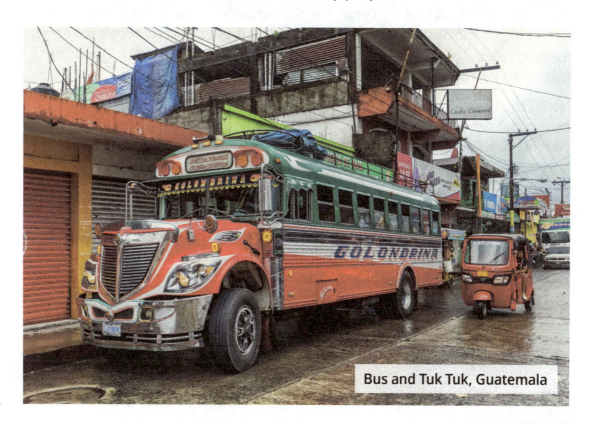

Bus and Tuk Tuk, Guatemala

How do improvements in technology and medicine affect the population and economy of Central America and the Caribbean?

....

....

....

....

READ

Government and Transportation

In society, people's right to vote has influenced creating the presidential system, a type of **government**. The majority of Central America and the Dominican Republic in the Caribbean use a presidential system. The citizens of the country elect presidents. This ensures people can participate in free and fair elections, a process known as democracy. Other parts of the Caribbean, like the Bahamas, Bermuda, and Jamaica, feature a constitutional monarchy. This system was created to allow people to vote for a leader, called a prime minister, while giving limited powers to monarchy, including kings and queens.

Not all countries allow people to vote. Some countries believe absolute power is necessary to govern a society. Cuba, for example, has a one-party system called Communism. Communism has a single leader called a dictator. There are no limits to how long a dictator can rule a society.

Despite technology improvements, many countries in Central America and the Caribbean are impoverished, meaning people do not have enough money to build roads and buy vehicles. In Central America, buses and small vehicles called tuk tuks are the main forms of **transportation**. Goods are transported by ship through the Panama Canal. There are no trains, and only a few flights are available due to the lack of airports. In the Caribbean, you can find buses, taxis, and ferries to travel from island to island.

REVIEW

In this lesson, you learned:

- The Taínov did not have written language. They used art to document their way of life.
- Cultural features of Central America and the Caribbean influence the population, economy, government, and transportation.
- Improvements in technology have led to the creation of vaccines and medicines, which have allowed people to live longer.
- People's shared beliefs in ideas like the right to vote have created government types in Central America such as presidential systems, which are led by a president.

Think About It

How can cultural features be exploited or taken advantage of in society?

WRITE

How do cultural features affect the types of governments and transportation in Central America and the Caribbean?

....

....

....

....

Circle all the correct answers for each question.

1. Pre-Columbian art was made from scarce materials such as _____.

   A. gold
   B. silver

   C. diamonds
   D. terracotta

2. Modern-day languages spoken in both Central America and the Caribbean include _____.

   A. Dutch
   B. Taíno

   C. French Creole
   D. Macoris

3. How are the religions in Central America and the Caribbean similar?

   ....

   ....

   ....

   ....

Cross-Country Study
Research cultural features such as art, language, and religion from a country of a previous continent that you have learned about, including Asia or Africa. Compare the same cultural features to a country in Central America or the Caribbean. How are these cultural features similar or different? Which one(s) do you think is/are the most influential in society? Present your findings by creating an online presentation or poster.

4. Complete the following table using your knowledge of Central America and the Caribbean:

Regions	Features That Influence Population	Features That Influence the Economy	Features That Influence the Government	Features That Influence Transportation
Central America and the Caribbean				

Central American Culture and Its Influence

By the end of this lesson, you will be able to:

- investigate the cultural geography of Central America
- explore influences of Central American culture on individuals and civilizations around the world
- discover the lasting impact of Central American culture on everyday aspects of life

Lesson Review

If you need to review the culture of Central America, please go to the lesson titled "Cultural Features of Central America and the Caribbean."

Academic Vocabulary

Read the following vocabulary word and definition. Look through the lesson. Can you find the vocabulary word? Underline the vocabulary word in your lesson. Write the page number of where you found the word in the blank.

- **cultural geography:** the study of human connection to natural resources, the economy, religion, government, and many other ways that humans interact with their world (page _____)

ONLINE CONNECTION

Central American Dishes

Have you ever walked through the international aisle of a local market and noticed that the types of spices, herbs, and sauces vary by geographic region? Perhaps you've noticed that the Central American section features herbs like cilantro and cumin while the Caribbean section features spices like allspice and cinnamon. These are some examples of cultural geography. Research famous dishes in Central America that use these herbs and spices. Then, compare them with your own favorite dishes. How are they the same or different? Create a poster to share your findings.

EXPLRE

Have you ever seen the tall, ancient Pyramids of Giza in Egypt? Pyramids around the world are all shaped similarly, but these structures have their own peculiarities in different cultures. For example, the Mayan pyramids are shorter than the Egyptian pyramids. Experts believe that this was to leave room for a temple on the top. As you research images of temples in Central America, be sure to look at pictures of famous Mayan stone pyramids, including Tikal in Guatemala, Tazumal in El Salvador, and Copán in Honduras. The ancient Mayans built two types of pyramids: some to use for rituals and some intended to remain untouched. These unique architectural features represent each region's **cultural geography**, as they vary by region in Central America. Take a look at these three Mayan pyramids. How are they different?

Tikal Pyramid, Guatemala

Tazumal Pyramid, El Salvador

Copán Pyramid, Honduras

Think about the types of architecture in your hometown or a place that you have visited. It may be a slanted skyscraper from a big city or a cathedral made from colorful stained glass windows. Think of the architecture and write down as many descriptive features as you can. How is it unique, and what do you think makes it influential?

....

....

....

....

....

....

....

....

....

Musical Instruments

Central American music was greatly influenced by Africa and Europe. Traditional music and musical instruments differ among countries of Central America due to European influences. Slavery also contributed to the evolution of Central American traditional music by introducing traditional African music, dances, and instruments to the natives in Central America.

Percussion instruments, like drums, xylophones, and rattlers, are played by striking with the hand, with mallets, or by shaking. Played throughout Central America, the *cabasa* drum originated from Africa. It has a handle and is made with loops of steel ball chain, which is wrapped around a cylinder. The cabasa produces sounds like a rattlesnake when twisted. In Guatemala, the national instrument is called the *marimba*, which is an instrument that consists of wooden bars that can be struck with rubber mallets to produce sound. The marimba is similar to a xylophone but produces softer tones.

Instruments like cabasas and marimbas have influenced the creation of popular musical genres like the samba and bossa nova of Brazil and the reggaeton of the Caribbean. These musical genres are popular in many regions of the world, including North America, South America, the Caribbean, and Europe. The cabasa is also frequently used in music therapy to help people who have trouble grasping objects with their hands.

Cabasa Instrument

What instruments are played in Central America, and what were their influences in the world?

....

....

....

Marimba Instrument

READ

Science and Technology

In Central America, the ancient Mayans were advanced in science and technology and created sophisticated written language, calendars, and pyramids.

The Mayans were skilled astronomers and mathematicians and developed the number zero. They also created two complex calendars: the Tzolk'in for religious ceremonies, and a solar calendar called the Haab' to track time. Like the Gregorian calendar we use today, the Haab' was a 365-day calendar that was used in agriculture and economics.

The Mayans built sophisticated pyramids and great cities using tools such as basalt axes and fire. They were also skilled in arts and crafts. They devised looms, which are instruments used to weave clothing, and created paints that were colorful and glittery from a mineral called mica.

The next time you start a stopwatch from zero or feel the frigid temperature at zero degrees Fahrenheit, you'll want to thank the Mayans, who were one of the first civilizations to develop the concept of the number zero. The number zero is universal, which means that it is used worldwide to measure time, distance, and space. Glitter, which you can find in any arts and crafts store, is also widely used among many parts of the world for decorative purposes.

WRITE How did science and technology influence societies in Central America and the world?

....

....

....

....

....

Mayan Calendar

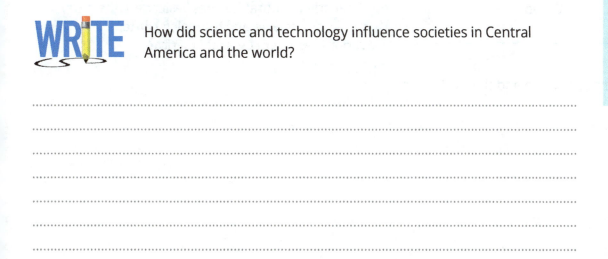

The religious calendar, or Tzolk'in, was a 260-day calendar. This calendar has two cycles, a 20-day cycle and a 13-day cycle. Each day has a name and a number. The name comes from the 20-day cycle, and the number from the 13-day cycle.

READ

Food

Corn, rice, beans, chili peppers, and tomatoes are important foods in Central America. These important crops have influenced the creation of many famous Central American dishes, like tamales, enchiladas, and empanadas, which are all made from corn dough. Many favorite foods in today's society came from the Mayans, including cacao beans, which they used to make hot chocolate! While the Mayans drank hot chocolate made from cacao beans that were mixed with water and chili peppers, later societies, like the Spanish, added sugar to their cacao beans for a sweeter flavor. The Spanish version of hot chocolate is similar to the sweet hot chocolate you might drink on a cold day!

Empenadas

Cacao

How did food influence societies in Central America and the world?

....

....

....

....

REVIEW

In this lesson, you learned:

- Cultural features like architecture, music, science and technology, and food in Central America have influenced civilizations around the world.

- The most famous civilization in Central America was the Mayans, who had great influence and achievements in science and technology.

- Mayan accomplishments, like the creation of the number zero, are universal and are used to measure time, distance, and space.

Think About It
What other cultural features besides architecture, music, and science and technology differ in various regions of Central America?

Discover! SOCIAL STUDIES • GRADE 5 • LESSON 31

PRACTICE

List three cultural features from your own life, such as music, food, religion, or language in the table below. Then, describe how these cultural features influence your daily life.

CULTURAL FEATURES FROM YOUR OWN LIFE	INFLUENCES ON DAILY LIFE

1. Which of the following are musical genres influenced by popular instruments in Central America? Circle all correct answers.

   A. soul

   B. gospel

   C. reggaeton

   D. pop

   E. samba

   F. bossa nova

2. An interesting feature of the cabasa instrument is that it is commonly used to _____.

   A. get rid of a toothache

   B. help people improve grasping objects with their hands

   C. encourage singing and dancing

   D. help people sleep

   E. reduce muscle aches

3. Name two ways science and technology from Central America have influenced countries around the world.

   ....

   ....

   ....

4. Important crops such as corn, rice, and cacao beans in Central America have influenced the production of all of the following except _____.

   A. hot chocolate

   B. tamales

   C. pizza

   D. empanadas

   E. enchiladas

ONLINE CONNECTION

Mayan Calendars

The Mayans had two major calendars, the Tzolk'in for religious ceremonies and a solar calendar called the Haab' to track time. Research how these important calendars were used. How did they influence the calendars that we use today?

....

....

....

....

....

....

Chapter 3 Review

By the end of this lesson, you will be able to:

- review the information from the lessons in Chapter 3, "Central America and the Caribbean."

Lesson Review

Throughout the chapter, we have learned the following big ideas:

- Different maps can tell you different stories—topographic maps show the physical features of land; geopolitical maps show a continent's boundaries and different countries within the continent; tourist maps help tourists navigate an unfamiliar city. (Lesson 23)

- Geographic factors such as climate and vegetation and geographic features such as volcanoes, the Pacific Ocean, the Caribbean Sea, rivers, and mountain ranges influence where people live in Central America. (Lesson 24)

- Natural resources influence people's relationship to the land in Central America and the Caribbean. For example, people make money by mining, but they can also overmine and lose valuable natural resources. (Lesson 25)

- People make changes and respond to changes in their environment through agriculture, deforestation, urbanization, dam building, and mining. (Lesson 26)

- Volcanoes, earthquakes, and erosion contribute to the availability and abundance of natural resources like gold, silver, fish, and forests. (Lesson 27)

- Gold, copper, and fish are key natural resources found in Central America. (Lesson 28)

- The Columbian Exchange impacted the distribution of people and resources across Central America. (Lesson 29)

- Key cultural features of Central America and the Caribbean include art, language, religion, shared beliefs, and technology. (Lesson 30)

- Cultural features like architecture, music, science and technology, and food in Central America have influenced civilizations around the world. (Lesson 31)

Go back and review the lessons as needed while you complete the activities.

ONLINE CONNECTION

Use an online search engine and look up a map of the world's natural resources. Which geographic features are they close to? On which continents are these natural resources found? What kind of climates are present in the continents of the world? Discuss your findings with your instructor.

REVIEW

Types of Maps

You learned different maps can tell you different stories. Maps can show us what countries or continents used to look like and how they look now. They can also tell us exciting locations to visit in a country and where some countries begin and end.

The image on the top right shows a **topographic map** of Central America, which highlights the physical features of the region. The brown on a topographical map indicates higher locations and the green indicates lower locations.

The image on the bottom right shows a **geopolitical map** of Central America, which defines the borders of the region's countries and cities.

WRITE

What stories do different maps tell? How do geographic features influence where people live in Central America? What types of natural resources can you find in Central America and the Caribbean?

....
....
....
....
....
....
....
....

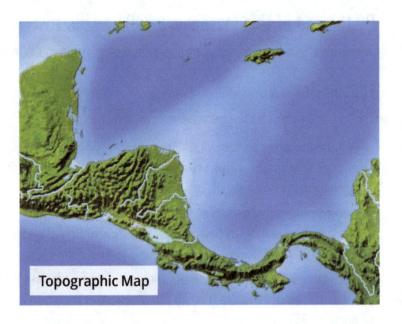
Topographic Map

Geopolitical Map

REVIEW

Geographic Features and Natural Resources

You also learned Central America has many geographic features such as volcanoes, the Pacific Ocean, the Caribbean Sea, mountains, coastlines, and rainforests that influence where people live. You may think that people wouldn't want to live near a volcano, but the lava from volcanic eruptions actually creates fertile soil and allows for plentiful agriculture. This makes it a very attractive location for farmers to live! Take a look at the lush green surroundings next to the volcano in Costa Rica in the image on the right.

Cities along the coastline in Central America, like Panama City in the image on the right, are also suitable locations for people to live in due to the easy access to fish, water, and transportation of goods.

Let's not forget about natural resources! You also learned that Central America and the Caribbean are abundant in gold, copper, silver, fish, timber, limestone, oil, lead, and aluminum. Volcanoes produce volcanic deposits that produce many of these resources like gold, copper, and aluminum! These resources are very important to the world and its economy.

Arenal Volcano, Costa Rica

Panama City

REVIEW

The Columbian Exchange and Cultural Features

Do you recall that Native Americans had never seen a horse before the 1400s? You learned about the Columbian Exchange, which was the widespread transfer of plants, animals, culture, human populations, technology, diseases, and ideas among the Americas, Europe, Asia, and Africa. One of the consequences of the Columbian Exchange was the transfer of diseases that many parts of the world had never seen before, such as measles, smallpox, and influenza. The Caribbean lost 99 percent of its native population as a result! These outbreaks led to the creation of medicine and advanced technology like vaccines, which prevent diseases in humans.

Art is one of the key features of Central America and the Caribbean. Before the arrival of the Europeans to the Americas in the 15th century, ancient civilizations in Central America and the Caribbean created Pre-Columbian art from scarce materials such as gold and obsidian and common materials such as rock and clay. The Mayans of Southern Mexico and Central America used picture symbols called hieroglyphics to write and create art that depicted mythical creatures to explain disasters like floods and disease.

In comparison, the Taíno of the Caribbean did not have a written language. Instead, they created *petroglyphs*, which were carvings done on rock surfaces for art. Their art expressed the importance of religion, astronomy, and their way of life.

The Country of Colombia in South America

As you read about the Columbian Exchange, it may be easy to confuse the word *Columbian* with the word *Colombian*. The word *Columbian* can refer to the explorer *Christopher Columbus* who was known for discovering the Americas, which includes North and South America. In contrast, *Colombian* can refer to the people or things of Colombia, a country in South America. While the Columbian Exchange made its way to South America, the spelling of the two words is not the same.

PRACTICE

Visualizing Vocabulary

Let's review important words from the chapter. First, read each word and write its meaning. (You can go back into the text to find the meanings.) Then, create a drawing to help you remember the meanings.

READ	WRITE	DRAW
Topographic map		
Geopolitical map		
Natural resources		
Culture		
Geographic features		
Columbian Exchange		

PRACTICE

Identifying and Understanding Cultural Features

Choose two key cultural features in Central America and the Caribbean that you learned about in this chapter. Include details from the text to show what you know about each cultural feature. Refer to the appropriate lessons as needed.

TYPE OF CULTURAL FEATURE:

Location	Use	Influence in Central America and the World

TYPE OF CULTURAL FEATURE:

Location	Use	Influence in the Caribbean and the World

REVIEW

As you fill in the table, think about how cultural features relate to your own life.

For example, this sentence is written in English. English was derived from Latin, French, and Dutch languages spoken in Northern Europe.

If we were to use language as a cultural feature, the table would look like this:

Type of Cultural Feature: Language (English)

Location: Derived from Northern Europe

Use: Many, examples include newspaper publishing and book publishing

Influence in the World: Most commonly spoken language

PRACTICE

Compare and Contrast

Use the Venn diagram to compare and contrast the geographic or cultural features of Central America and the Caribbean. Place the name of one region on the line above the left circle and the name of the other region above the right circle. Under each region's name, write facts that are unique to that region. Some aspects of the region will be the same, and those can be written in the center of the Venn diagram.

_____   _____

BOTH

Chapter 4
Europe

Bonjour mon amie! It is Pierre, the magnifique, world-traveling frog!

Last time, we traveled to the Mayan Mountains in Belize. Monsieur Jean guided us. We found a Mayan temple in the middle of the jungle. It is incredible how well they built it. The temple still stood even though it was built over 1000 years ago!

We then went to the Cockscomb Basin Wildlife Sanctuary. That is a place made to protect animals. But we were in for a nasty surprise.

It turns out the sanctuary was created to protect one animal in particular—the jaguar. Have you ever seen a jaguar? They are the fastest and deadliest animal.

They wanted to protect the jaguar, but what about protecting us? Sacre bleu!

Chang felt lost and sad. I said, "Listen, mon amie. Stay with me in France. I know it's cold there. But we will come up with a new plan." Chang agreed.

We landed in Paris, and Monsieur Jean took us to the Louvre. The Louvre is the most famous art museum in the world. It has 38,000 pieces of art, and it is the most visited art museum in the world. I am so proud of my beautiful country.

There is so much to see here that it even cheered Chang up for a little while.

But I had not given up. I was determined to find a home for my friend. Allons-y!

What Will I Learn?

This chapter focuses on Europe. It examines the geography and resources of the area as well as its cultural and human history.

Lessons at a Glance

Stories in Maps of Europe

By the end of this lesson, you will be able to:

- examine different maps of Europe
- determine a story a map can tell about Europe
- compare and contrast the major cities in Europe and the cities in your state or country

Academic Vocabulary

Read the following vocabulary words and definitions. Look through the lesson. Can you find each vocabulary word? Underline the vocabulary word in your lesson. Write the page number of where you found each word in the blanks.

- **continent:** one of seven large land masses on the globe that is generally surrounded by large bodies of water (page _____)

- **geopolitical maps:** maps that show boundaries of countries, states, cities, and counties (page _____)

- **topographic maps:** maps that show the elevation and shape of Earth's surface (page _____)

- **tourist maps:** maps that show destinations that are popular for tourists, help tourists determine various destinations to visit, and assist with planning daily activities in a particular place (page _____)

CREATE

Think about your neighborhood, city, state, and country. What are the important places that exist in each of these locations?

Next, choose either your neighborhood, city, state, or country and create a map to represent it. Label the important places of your location on the map.

EXPLORE

Do you take pictures? Why do people take pictures? When people take pictures, those pictures tell a story. They might tell about a birthday party or a fantastic vacation to a tropical island. Maps, just like pictures, tell a story too. Different maps can tell different stories. Maps of the same place created over time can tell different stories about the same location.

This is a map of Europe. When you view this map, what stories do you see? What can you learn about Europe?

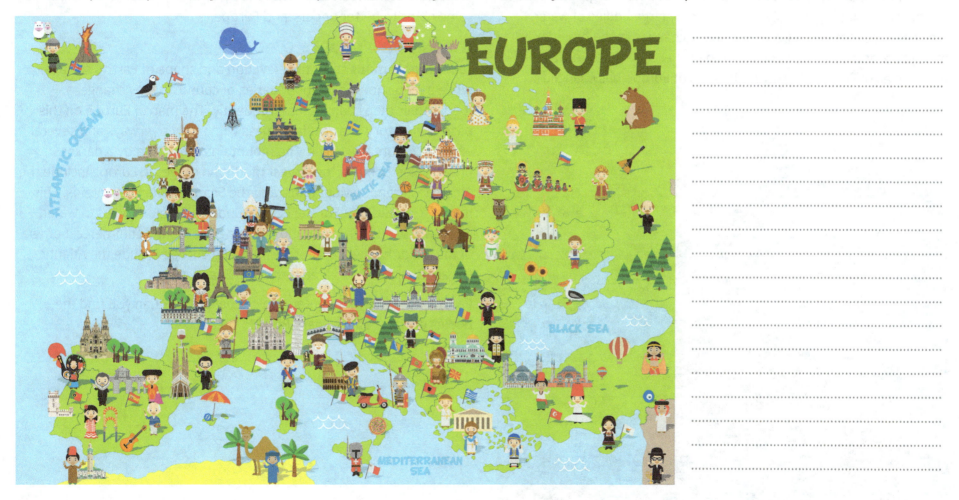

Maps show different types of information. What information do you think you can learn about Europe by looking at different maps?

Europe

If you were given a map, could you find Europe? What does it look like? Where is it located in the world? Europe is the second smallest continent on our planet. A **continent** is one of seven large land masses on the globe that is generally surrounded by large bodies of water. It is a continent that has experienced many changes to the boundaries or borders of the countries within. Today, there are 44 countries that make up all of Europe. However, the map of Europe has changed

frequently. Throughout history, maps of a continent have changed often. Examining maps of the same location over long periods of time helps us better understand what the story of that place is. Let's look at some maps to better understand Europe.

TOPOGRAPHIC MAPS OF EUROPE

Topographic maps show the elevation and shape of Earth's surface. While a map showing the boundaries of countries may change, a topographic map changes less frequently. The map of Europe on this page tells a story of a vast land mass with many riverways and several extreme mountain ranges. The mountains are shown by a darker brown color. Some of the largest mountain ranges in Europe include the Alps, the Pyrenees Mountains, and the Scandanavian Mountains. This map also shows that Europe is surrounded by major bodies of water, which are useful for exploration, trading goods, and commerce. Some of the major bodies of water surrounding Europe include the Atlantic Ocean, Baltic Sea, and Mediterranean Sea.

Can you find where mountains might be located? Can you find the bodies of water on the map? Point to them.

Discover! SOCIAL STUDIES • GRADE 5 • LESSON 33

READ

Geopolitical Maps of Europe

Geopolitical maps show boundaries of countries, states, cities, and counties. The map to the right shows the current geopolitical boundaries of each country within Europe. This map also marks the major cities and capitals within present-day Europe. The capital of each country is indicated by a star. Major cities in Europe are indicated by circles. This map changes frequently as boundaries change and new countries form or dissolve. This map can tell a story about the countries that make up the continent. It can tell about the important cities and where they are located.

Many of the major cities on the map are located on or near bodies of water. Why do you think many cities are located there?

....

....

Tourist Maps of Europe

Tourist maps show destinations that are popular for tourists. These maps help tourists determine various destinations to visit based on their needs and interests and assist with planning daily activities in particular places. Below is a tourist map of France, one of the larger countries in Europe. It tells a story of the important places and things in France. For example, you can see different foods on the map, such as breads, coffee, and honey. This tells you that France has special foods that are important to or popular in the country.

As you take a look at this map, circle an attraction that you would want to visit.

 WRITE What is something you can learn about France from this map? What is a story that the map is telling?

....

....

....

....

....

....

READ

Telling Stories About Europe

Comparing maps from different time periods can help us tell a story about how a continent has changed. Look at the map below. This map shows Europe in 1092. It lists the different groups and countries that made up Europe at the time. You might notice that the borders or shapes of the countries look different from the other maps you have seen of Europe today. The names of the different areas on the map might have changed since the map was created. For example, on this map, there is no Spain. Instead, it is divided into multiple different kingdoms. By comparing this map to a map of present-day Europe, we can tell that borders and names of countries have changed over time.

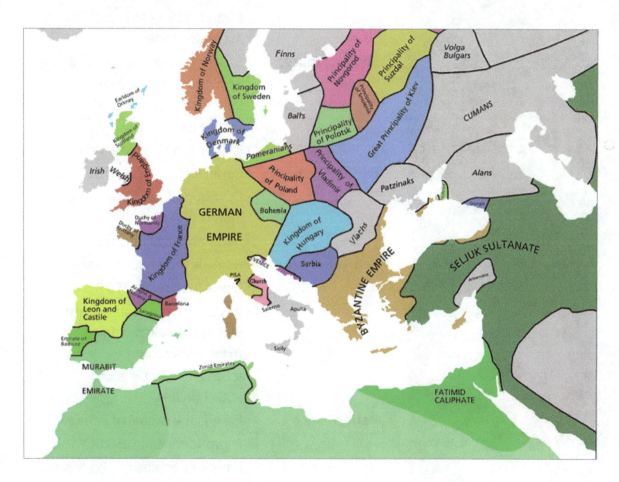

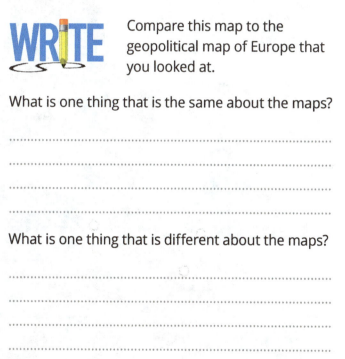

Compare this map to the geopolitical map of Europe that you looked at.

What is one thing that is the same about the maps?

....

....

....

What is one thing that is different about the maps?

....

....

....

READ

Cities in Europe

Many major cities are located throughout the continent of Europe. These cities have many similarities and differences. Read about some of the major cities in Europe. As you read about each major city, think about which one you would want to visit most and why. Then, find each city on the map below.

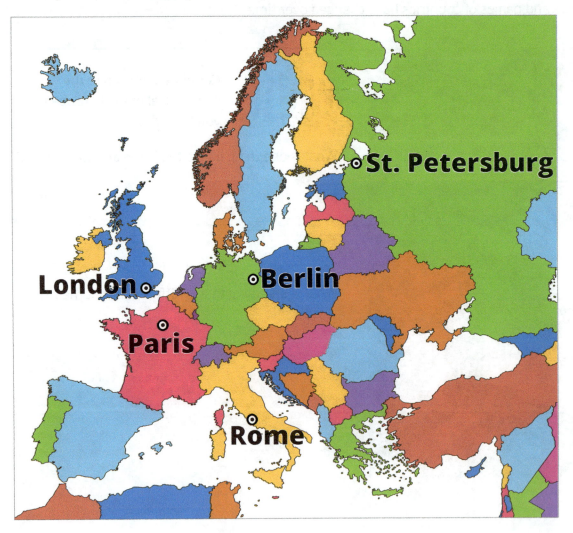

Major City in Europe	Characteristics
London, United Kingdom	• London is the capital of England. • Its history stretches back to the time of the ancient Romans. • Major attractions include Big Ben, the Houses of Parliament, the Tower of London, and Westminster Abbey. • Over 300 languages are spoken in London today.
St. Petersburg, Russia	• St. Petersburg was founded in 1703 by Peter the Great. • It is located next to the Baltic Sea. • It has been renamed three times.
Berlin, Germany	• Berlin is the capital of Germany. • Its history dates back to the 13th century. • It has about 175 museums.
Rome, Italy	• Rome is the capital of Italy. • It was founded in 753 BC. • It is the most populated city in Italy with almost three million residents. • It has 250 fountains and 900 churches.
Paris, France	• Paris is the capital of France. • It was founded in 259 BC. • Paris was originally a Roman city called "Lutetia."

PRACTICE

Comparing Cities

Choose one of the cities on the previous page. How is the city you selected similar to the city or town where you live? How is it different? Consider the location, size, population, topography, attractions, and other characteristics.

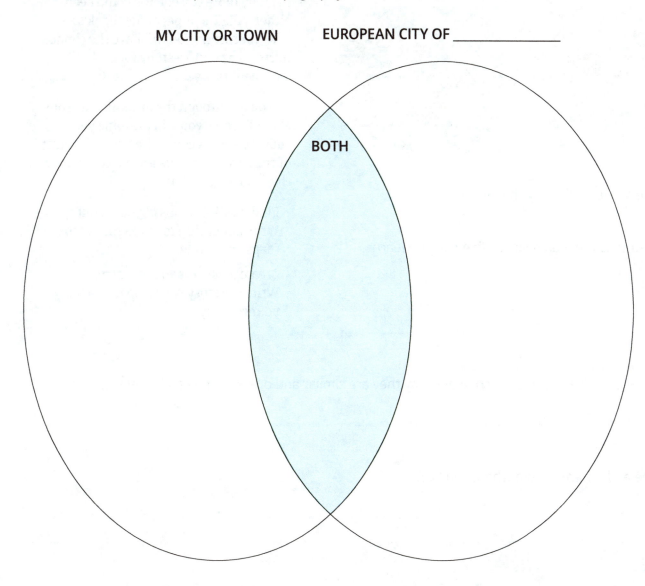

MY CITY OR TOWN   EUROPEAN CITY OF _____

BOTH

REVIEW

In this lesson, you learned:

- There are many different maps of Europe.

- Each map of Europe tells a different story.

- There are similarities and differences between the major cities in Europe and cities in your state and country.

Think About It

How do the geographic features in Europe, like mountains and rivers, influence where people live?

Choose the correct answer for each question.

1. Which of these maps is a topographic map of Europe? Circle the map.

2. True or False: Europe is a continent that has experienced many changes to its countries' borders.

3. Pick one of the maps from question 1. What story is the map telling? What can you learn about Europe from looking at it?

....

....

4. Choose two of the major cities in Europe that you learned about. Describe one way they are similar and one way they are different.

One way they are similar is ....

One way they are different is ....

5. Choose a city from Europe. How is it the same and different from where you live?

One way they are the same is ....

One way they are different is ....

Lesson 34

Geographic Features of Europe

By the end of this lesson, you will be able to:

- analyze geographic factors that influence where people live in Europe
- identify geographic features of Europe
- identify geographic connections between the continents

Lesson Review

If you need to review map types, please go to the lesson titled "Stories in Maps of Europe."

Academic Vocabulary

Read the following vocabulary words and definitions. Look through the lesson. Can you find each vocabulary word? Underline the vocabulary word in your lesson. Write the page number of where you found each word in the blanks.

- **canal:** a man-made waterway which allows for the passage of boats or ships (page ____)

- **channel:** a length of water that connects two larger bodies of water (page ____)

- **foothill:** land usually found at the base of a mountain with gradual incline and higher elevation (page ____)

- **geographic features:** naturally created or man-made features of the Earth's surface (page ____)

- **marsh:** a type of wetlands where water covers the land for long periods of time (page ____)

- **plains:** a broad area of land that is usually very flat (page ____)

- **plateau:** an area of highland consisting of flat terrain (page ____)

Think about your ideal area to live. Would there be hills, a lake, or an ocean? Would you like to live near mountains so you can go skiing in the winter and hiking in the spring? Maybe you would enjoy living near a desert so you can stargaze at night and learn more about desert animals. Make a list of features you would like to live near. Then, draw a picture of those features on a separate piece of paper. Make sure you include yourself in the drawing!

....

....

....

....

Our world is filled with many beautiful flowing rivers, soaring mountains, deep oceans, and vast deserts. Europe is no exception. It is a continent filled with many rivers, mountains, and deserts. The pictures on this page show examples of them. Maybe you have wondered what it would be like to live near the ocean. Have you ever visited a mountain and seen the locals that live nearby? Perhaps you've played by a river on vacation and imagined what it would be like to have it in your own backyard everyday?

If you could choose any of the areas in Europe shown in the pictures below, which area would you want to live near? Circle your choice. Then, write about why you would choose that area based on what is shown in the picture.

Every continent on our planet is connected to an ocean. Oceans connect continents to one another. Europe is connected to North America by the Atlantic Ocean. South America and Australia are connected by the Pacific Ocean. The Mediterranean Sea connects the continent of Europe to Africa.

Europe and Asia are two continents that are directly connected, but not by an ocean. Examine the map below. How are they connected? The Ural Mountains act as a border between the continent of Europe and the continent of Asia.

Ural Mountains

....

....

Do you think everyone wants to live in the same location? Why do you think people live in different areas of Europe?

Geographic Features of Europe

Have you ever wondered why people choose to live in certain places? People have all different reasons for choosing to live in a particular place. One reason people choose to live somewhere is the geographic features of an area. **Geographic features** are naturally created or man-made features of the Earth's surface. Europe has many different geographic features. For example, **plateaus** are areas of highland consisting of flat terrain. The Iberian Plateau is a plateau in Spain. Europe also has a large area of plains. **Plains** are broad areas of land that are usually very flat. This area stretches from the border of France and Spain towards Russia. Additionally, Europe also has many marshes. **Marshes** are a type of wetlands where water covers the land for long periods of time.

WRITE

Pick two of the geographic features on this page. What is one way they are similar? What is one way they are different?

....

....

....

....

CREATE

Pick one of the geographic features on the page and draw a picture to help you remember it. Include as many details as you can.

More Geographic Features of Europe

Europe has many more geographic features. For example, mountains are a geographic feature in Europe. You already know about the Ural Mountains, which separate Europe from Asia. This is a picture of another mountain range in Europe called the Dolomite Mountains, which are in the country of Italy. At the base of the mountains are usually **foothills**, which have more of a gradual incline or higher elevation than the other land around them.

Deserts are another geographic feature in Europe. This is the Tabernas Desert in Spain. It is very dry land.

Europe has oceans and seas. This is a picture of the Mediterranean Sea from the shores of Santorini, Greece. Europe is also bordered by the Arctic and Atlantic Oceans.

Europe also has other types of geographical features that involve water. Some cities in Europe, like Venice, Italy, have canals. A **canal** is a man-made waterway which allows for the passage of boats or ships. In Venice, many people travel by boat throughout the city instead of using the roads. Europe also has the English Channel. A **channel** is a length of water that connects two larger bodies of water. This channel is located between England and France. Finally, Europe has a lot of lakes, such as Lake Annecy in France.

READ

Why Do People Live Where They Do?

People everywhere have to make choices about where they live. Many factors go into those choices. Just as there are a variety of geographic features, there are also a wide range of reasons to live near or far from each type. For example, people may choose to live near water because water is a good transportation source, sustains life, and provides an area for recreational activities. Danger, like flooding, can also come from living near water. Some people like to live near mountains because they enjoy the snow and activities like skiing. However, snow can also be dangerous with the possibility of avalanches. Still, people prefer to live in or near a desert. They might prefer the dry temperatures for health reasons or own animals that cope better with the temperatures of the desert. But despite these reasons, deserts lack life-sustaining water and can be dangerous for this reason.

WRITE

Pick one of the geographic features below. Write one advantage and one disadvantage of living in that location.

- Alps Mountain Range
- English Channel
- Tabernas Desert

Advantage:

....
....
....

Disadvantage:

....
....
....

REVIEW

In this lesson, you learned:

- Geographic factors influence where people live in Europe.
- There are a variety of geographic features in Europe, such as plains, mountains, canals, and marshes.
- Geographic features, such as oceans and mountain ranges, serve as connections between the continents.

Think About It
What geographic feature in Europe would you choose to live near? Why?

READ

Connecting Continents

Major geographic features exist on all continents. They connect various continents on our planet. Look at the map below. Do you see any large bodies of water that connect continents? Are there any landforms that connect them? You will notice there are several geographic features labeled. All of these connect continents on Earth.

Continents can be connected by land. We know that the Ural Mountains connect Asia and Europe. North America and South America are also connected by land. They are connected by a narrow strip of land where the country of Panama is located.

Continents can also be connected by bodies of water. For example, the Pacific Ocean connects North America and Asia. The Indian and Pacific Oceans connect Asia and Australia.

PRACTICE

Can you find two other geographic features that connect continents on the map? Write the geographic feature below and the continents it connects.

Geographic Feature	Continents Connected

1. Name three types of geographic features that can be found in Europe.

1. ....
2. ....
3. ....

2. Look at the map below. Write three types of geographic features you see on the map.

1. ....
2. ....
3. ....

3. Choose one geographic feature in Europe and describe why someone may want to live near it.

....

....

4. If someone worked on a fishing boat, what geographic feature in Europe might they live near?

A. Alps Mountain Range

B. Tabernas Desert

C. Iberian Plateau

D. Atlantic Ocean

5. What geographic feature connects Europe to Asia?

A. Panama

B. Ural Mountains

C. Mediterranean Sea

D. Atlantic Ocean

Country Study

Let's dig in and get to know the country we selected in the last lesson a little better.
Try to find a map of your country that shows the different geographic features. What geographic features are present in your selected country? Write about it in your journal using the specific names of your geographic features. Be sure to put a copy of the map in there too!

Human Settlement in Europe

By the end of this lesson, you will be able to:

- compare and contrast human settlements of different regions in Europe
- analyze how the environment influenced settlements in Europe

Lesson Review

If you need to review the physical geography of Europe, please go to the lesson titled "Geographic Features of Europe."

Academic Vocabulary

Read the following vocabulary words and definitions. Look through the lesson. Can you find each vocabulary word? Underline the vocabulary word in your lesson. Write the page number where you found each word in the blanks.

- **erosion:** the wearing away of the land by forces such as water, wind, and ice (page _____)
- **seaports:** places where ships can dock and load or unload supplies (page _____)
- **settlement:** a specific geographic region where a community of people live, such as mountains, lowlands, or coasts (page _____)
- **stilt houses:** houses built on elevated platforms, usually over water or land, to prevent against flooding (page _____)

ONLINE CONNECTION

Using an online search engine, research images of mountain regions and coastal cities in Europe. Select two cities in Europe—one depicting a mountain region and the other depicting a coastal city. Compare and contrast the features of both cities. How are they different? Which region would you want to live in? Share your findings by creating a poster.

EXPLRE

Think about the environment in your hometown. Do you live in the mountains, next to the coast, or in a desert area? The specific region where a community of people live is known as a human settlement. A **settlement** is a specific geographic region where a community of people live, such as mountains, lowlands, or coasts. In Europe, settlements exist in different types of environments that include mountains, plains, and coasts. Take a look at these images of settlements in Europe. What similarities and differences can you spot? Which one would you live in and why? Write your ideas on the lines provided

The Dolomite Mountains, the Alps

The Lowlands, Croatia

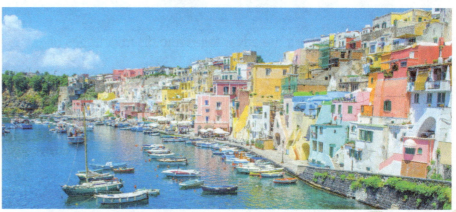

The Coastline of Procida, Italy

Mountain Settlements

THE ALPS

About 17 percent of Europe's population live in mountain areas. Mountain ranges such as the Alps, which stretch from France in western Europe to Slovenia in eastern Europe, are important geographic features of European settlements. Humans have been living in the Alps since Paleolithic times. Today many people who live in cooler regions of the Alps grow crops or raise livestock. Drier, hotter parts of the Alps, like the Rhône Valley in Switzerland, are popular for harvesting fruits and vegetables and are good for growing grapes for wine. People who live in the Alps typically reside in houses called chalets, which are made of wood, have a sloping roof, and are often more than one story tall. While the Alps seem like a good place for farmers, these isolated settlements make it hard for them to access medicines and technology.

THE URALS

The Ural Mountains of Russia, stretching north to south, form the boundary between Europe and Asia. Russians entered the northern Urals in the late 1000s and developed farming communities. They grew wheat, buckwheat, millet, potatoes, and vegetables. The Urals became one of Russia's most important industrial areas. Mines produce iron ore, copper, chromite, gold, silver, and platinum. Ural forests provide valuable wood for building houses. However, the Urals are difficult to live in due to extreme cold and large distances, which make it hard for people to transport goods to different regions in Europe.

The Ural Mountains

What are the advantages and disadvantages of mountain settlements?

....

....

....

....

Chalets of Switzerland

Coastal Settlements

If you have been to a coastal city, you may have noticed large amounts of people, shops, restaurants, and houses. Coastal cities are popular areas where people establish permanent residences due to easy access to resources such as food and water. They are also popular places to establish seaports. **Seaports** are places where ships can dock, load, or unload supplies. When a city has a seaport, it is able to make money through the trading of materials, including cars, which are the primary exports of Europe. Other items that are traded include medication, petroleum, crops, fish, and electronics. The climate of coastal cities is generally temperate, which makes them comfortable locations for people to live in. Popular coastal cities in Europe include Porto in Portugal, Copenhagen in Denmark, Nice in France, Mykonos in Greece, Dubrovnik in Croatia, and Podgorica in Montenegro. However, coastal settlements can be met with extreme weather conditions that can cause coastal **erosion** and rising sea levels. This has led people to build **stilt houses**, which are houses raised over the water surface and built to protect against flooding. Coastal stilt houses can be found in Austria, France, and Germany.

Stilt houses of Mykonos, Greece

What are the advantages and disadvantages of coastal settlements? Write your ideas using the table provided below.

Advantages	Disadvantages

READ

Settlements in the Plains

Similar to the Midwestern plains of the United States, there are plains in northwest and eastern Europe. These plains are located in countries like Germany, France, Ireland, Scotland, Ukraine, and Russia. They contain either short or tall grasses and plenty of space for farmland. The plains of northwest Europe have warm summers and cold winters. This is different from a temperate climate. A temperate climate has mild summers and winters. The temperature stays pretty much the same all year round. A temperate climate is ideal for growing crops like wheat, rye, and barley. Many people who live in the European plains work as farmers and raise livestock. Others live near the farms in towns and work in factories or mines. Many of the European plains are also next to major rivers like the Rhine in Germany and the Oder in Poland. These rivers make it easy for trading goods between regions, but long periods of rain may cause rivers to overflow, which leads to flooding. While flooding can be a problem, it can also keep the plains fertile.

WRITE

What are the advantages and disadvantages of settlements in the plains?

....
....
....
....
....
....
....
....
....
....

REVIEW

In this lesson, you learned that:

· Settlements in Europe include mountains, plains, and coasts.

· Many people who live in cooler regions of the Alps grow crops or raise livestock.

· Drier, hotter Alpine regions are popular for harvesting fruits and vegetables and growing grapes for wine.

· Many people who live on European plains work as farmers or industrial workers or miners.

· Coastal cities are often seaports and are popular due to easy access to resources.

· Coastal city climates are generally temperate.

Think About It
How might cultural features influence human settlement patterns in Europe?

1. What regions or cities in Europe can you find human settlements in the mountains, plains, and coasts?

....
....
....

2. Which of the following are features of human settlement in the mountains? Circle all the correct answers.

   A. isolation

   B. nutrient-rich soil

   C. extreme weather

   D. chalets

3. How does the climate in the European plains influence human settlement? Circle all the correct answers.

   A. It prevents people from getting jobs as industrial workers in nearby towns.

   B. It limits the type of crops that can be grown, such as rye.

   C. It allows certain crops to grow year round, such as wheat, rye, and barley.

   D. It allows people to trade goods through rivers from different regions.

Pretend you are getting ready to take a trip to one of the types of settlements in Europe. Create a survival guide handbook of the items that you think you will need to take with you. Why did you choose these items?

4. Which of the following is NOT a way that the climate in European coastal cities has influenced the way people live?

   A. Climate causes extreme weather, which has led to the development of stilt homes.

   B. Climate has led to the creation of seaports, which are important for the trading of materials, such as cars.

   C. Climate has created more jobs for people as industrial workers, such as coal miners.

   D. Climate has allowed people to create permanent residences.

   E. Climate has led people to have easy access to food and water.

Physical Geography and Natural Resources of Europe

By the end of this lesson, you will be able to:

- identify features of the physical geography of Europe
- analyze the influence of people's relationship to natural resources and its effects on the development of various European civilizations

Lesson Review

If you need to review European settlements, please go to the lesson titled "Human Settlement in Europe."

Academic Vocabulary

Read the following vocabulary words and definitions. Look through the lesson. Can you find each vocabulary word? Underline the vocabulary word in your lesson. Write the page number of where you found each word in the blanks.

- **peninsula:** a piece of land surrounded by water on three sides (page _____)
- **physical geography:** the study of Earth's surface such as continents, oceans, and mountains, often using maps (page _____)

ONLINE CONNECTION

Physical Geography
Think about the physical geography, such as mountains, oceans, and rivers, of the town or city that you live in. Research the names, heights, depths, and lengths of these geographic features and study your area's climate. Then compare these findings with the physical geography of Europe. How do the geographical features in your hometown differ from those in Europe? Share your findings by creating a poster.

Did you know that Europe is the second-largest continent in the world after Asia? It is a continent of several geographic features, including oceans, seas, peninsulas, and mountains. The study of these geographic features is known as **physical geography**, and scientists often study them by using maps. For example, we can use a physical map to find and outline the boundaries of Europe. These include the Atlantic Ocean to the west, the Ural Mountains in Russia to the east, the Arctic Ocean to the north, and the Mediterranean Sea to the south.

READ

Mountains

THE ALPS

You have already learned about different types of human settlements in Europe and how they are influenced by the environment. The Alps, which make up the highest mountain range in Europe, stretch 750 miles (1,207 kilometers) from France in the west to Slovenia in the east. The highest peak is Mont Blanc in France, which has a height of 15,776 feet (4,809 meters). The Alps' climate varies by location and elevation. Alpine regions typically have a temperate climate, which features cool to warm summers and mild winters. Temperate climates allow for the growth of crops such as olives, citrus fruit, figs, apricots, and grapes. Other regions in the Alps, such as the Mediterranean Sea, have subtropical climates, which feature hot, dry summers and cool, wet winters. Higher elevations like Mont Blanc are typically covered in snow and ice.

To the right is a physical map of the European Alps. Trace the regions of Europe where the Alps cross with a colored pen or highlighter.

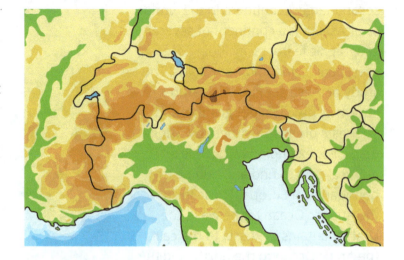

THE CARPATHIANS

The Carpathians are the second-longest mountain range in Europe and sit next to the Alps. They stretch in an arc about 900 miles (1,448 kilometers) west to east, from the Czech Republic to Romania. The Carpathians provide habitats for the largest European populations of brown bears, wolves, chamois, and lynxes. They also provide one-third of all European plant species. Like the Alps, the Carpathians have a temperate climate. The highest peak is Gerlachovský Štít at 8,711 feet (2,655 meters).

Mont Blanc in the Alps (France)

WRITE

What are the differences between temperate and subtropical climates?

....

....

....

READ

Oceans, Seas, and Rivers

Europe is a **peninsula**, which is a piece of land surrounded by water on three sides. Europe is bordered by the Arctic Ocean to the north, the Atlantic Ocean to the west, and the Mediterranean, Black, and Caspian Seas to the south. Oceans and seas influence Europe's climate variety of climates. Most of Europe has a temperate climate, which features cool to warm summers and mild winters. This is due to the Gulf Stream that originates in the warm Gulf of Mexico. As the Gulf Stream crosses the Atlantic Ocean into Europe, it brings warm air currents. Northern European countries such as Russia, Finland, and Sweden have a continental climate, which features warm to cool summers and very cold winters. There are also five major rivers in Europe: the Danube, the Volga, the Loire, the Rhine, and the Elbe, which have all been important in trade. For example, the Rhine River in Germany has been described as a superhighway of the ancient Roman Empire as it was used to trade with nearby countries including Austria, Germany, Switzerland, France, and the Netherlands. Many rivers and mild temperatures also allow for growth of crops like wheat, rye, barley, potatoes, and corn, which are all important natural resources in Europe.

Mediterranean Sea (Croatia)

Rhine River (Germany)

WRITE

What oceans and seas define the borders of Europe?

....

....

....

....

....

Natural Resources and Early Civilizations

CELTIC PERIOD

At the beginning of the Iron Age, the ancient Celts from central Asia began making advanced iron weapons, along with drinking cups, plows, and battle helmets. One of the most important iron uses was in making chariots, which helped the Celts defeat the Neolithic peoples. Chariots expanded the Celtic civilization from central Europe to Ireland and Scotland in the northwest. The Celts also created steel from heating iron and carbon, a process known as smelting. Steel was typically used to make stronger swords. Celtic warriors used steel swords during battles with larger civilizations like ancient Rome.

ROMAN PERIOD

Ancient Romans were known for their impressive architecture and use of natural resources such as travertine, granite, and marble. Travertine is a type of limestone formed by mineral deposits from natural springs and is often used as a building material. The Romans mined travertine deposits for building temples, aqueducts, monuments, bath complexes, and amphitheaters such as the Colosseum. The Romans also extracted marble and granite from Alpine quarries. Marble was used to create statues and make shiny, hard floors in temples that could last a long time. Granite was used to create paving stones and temple columns, for buildings such as the Pantheon. Romans also made iron clamps that held stones together on bridges. These natural resources made the Romans one of the most powerful and long-lasting civilizations of ancient times.

WRITE What were the influences of natural resources on the Celtic and Roman civilizations?

....
....
....
....

In this lesson, you learned:

- Mountains, oceans, seas, and rivers are major features of physical geography in Europe.

- The Alps form the highest mountain range in Europe.

- The Alps cross eight countries, including Switzerland, Monaco, Italy, Liechtenstein, Austria, Germany, France, and Slovenia. The highest peak is Mont Blanc in France at 15,776 feet.

- Europe is bordered by the Arctic and Atlantic Oceans and the Mediterranean, Black, and Caspian Seas.

- Most of Europe has a temperate climate, with cool to warm summers and mild winters.

Think About It

What other land or water features make up the physical geography of Europe?

SHOW WHAT YOU KNOW

1. Which of the following are features of the Alps? Circle all the correct answers.

   A. temperate climate

   B. provides habitats for the largest European populations of brown bears

   C. continental climate

   D. stretch from France to Slovenia

   E. stretch from Czech Republic to Romania

2. The Carpathians have a _____ climate, which features mild summers and winters.

3. Which bodies of water define the boundaries of Europe? Circle all the correct answers.

   A. Caspian Sea

   B. Atlantic Ocean

   C. Black Sea

   D. Balkan Sea

   E. Arctic Ocean

   F. Mediterranean Sea

4. Which of the following was NOT an influence of iron in the development of the Celtic civilization?

   A. Iron was used to make weapons.

   B. Iron was used to make clothing.

   C. Iron was used to make plows.

   D. Iron was used to make drinking cups.

ONLINE CONNECTION

The Iron Age

Using an online search engine, research famous iron objects in different regions of the world, such as ancient China or Africa, during the Iron Age. Then compare your findings with famous iron objects created by early European civilizations, such as the Celts and Romans, during the Iron Age. Record your findings by creating a compare-and-contrast table.

5. Which of the following natural resources is NOT correctly matched with how they were used in ancient Rome?

   A. iron—money

   B. travertine—Colosseum and temples

   C. granite—roads

   D. marble—statues and temple floors

Humans' Environmental Impacts in Europe (Part 1)

By the end of this lesson, you will be able to:

- identify ways that people in Europe have made changes to their environment
- identify examples of how people in Europe responded to changes in the environment
- describe the effects of land use conversion from forests to farmland and the depletion of Britain's forests due to World War I

Academic Vocabulary

Read the following vocabulary words and definitions. Look through the lesson. Can you find each vocabulary word? Underline the vocabulary word in your lesson. Write the page number of where you found each word in the blanks.

- **acid rain:** rain, snow, or hail mixed with air pollutants, typically smog (page ____)
- **deforestation:** the cutting down of large groups of trees or forests (page ____)
- **reforestation:** the act of renewing forest growth by planting seeds or young trees (page ____)
- **smog:** a type of air pollutant caused by the combination of smoke and fog (page ____)

Environmental changes may be beneficial, such as planting more trees to increase oxygen levels, or harmful, such as cutting down trees and destroying animal habitats. Think about one beneficial and one harmful way that people have made changes to the environment in your community. How have people responded to these changes? Discuss your answers with your instructor.

Have you ever seen large amounts of algae on the surface of rivers or lakes? Perhaps you have seen these green or red slimy growths known as algal blooms, in photos or in person. Many algal blooms are a consequence of human activity. The waters they grow on are filled with nitrogen, which is washed away from farmland, and can harm the environment, including plants and fish. Take a look at these images of human activities that have impacted the environment. What are some rules and regulations that people can implement to protect the environment? Write down your ideas on the lines below.

Algal Bloom in Rivers

Deforestation

Plastic Pollution

READ

Air and Water Pollution

Have you been to a city and felt a thick, heavy atmosphere? If so, you may have observed air pollution. In Europe, air pollution has been a problem since the Industrial Revolution of the 18th century. It is caused by toxic gases like nitrogen dioxide and carbon monoxide released from factories and vehicle exhaust. Carbon dioxide is released from burned fossil fuels. **Smog**, or toxic gases mixed with fog, can remain in the air for weeks. Nitrogen dioxide can harm vegetation. **Acid rain**, or toxic gases mixed with rain, can fall in lakes and rivers, killing fish such as brown trout and Atlantic salmon. These gases can also contribute to temperature increase, or global warming. Today, the United Kingdom, Germany, France, Italy, and Spain have the highest levels of nitrogen dioxide as they have large populations relying on vehicles or working in factories.

Water pollution is also a big problem. About 60 percent of Europe's waters are polluted with nitrates, which are used in fertilization and formed when nitrogen is not fully used by crops. These then get into soil and surface water. High amounts of nitrates are toxic to aquatic life because they reduce the water's oxygen. Nitrates can also pollute the groundwater that people drink. Because nitrates are tasteless, they are often ingested without notice and are harmful to people's health.

Air pollution (smog) in London.

WRITE

What kinds of human activities have caused air and water pollution? Describe how pollution has affected the environment.

....

....

....

....

Environmental Laws

People have created many laws to reduce air pollution and improve air quality. The Clean Air Package, created in 2013 by European countries, limits the amount of toxic gases, such as nitrogen dioxide and carbon monoxide, released into the air from factories. It also limits the amount of fossil fuels that are burned and promotes safer energy alternatives such as solar energy, or energy from the sun, to power cars and homes. Laws have also been created to reduce water pollution. In 1992 the Nitrates Directive was used to identify rivers, lakes, and streams with large amounts of nitrates. This law also limits the amount of nitrogen that can be used by farmers to fertilize crops. While both laws have reduced air and water pollution, pollution remains a problem due to a growing population.

World War I and the Environment

Wars not only have an impact on people. Wars can also have a major impact on the environment. During World War I (1914–1918), many forests' trees were cut down and used as timber to build houses, forts, shelters, and tunnels. Timber was also used as firewood. Trees were also cut down to create farmland where soldiers created military camps and grew crops. The overcutting of large groups of trees, or **deforestation**, was harmful to the environment. It destroyed animal habitats and killed several forest plants and vegetation. Deforestation in England was especially severe. By the end of World War I, only three percent of Britain's forests remained. Many soldiers also hunted animals, like bison, moose, and deer, for food. This decreased the number of animals in the environment. After World War I, people passed laws to protect European forests by promoting **reforestation** and made the cutting down of trees illegal in some areas. In England, reforestation efforts increased Britain's forests between 10 and 12 percent in 2010.

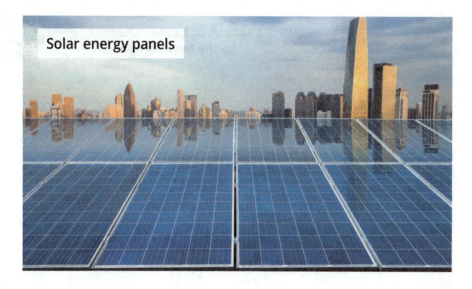
Solar energy panels

WRITE

How did the Clean Air Package and Nitrates Directive affect the environment?

....

....

....

How did World War I impact European forests?

....

....

....

Use the information from the lesson to fill in the table below about humans' environmental impacts in Europe.

Environmental Features	Features of Human Changes to the Environment	Features of Human Responses to the Environment
Air Pollution		
Water Pollution		
Forests (during World War I)		

REVIEW

In this lesson, you learned:

- Air and water pollution are due to human activity. Air pollution is caused by toxic gases released from factories and vehicle exhaust, and fossil fuels.

- Smog can remain in the air for weeks, and acid rain can harm the environment by killing fish.

- About 60 percent of Europe's waterways are polluted with chemicals. High nitrates are toxic to aquatic life and can pollute the groundwater.

- During World War I, many trees were cut for timber. Deforestation so devastated European forests that only three percent remained after World War I.

Think About It
How have people made and responded to environmental changes in different regions of the world?

SHOW **WHAT** **YOU** **KNOW**

Match the pollutants to their effects on the environment.

1. _____ nitrogen dioxide

2. _____ nitrates

3. _____ carbon monoxide

A. remove oxygen from surface water

B. creates acid rain

C. creates smog and acid rain

4. Fill in the blank: The environmental law known as _____
was created by European countries to limit the amount of toxic gases released into
the air from factories and create safer energy alternatives.

Circle all correct answers.

5. What types of human activity can lead to air pollution?

A. the burning of fossil fuels

B. the release of toxic gases
from factories

C. the heating of foods and liquids

D. the release of carbon monoxide
from vehicle exhaust

6. Why was the Nitrates Directive used?

A. to identify rivers, lakes, and
streams with large amounts
of nitrates

B. to control the amount of nitrogen
released into the air to prevent
global warming

C. to limit the amount of nitrogen
that can be used to fertilize crops

D. to limit the amount of carbon
monoxide that can get into crops

ONLINE CONNECTION

Using an online search engine, pull up images of different European cities that are known for having clear air, such as Zurich in Switzerland, Tallin in Estonia, Uppsala in Sweden, Trondheim in Norway, Edinburgh in Scotland, and Funchal in Portugal. Research why these cities have the lowest amounts of air pollution in Europe and if there are any rules or regulations that have been created to promote good air quality. Share your findings by creating a poster.

7. What were some of the environmental effects caused by deforestation in World War I?

....

....

....

....

Humans' Environmental Impacts in Europe (Part 2)

By the end of this lesson, you will be able to:

- identify the physical processes that contribute to the availability and abundance of a natural resource
- compare and contrast the availability and distribution of natural resources in Europe across regions

Lesson Review

If you need to review humans' environmental impacts in Europe, please go to the lesson titled "Humans' Environmental Impacts in Europe (Part 1)."

Academic Vocabulary

Read the following vocabulary words and definitions. Look through the lesson. Can you find each vocabulary word? Underline the vocabulary word in your lesson. Write the page number of where you found each word in the blanks.

- **abundance:** a large amount of something (page _____)
- **aquaculture:** the farming of fish, crustaceans, and aquatic plants in controlled environments (page _____)
- **availability:** able to be used or possible to get (page _____)
- **mining:** the process of digging underground to retrieve valuable resources (page _____)

IN THE REAL WORLD

Using an online search engine, choose a region in Europe and investigate the natural resources that are present, including their availability and abundance. The availability of natural resources means that they are able to be used or are possible to get. The abundance refers to something existing in large amounts. Compare and contrast these natural resources with the ones in your region or community. How available and abundant are they? Discuss your findings with your instructor.

Have you ever wondered about the natural resources in Europe? Europe is the second-largest continent in the world and features major natural resources such as timber, water, fish, coal, natural gas, oil, and gold. Take a look at these images of some of the natural resources in Europe. How do you think they can be used by people in society, including in your own life? Write your ideas on the lines below.

Iron Ore

Timber

Water

READ

Mining and Drilling

Did you know that gold, chromium, copper, lead, silver, zinc, iron ore, and coal are mined in Europe? **Mining** is the process of digging underground to retrieve valuable resources. Mining and drilling are used in construction and the production of steel, medicines, fertilizers, and vehicles. Sweden produces 92 percent of Europe's iron ore. Gold is also available and abundant in Europe. Russia produces 83 percent of the gold used by several European countries. **Availability** and **abundance** of natural resources have also influenced Europe's trade with other major countries. However, frequent mining of iron ore can release toxic substances in the environment, such as carbon monoxide and heavy metals. These can cause air and water pollution.

Oil and natural gas are important natural resources for energy and fuel. Some of the largest natural gas deposits in Europe are found in Russia, Norway, and the United Kingdom. Because oil is frequently distributed to countries around Europe, Europe has to rely on oil imported from regions like the Middle East. Much of Europe's natural gas is produced in Russia, the world's largest natural gas exporter. While widely used for electricity and heat, natural gas creates some problems. It releases carbon dioxide into the air, which can pollute the environment. Also, since Europe's supply is primarily in Russia, it is not always easy to access. To increase availability for distribution, Europe imports natural gas from the Middle East.

Coal Mining

WRITE

How do mining and drilling influence the availability and abundance of natural resources in Europe?

....

....

....

Discover! SOCIAL STUDIES • GRADE 5 • LESSON 38

READ

Aquaculture

Europe is surrounded by many oceans and seas that provide easy access to large amounts of fish. If you've seen large fish tanks on a farm, then you probably know that fish, which are an important natural resource in Europe, can be farmed! The farming of fish, crustaceans, and aquatic plants in controlled environments is known as **aquaculture**. Farmers typically use aquaculture to raise fish such as bluefin tuna and rainbow trout. These wild fish are captured from the Mediterranean and Adriatic Seas and then bred on farms. This saves farmers time and money, and increases fish availability for distribution. The more fish are raised in aquaculture, the more they are distributed to other countries, such as Spain, Portugal, Sweden, Norway, Finland, Italy, Greece, and Iceland, where people consume large amounts of fish. This also creates demand, and has led to the increase of aquaculture. However, the availability and frequent distribution of fish in Europe is an issue. Due to overfishing, it is estimated that bluefin tuna may become extinct in the Mediterranean by 2050.

Bluefish Tuna

WRITE

How does aquaculture influence the availability and distribution of fish across Europe?

....

....

....

....

....

....

....

....

Fish Farm Aquaculture

PRACTICE

Using your knowledge of the natural resources in Europe, complete the bubble diagram shown below.

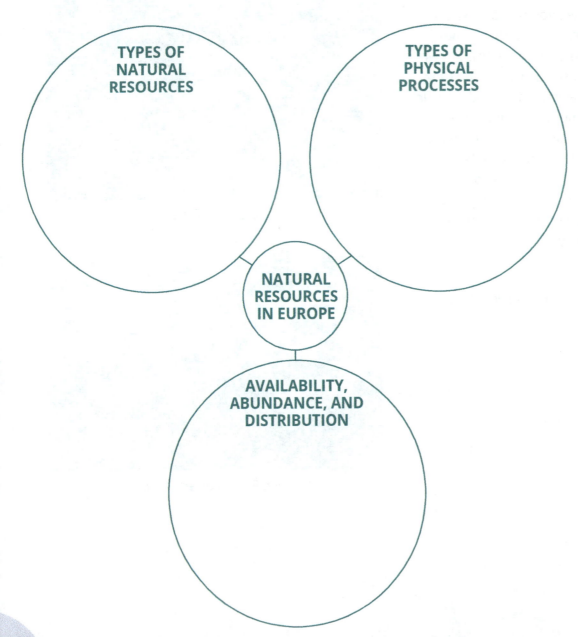

TYPES OF NATURAL RESOURCES

TYPES OF PHYSICAL PROCESSES

NATURAL RESOURCES IN EUROPE

AVAILABILITY, ABUNDANCE, AND DISTRIBUTION

REVIEW

In this lesson, you learned:

- Iron ore, gold, natural gas, and fish are important natural resources of Europe.

- Mined minerals are used in construction and the production of many goods.

- Some of the largest oil deposits in Europe are found in Russia, Norway, and the United Kingdom. Oil use releases carbon dioxide into the atmosphere and can cause pollution.

- Aquaculture is the farming of aquatic life in controlled environments.

Think About It

When people overuse natural resources, it can cause pollution or loss of fish from the sea. How can Europe prevent these problems from happening?

SHOW WHAT YOU KNOW

1. Which of the following countries in Europe have large amounts of iron ore?

   A. Sweden

   B. Russia

   C. The Netherlands

   D. Bulgaria

   E. Poland

2. Which of the following countries in Europe does not have large amounts of natural gas? Circle all correct answers.

   A. Russia

   B. Belgium

   C. The United Kingdom

   D. Norway

   E. The Netherlands

3. How do the availability and distribution of fish affect different regions in Europe? Circle all correct answers.

   A. They provide food for people.

   B. They have influenced the development of aquaculture.

   C. They have led to overfishing.

   D. They have created competition among European countries for fish supply.

TAKE A CLOSER LOOK

Using an online search engine, research a major or minor natural resource in Europe. Investigate its unique features, availability, abundance, and distribution in Europe and around the world. Share your findings by creating a poster.

4. Describe the physical processes of mining and drilling. How do they contribute to the availability and abundance of natural resources in Europe?

....

....

....

....

....

....

....

....

....

....

....

Lesson 39

Europe's Relationship with Natural Resources

By the end of this lesson, you will be able to:

- identify key natural resources found in Europe
- describe how the use, distribution, and importance of natural resources can affect different groups
- identify the impact of trade on the availability of natural resources

Lesson Review

If you need to review how physical processes impact the availability of natural resources in different parts of Europe, please go to the lesson titled "Physical Processes and Natural Resources in Europe."

Academic Vocabulary

Read the following vocabulary words and definitions. Look through the lesson. Can you find each vocabulary word? Underline the vocabulary word in your lesson. Write the page number of where you found each word in the blanks.

- **agricultural resources:** the land, soil, plants, and animals needed to grow crops and raise livestock (page _____)
- **demand:** the amount of people who want to buy a good or service (page _____)
- **export:** a good that is sold and sent to other countries (page _____)
- **fossil fuel:** a nonrenewable resource made from decomposed plants and animals; these fuels are burned for energy (page _____)
- **labor:** manual workers; physical work (page _____)
- **migrant workers:** temporary workers who move from place to place where labor is needed (page _____)
- **mineral deposits:** large quantities of a particular mineral (page _____)
- **service-based economy:** an economy in which the majority of wealth is accumulated through service jobs (page _____)

TAKE A CLOSER LOOK

In Europe, there is growing demand for tropical fruits and soybeans. These products are not native to the continent, but customers enjoy them. How do natural resources grown in other parts of the world find themselves on the shelves of European markets year-round? How do you think these agricultural products get to Europe? Discuss your ideas with your instructor.

- **surplus:** an abundance or excess (page _____)
- **trade:** the action of exchanging something for something else buying and selling of goods and services (page _____)

EXPLORE

Windmills in the Netherlands have been used for more than 1,000 years to harness an important natural resource—wind! The first windmills were used to pump water away from canals to help farms and villages avoid floods. Today many wind turbines convert wind energy into electricity. These turbines harness power created when wind turns the turbines' sails.

Europe's strong economy still depends on natural resources found in the air, on land, and at sea. These resources provide energy, food, water, and materials that communities need to thrive. But Europe has had to change where it finds its resources and how it uses its resources.

Do you think countries must think differently or creatively about how they use their natural resources? Why do you think this? Discuss your answers with your instructor.

Germany has embraced the need for alternative energy sources and produces more energy from wind than any other European country.

A windmill in the Netherlands

Wind turbines

Important Resources in Europe

Europe has a temperate climate and fertile soil, which means it has a lot of agricultural resources. **Agricultural resources** are the land, soil, plants, and animals needed to grow crops and raise livestock. France is a leading producer of agriculture, growing wheat and grapes and raising livestock such as sheep and cattle for meat and cheese. There is demand for French wines from grapes and cheeses from cows' and sheeps' milk all around the world. **Demand** means many people want to buy the goods. High demand encourages farmers to produce a **surplus**, or an excess. French agricultural products then become **exports**, which means they are traded to other nations. **Traded** means sold and shipped. The Netherlands is a small country with one of the world's largest surpluses of agricultural resources. The Netherlands exports tomatoes, apples, pears, wheat, and potatoes.

Even with the high demand, fewer people work as farmworkers in these countries. Technology allows robots to care for and harvest crops. Europe's economy has become more service-based. **Service-based economies** have many citizens who earn an income providing services instead of goods. Services provided in service-based economies include finance, tourism, education, and technology.

Fewer farmworkers lead farmers to rely on migrant workers to care for and harvest crops. **Migrant workers** are people who help harvest crops in a region and then move to another region where a different crop is ready for harvest. High-paying jobs are more difficult to find in eastern European countries like Ukraine, Romania, and Bulgaria. People from these regions relocate to western Europe to work on farms.

Automation and Robotics in Agriculture

Using technology to do work previously done by people, Europe can increase the amount of food it grows and support a population moving away from rural areas and into urban areas. Drones help monitor crops, and robot systems plant sprouts.

Robot system preparing seedlings

WRITE

How do migrant workers affect the natural resources in western Europe?

READ

Minerals and Energy

Europe's mineral deposits and fossil fuels are important natural resources. **Mineral deposits** are large amounts of particular minerals used to make goods like metal or medicine. **Fossil fuels** are natural resources made of decomposed plant and animal matter that create energy when burned. Several European countries mine for various mineral deposits and drill for natural gas, a fossil fuel used to heat homes and generate electricity.

Norway and Sweden mine iron ore, which is used to make steel. The iron ore deposits in Europe provide some of the steel necessary to make cars in factories throughout Europe. Iron is also imported from other countries like Australia and Brazil, where **labor**, or a human workforce, is less expensive.

Norway, England, and the Netherlands drill for natural gas. Russia is the largest producer and exporter of natural gas. Part of Russia is in Asia, not Europe. Most of Russia's natural gas is located in Asia. Many European countries depend on Russia for energy resources.

While Europe's natural resources are plentiful, the majority of its population lives in urban centers throughout the continent. While several countries mine for mineral deposits and drill for natural gas, much of Europe depends on trade with other nations to provide enough of these resources to satisfy the need from industries and citizens.

WRITE

What must many European countries rely on to ensure natural resources such as metal and fossil fuels are available?

....

....

....

....

....

Energy Debate

Solar energy panels in Wales, UK

Russia exports large quantities of petroleum, the fossil fuel used to power vehicles, to other European countries. Norway and England also produce significant quantities of petroleum. While this resource is incredibly valuable, the burning of this fossil fuel causes pollution. The cost to most nations of importing this resource is also significant. Many countries such as Germany and England have begun investing in alternative forms of energy. Do you think countries should begin using alternative forms of energy? Discuss your thinking with your instructor.

PRACTICE

What important natural resource is found in each of the numbered countries?

1. Russia _____

2. Norway and Sweden _____

3. Germany _____

4. France _____

5. The United Kingdom / Great Britain _____

6. Explain how trade helps keep resources available for populations in Europe.

....

....

....

REVIEW

In this lesson, you learned:

- Agricultural products such as wheat, wine, and cheese are important resources in Europe.

- Europe depends on migrant workers from eastern Europe to provide labor for farms as western European populations move to cities.

- Mineral deposits, petroleum, and natural gas are also key resources.

- Europe must import metals needed for manufacturing cars and fossil fuels needed to power vehicles.

- Some countries in Europe are trying to produce alternative forms of energy to limit dependence on countries such as Russia for fossil fuels.

- Trade with other nations allows Europe to sell a surplus of its natural resources and buy imports to make sure products in demand are available.

Think About It

Advancements in technology are making it easier to farm and use alternative forms of energy. How do you think this will change the use of natural resources in Europe in the future? How might this affect Europe's economy and trade with other nations? Discuss your thinking with your instructor.

SHOW WHAT YOU KNOW

Fill in the blank using a word from the Word Bank.

Word Bank: Agricultural resources   Iron ore

1. _____, such as grapes, wheat, and cheese are important natural resources in France.

2. _____ is an important natural resource in Norway and Sweden. This resource provides the material needed to build cars and machinery.

Circle the correct answer.

3. Which group of people moved to western Europe temporarily to work on farms?

   A. computer engineers

   B. teachers

   C. migrant workers

   D. mine workers

4. How does Europe get most of the iron ore it needs for manufacturing cars and machinery?

   A. trade with other nations

   B. mines in France

   C. mines in Portugal

   D. Europe's surplus of iron ore

IN THE REAL WORLD

Spain, Denmark, England, and France take advantage of the natural resources swimming in the ocean waters that border their countries. The fish that swim in the Atlantic Ocean and Mediterranean Sea are caught and sold throughout Europe and to other countries as well. Overfishing these waters affects the ocean ecosystem, and some fish species, such as the bluefin tuna, are nearing extinction.

How should those working with this natural resource react to these environmental issues? Should fishing seek to meet the demand when it can harm wild species? Write your answer on the lines below.

....

....

....

....

....

....

Lesson 40

Migration in Europe

By the end of this lesson, you will be able to:

- explain how cultural attitudes, political unrest, economic downturns, and natural disasters influence the behavior of people in a region
- differentiate between voluntary and involuntary human migration
- identify the factors that led to the migration of people from one region in Europe to another
- describe the influences and contributions of the migrants to the new region

Lesson Review

If you need to review human settlement patterns, please go to the lesson titled "Human Settlement in Europe."

Academic Vocabulary

Read the following vocabulary words and definitions. Look through the lesson. Can you find each vocabulary word? Underline the vocabulary word in your lesson. Write the page number of where you found each word in the blanks.

- **democratic:** a type of government where representatives are elected by the people (page ____)
- **free-market economies:** economies not controlled by their government, but based on the public's supply of and demand for goods (page ____)
- **inflation:** when goods and services are more expensive than their actual value (page ____)
- **innovations:** new ideas, inventions, or advancements (page ____)
- **involuntary:** forced, not done freely (page ____)
- **labor:** manual workers; physical work (page ____)
- **migration:** the movement of people, either for a short time or permanently, from one place to another (page ____)

ONLINE CONNECTION

While not the official flag of the European Union, the Flag of Europe often represents Europe as a whole. Make a prediction. What do you think this flag represents or symbolizes? Now conduct research online. What is the meaning behind this flag?

- **nationalism:** the support of a country at the expense of others (page ____)
- **nation states:** countries with their own government, language, and traditions (page ____)
- **natural disasters:** naturally occurring events causing damage and death (page ____)
- **persecution:** mistreatment of populations due to their language, religion, and culture (page ____)
- **political unrest:** conflict within the government or about the government (page ____)
- **recession:** a decline in economic activity such as trade (page ____)
- **refugees:** migrants fleeing involuntarily (page ____)
- **voluntary:** not forced; done freely (page ____)

EXPLORE

The European Union has 27 member nations. This union allows these countries to trade freely with one another. It also allows **migration**, or movement of citizens from country to country. These 27 countries work or act together when entering into trade agreements or treaties with other nations around the world. They share a currency, or common system of money. The euro is used throughout the European Union to pay for goods and services.

The United Kingdom, made up of England, Wales, Scotland, and Northern Ireland, left the European Union in 2020. Citizens of this nation were divided. Many wanted to remain part of the union. Forming new agreements for trade and migration has been challenging for the United Kingdom.

Why do you think some countries have chosen to remain independent rather than join the union? Why do you think some countries have not been permitted or allowed to join the union? Discuss your ideas with your instructor.

The continent of Europe is composed of nation states, or countries with their own government, language, and traditions. Italy is an example of a nation state. Most Italian citizens speak Italian and take pride in Italian food and history. With a common language, government, and history, the populations of nation states have identities strongly tied to their countries.

Changes in Europe

Unfortunately, strong ties to one's nation can lead people to embrace **nationalism**, or the support of a country at the expense of others. Nationalistic movements throughout the centuries have often resulted in conflicts between countries. After the chaos and destruction of World War II, western European countries began to search for new ways to cooperate and avoid new wars. This spirit of cooperation first created the European Economic Community (EEC) to strengthen economic ties between countries. More countries joined, until finally the European Union (EU) was formed. The EU requires that each member nation share certain basic rules and laws, as well as the euro for currency. In turn, each nation can depend on help from all the other members of the union. While the idea of cooperation is a good one, anything as large, diverse, and complicated as the EU is bound to face problems.

As the European Union began its cooperative effort, several eastern European countries, once a part of the Soviet Union, declared their independence. They struggled to develop democratic forms of government and embrace free-market economies. These are requirements to join the European Union. **Democratic** governments have representatives elected by the people. **Free-market economies** are not controlled by their government, but based on the public's supply of and demand for goods. Many of these countries have made these transitions and joined the European Union in recent years.

Ukraine's Struggles

The country of Ukraine declared its independence from Russia in 1991 but still struggles to maintain its independence and provide free elections for the people. Portions of the population feel strong connections to Russia and desire a reunification with the country. Others seek democracy and entry into the European Union. This political unrest is a sign of continued instability in Ukraine that has led to demonstrations and violence. Many Ukrainian citizens choose to leave their country and migrate to other countries across Europe.

WRITE How has Europe changed since the formation of the European Union?

....

....

....

READ

Voluntary and Involuntary Migration

Voluntary migration to a new country may happen for education or work opportunities. **Voluntary** means a person or people choose to make a decision freely. Some migration is involuntary. **Involuntary** means people do not have a choice. They move for survival. **Political unrest** can lead to involuntary migration, as people fear for their lives during violence.

Recently, the eastern European countries of Bosnia, Croatia, Macedonia, Montenegro, Serbia, and Slovenia have endured war. These nations were previously one nation called Yugoslavia. The **persecution**, or mistreatment, of populations due to their language, religion, and culture within this region resulted in violence. Migrants fleeing involuntarily are called **refugees**. Refugees seek shelter in safer nations within Europe and beyond.

Some refugees flee destruction from **natural disasters**, naturally occurring events that cause damage and death. Earthquakes, flooding, drought, and famine are natural disasters that can cause migration.

Migrant populations move for many different reasons, but they all have an impact on their new communities. They bring a workforce, or **labor**, to fields such as farming and manufacturing. They share **innovations**, or new ideas, languages, and cultures.

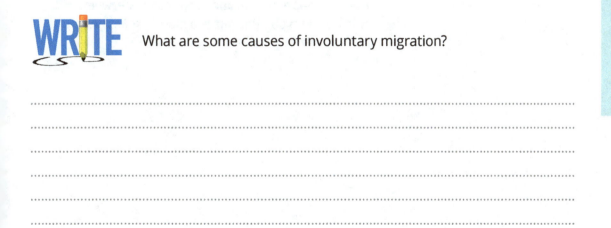

WRITE

What are some causes of involuntary migration?

....

....

....

....

....

TAKE A CLOSER LOOK

What Is a Recession?
In 2008 a recession, or a decline in economic activity such as trade, affected countries worldwide. Eastern European countries such as Poland, Romania, and Bulgaria saw many young people migrate to western Europe, which was not as severely affected by the recession.

In a recession, goods and services can become more expensive. This is called inflation. When goods and services are more expensive, employers may not be able to afford as many workers or pay their workers higher wages. Populations may struggle to earn the money needed to pay for housing and food.

PRACTICE

Why do populations decide to migrate? Write at least three causes of migration.

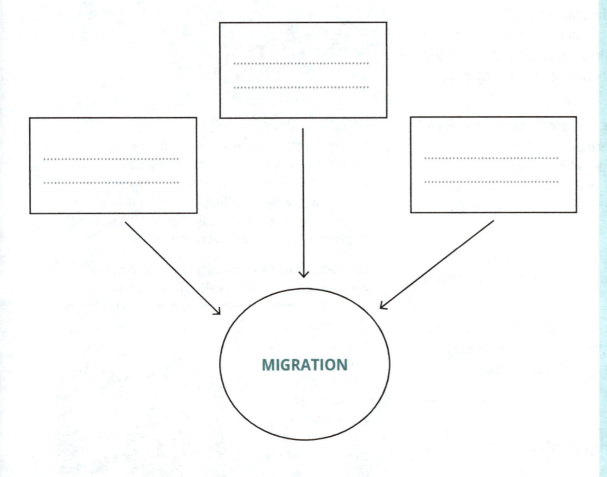

REVIEW

In this lesson, you learned:

- Changes in cultural attitudes led to the formation of the European Union.

- The cooperation between nations of the European Union has influenced trade and migration on the continent.

- Recessions are periods of economic struggle that can affect the availability of resources and jobs.

- Individuals voluntarily migrate to take advantage of educational and job opportunities.

- Populations in eastern Europe have migrated involuntarily to escape political unrest and economic struggles.

Think About It

How can appreciation and cooperation between cultures help populations prosper? Discuss your thinking with your instructor.

Why do populations migrate during periods of recession?

Circle True or False for each sentence.

1. True or False   Europe's nations want to take land from each other, so they formed the European Union.

2. True or False   During natural disasters or political unrest, populations migrate involuntarily to survive.

3. True or False   Innovations have led the citizens of Ukraine to migrate to other nations.

Answer the following question in complete sentences.

4. How do migrants contribute to their new communities?

....

....

....

....

....

....

....

....

CREATE

Europe is the second smallest continent but is composed of 44 nations! Dozens of languages are spoken across the continent. Today, nations of the European Union encourage citizens to learn multiple languages, not only the official language of their country but also languages spoken in other nations.

Create a list of all the ways people say *hello* in Europe. Conduct research online and write the name of each language you find along with the word used to greet someone. How many greetings can you collect?

Cultural Features and Europe

By the end of this lesson, you will be able to:

- identify the location of key cultural features and relate their significance
- relate how cultural features in a region influence population, the economy, government, and transportation

Lesson Review

If you need to review cultural influences of migrants, please go to the lesson titled "Migration in Europe."

Academic Vocabulary

Read the following vocabulary words and definitions. Look through the lesson. Can you find each vocabulary word? Underline the vocabulary word in your lesson. Write the page number of where you found each word in the blanks.

- **architecture:** design and building (page ____)
- **colonialism:** settling and taking control of other lands (page ____)
- **cultural features:** unique traditions or aspects of a culture, such as language, religion, and dress (page ____)
- **democracy:** a government that allows the people to vote and elect their representatives (page ____)
- **independent:** under its own control (page ____)
- **religion:** belief in a power, God, or gods (page ____)
- **revolution:** an overthrow of the government (page ____)
- **tourist:** a person who is visiting or traveling to a place for enjoyment (page ____)
- **transportation:** the way something or someone moves from place to place (page____)

CREATE

Make a cultural museum focused on your family! Look around your home and select items that show what life is like in your family. What do you like to eat and what language do you speak? Do you practice a particular religion or belong to a certain political party? Perhaps there is a sports team your whole family likes to cheer for. All of these traditions are part of your family culture! Lead a family member or friend through your museum when it is complete.

EXPLORE

In Europe, many people speak multiple languages and travel to different countries nearby. This is part of European culture. To help populations move and travel, the Channel Tunnel, or Chunnel, was built in 1994. This tunnel runs underground, across the Strait of Dover, the water between the United Kingdom and France. Migrants and **tourists**, or people who are visiting or traveling to a place for enjoyment, can drive or take a train from the mainland of Europe to England using this tunnel. Europe's culture has influenced transportation in this way. Because populations wanted to travel easily between France and England, the Channel Tunnel was constructed.

Cultural features can affect the people, economy, government, and transportation in a region. How do you think a desire to travel and visit other countries affects Europe's economy? Discuss your thinking with your instructor.

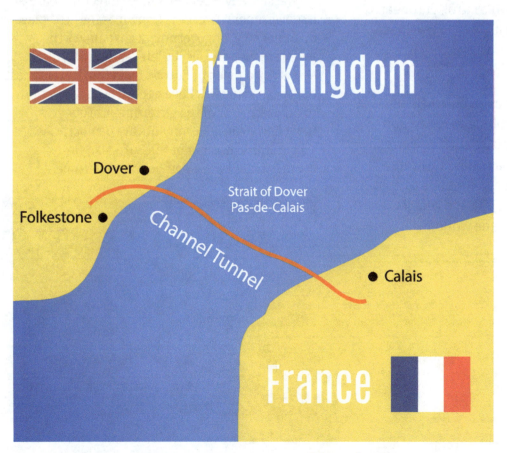

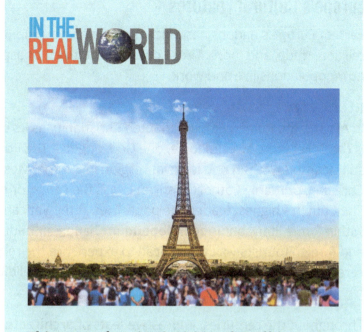

IN THE REAL WORLD

This group of tourists is visiting the Eiffel Tower in Paris, France. Travelers spend money on tours, food, hotels, and more. Making it easy for tourists to visit is good for France's economy.

Europe's Cultural Features

Each of Europe's nations has a rich history of government, art, architecture, language, religion, trade, and more. These **cultural features**, or aspects of a culture, influence how populations live and work.

RELIGION

In AD 313, the Roman Empire adopted Christianity as its official religion. A **religion** is the belief in a powerful force, one God, or gods. The Roman Empire's influence is still clear today when one looks at religion in Europe. Most of Europe's population is Christian, primarily Catholic. Vatican City is the center or capital of the Catholic Church. The Church's highest leader, the pope, lives at the Vatican. This unique city is located within Rome, Italy, but is an **independent** nation, or under its own control. Europeans and foreign tourists visit the Vatican to experience the religious city, attend religious ceremonies, or view artwork found in the historical buildings.

ARCHITECTURE

Throughout the centuries, impressive feats of **architecture**, or design and building, have taken place throughout Europe. Many of these structures still stand today, and the importance of Christianity is apparent in many of them. Churches such as Notre Dame in Paris, France, and Saint Paul's Cathedral in London, England, demonstrate the importance of religious life in the past. These historical buildings continue to hold great importance for Europe's populations today, as they are repaired and kept in operation for the local population as well as tourists from around the world.

How has religion influenced life in Europe?

....

....

....

Government

The Parthenon in Athens, Greece, was completed in 432 BC and is part of the Acropolis of Athens, Greece. The Parthenon illustrates ancient Greece's impressive advancements in architecture and also in government. Greece is known as the birthplace of democracy, or government that allows the people to vote and elect their representatives. Kings ruled much of Europe for centuries, but most European countries have experienced revolutions, or an overthrow of the government. Today most European governments are democracies. To become a member of the European Union, a country must have a democratic government.

Changing Cultural Features

Europe was the home of famous artists such as Monet, Picasso, Van Gogh, and Leonardo da Vinci Europe protects its art heritage in many museums, such as the Louvre in France, the Picasso Museum in Spain, and the Uffizi Gallery in Italy.

Many European countries, including France, Spain, and England, have histories of **colonialism**, or settling and taking control of other lands. As colonies were formed, valuable artifacts were taken and displayed in Europe. Many museums still display African art taken during colonization. Today a debate about ownership surrounds many pieces of art, and some are being returned to the country they came from.

Many historic European streets are paved with cobblestones. Cobblestone roads are made of small, flat, smooth stones. These cobblestones can be hundreds of years old and demonstrate the value placed on history in Europe. Much like historical buildings, maintaining cobblestone roads is costly and inefficient. The stones are easily damaged by cars and difficult to replace. Some historic streets are being replaced with asphalt roads to accommodate traffic.

Transportation

Cobblestone roads remind Europeans and tourists of a time when primary modes of transportation were walking and using horse-drawn carriages. Today in busy cities such as Paris and London, modes of public transportation such as subways, trains, and buses help people move from place to place. Outside of major cities, most people travel by car. A dependence upon the automobile has helped fuel European economies. One of the most important industries in Europe today is the automobile industry.

WRITE How are some cultural features changing in Europe?

....

....

....

....

....

PRACTICE

Describe each cultural feature and how it affects the way people live in Europe.

CULTURAL FEATURE	DESCRIPTION AND INFLUENCE IN EUROPE
Christianity	
Democracy	
Art	
Architecture	
Channel Tunnel	
Cobblestone Roads	

SHOW WHAT YOU KNOW

Circle the correct answer for each question.

1. European travel and tourism led to the building of _____.

   A. the Acropolis

   B. the Channel Tunnel

   C. Vatican City

   D. the Parthenon

2. Most European populations feel _____.

   A. people should be able to vote for their representatives in government

   B. a king should be in power

   C. government should be controlled by one person

   D. governments should not be democracies

3. What is the most common religion in Europe?

   A. Hinduism

   B. Islam

   C. Christianity

   D. Judaism

4. How can you tell that art is highly valued in European countries?

   ....

   ....

   ....

   ....

CREATE

The cuisine, or food, commonly eaten in a region is also a cultural feature. Italy is known for its pasta, France is known for its cheese, and Germany is known for its sausages. Tourists visit these countries in part to experience their cuisines. These famous foods are important to the local population, as many recipes have been handed down from generation to generation. Traditional foods also keep economies strong, as these products are in high demand locally and abroad.

What food is part of your culture? Create a family recipe book of your traditional foods.

Lesson 42

Cultural Geography and Europe

By the end of this lesson, you will be able to:

- investigate the cultural geography of Europe
- explore broader influences of European culture on individuals and civilizations around the world
- discover the lasting impact of European culture on everyday aspects of life

Lesson Review

If you need to review the culture of Europe, please go to the lesson titled "Cultural Features and Europe."

Academic Vocabulary

Read the following vocabulary words and definitions. Look through the lesson. Can you find each vocabulary word? Underline the vocabulary word in your lesson. Write the page number of where you found each word in the blanks.

- **adapt:** to change one's way of life (page ____)
- **architecture:** the artistic or scientific way of building (page ____)
- **cuisine:** food (page ____)
- **cultural geography:** the study of human connection to natural resources, the economy, religion, government, and many other ways that humans interact with their world (page ____)
- **dikes:** areas of raised land (page ____)
- **immigrants:** people who leave one country to settle permanently in another country (page ____)
- **myth:** a story of a person, event, or thing that is unable to be proven as true (page ____)
- **natural resources:** any useful substance that can be found in nature (page ____)
- **population:** a particular section, group, or type of people or animals living in an area or country (page ____)

TAKE A CLOSER LOOK

Europe is the second smallest of the world's seven continents. But even though it is small, it has the third-highest population! Population is a particular section, group, or type of people or animals living in an area or country. Many countries make up Europe. Can you guess how many? Europe has 51 countries!

- **symbol:** images or objects that represent something else (page ____)

Discover! SOCIAL STUDIES • GRADE 5 • LESSON 42

EXPLORE

How many of Europe's countries have you heard of? Maybe you live in Europe, or you have looked up the countries that make up Europe. Is there one you recognize? How about Spain, France, Italy, or Germany?

Though Europe is made up of many countries, there are some things that bring unity. For example, football, sometimes called soccer, was first played in Europe in the 12th century.

Football is one of the many ways that Europe influenced many parts of the world! The immigrants brought this sport to the United States in the late 1800s. **Immigrants** are people who leave one country to settle permanently in another country.

Food, or **cuisine**, is another way that Europe influenced many parts of the world! The bagel is a bread that originated in the 16th century with the Jewish communities of Poland. The bagel is now very popular in North America. Dry pasta, such as the kind used to make spaghetti, originated in Sicily, Italy, in the 12th century.

This picture shows the Madrid and Barcelona soccer teams during a match in Madrid, Spain, on July 12, 1912.

IN THE REAL WORLD

The architecture in Europe is amazing. Europeans influenced architecture, which is the artistic or scientific way of building. Many cathedrals, castles, and other buildings were both artistic and dramatic. Ancient architecture shows that both beauty and functionality were combined to serve many purposes.

The Parthenon on the Acropolis, Athens, Greece

The Eiffel Tower, Paris, France

READ

Europe's Cultural Geography

You have already learned about Europe's geographical features. **Cultural geography** is the study of an area's geographical features and how they relate to the cultures that develop there. Europe's populations used the available **natural resources**, which are any useful substance that can be found in nature. Europeans **adapted**, or changed their way of life, to meet challenges like climate and natural disasters. As populations learned how to interact with their environments, traditional practices helped people survive and became culture.

In ancient Greece, people used the ocean's resources to survive. Ancient Greece's religion inspired stories called myths and many writings, such as the *Iliad* and the *Odyssey* by Homer. A **myth** is a story of a person, event, or thing that is unable to be proven as true. Many ancient Greek myths explained the dangers of the sea and became popular with fishermen and merchants. Poseidon, the god of the sea, helped provide explanations for storms.

In the Netherlands, the sea often flooded the low land. People solved this problem by building **dikes**, or areas of raised land, to prevent flooding. They used windmills, first invented in Asia, to harness wind power. The windmills pumped water away from crops and homes. Windmills became a symbol of the Dutch culture. **Symbols** are images or objects that represent something else. When Dutch people migrated, they brought windmills to other countries. This technology is still used today to convert wind power into energy.

Did You Know?
Ancient Athens had beautiful architecture, statues, and paintings that can still be seen today. Athens is known for its famous artists, writers, and sculptors. Many immigrated to to Athens because of their strong focus on education for boys and men. This led to many mathematicians and astronomers who taught us about the planets, geometry, and physics!

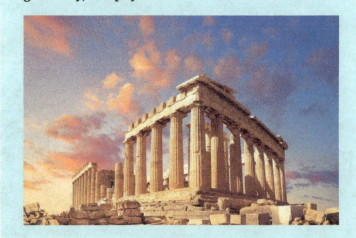

READ

Europe's Influence

Europe impacted most areas of the world, perhaps most notably during the exploration and colonization of the Americas. Christopher Columbus was a European who has perhaps the most recognizable name in the discovery of the Americas. It was his discovery that paved the way for eventual colonization and trade with the Native Americans. The Native Americans would inevitably trade for firearms, livestock, and metals. These goods changed how the Native Americans hunted and interacted with their world.

European influence can be seen in many other areas too. Without the influence of the Europeans we would not read and write from left to right, which could affect the way we communicate! Science would not have the scientific process, which is a process where scientists investigate and verify facts. Technology was also influenced by Europeans. They influenced the invention of eyeglasses and gunpowder.

Perhaps most notable is the way Europe influenced art! There were many famous artists and paintings that were created. Do you remember seeing the *Mona Lisa*, painted by Leonardo da Vinci? He was not only an artist, but he also had many notes on scientific inventions. Paintings from Europe not only preserved history in the art, but they also became a way to emphasize emotions. Without it, we would not understand each other's cultures.

WRITE

What is one specific way that the world has benefited from the cultural geography of Europe?

....

....

....

....

ONLINE CONNECTION

Use your favorite search engine and read about all the famous explorers who came from Europe. You can start by reading about a period of time called the Age of Discovery or the Age of Exploration in Europe.

PRACTICE

Make a chart using the topics provided and identify how the world would be different without European influence.

CATEGORY	WITHOUT EUROPE'S INFLUENCE
Architecture	
Arts	
Communication	
Culinary	
Science	
Technology	

SHOW WHAT YOU KNOW

Circle all the correct answers for each question.

1. In what ways has Europe had cultural influences on civilizations around the world?

  A. Europe influenced China with tea.

  B. Europe influenced the Native Americans with guns and metal.

  C. Europe made the airplane.

  D. Europe influenced science, as in the instance of eyeglasses.

2. In what areas did Europe influence the world?

  A. communication

  B. science

  C. technology

  D. cuisine

  E. sports

  F. architecture

  G. art

3. True or False   Europe's populations used natural resources, which are materials supplied by nature.

PLAY.

European inventors have created so many things! Do a scavenger hunt to find things invented in Europe.

- a hole punch, invented by Friedrich Soennecken from Germany
- a mop, invented by Mauel Jalón from Spain
- a digital calculator, invented by Leonardo Torres y Quevedo from Spain
- a hot-air balloon, invented by Jean-François Pilâtre de Rozier from France
- a motorcycle, invented by Gottlieb Daimler from Germany

Match the correct term with the correct definition.

4. _____ the number of people who live in a specific area, town, or country

5. _____ to change one's way of life

6. _____ a story of a person, event, or thing that is unable to be proven as true

7. _____ images or objects that represent something else

8. _____ areas of raised land

9. _____ materials that are supplied by nature

10. _____ people who leave one country to settle permanently in another country

11. _____ the study of human connection to natural resources, the economy, religion, government, and many other ways that humans interact with their world

12. _____ food

13. _____ the artistic or scientific way of building

A. adapt

B. dikes

C. cuisine

D. architecture

E. cultural geography

F. population

G. symbol

H. myths

I. natural resources

J. immigrants

14. What is cultural geography?

....

....

....

....

....

Chapter 4 Review

By the end of this lesson, you will:

- review the information from the lessons in Chapter 4, "Europe."

Lesson Review

Throughout the chapter, we have learned the following big ideas:

- Different maps of Europe can tell us different stories about the continent. (Lesson 33)
- Europe has many geographic features throughout. (Lesson 34)
- Human settlement had patterns in Europe. (Lesson 35)
- There is different physical geography and natural resources throughout Europe. (Lesson 36)
- Humans have had an impact on the environment in Europe. (Lesson 37)
- There are different physical processes in Europe, and they impact the natural resources. (Lesson 38)
- Europe has a relationship with the natural resources on the continent. (Lesson 39)
- There were different migration patterns caused by different factors in Europe. (Lesson 40)
- There are many cultural features of Europe. (Lesson 41)
- Cultural geography in Europe has influenced the rest of the world in many ways. (Lesson 42)

Go back and review the lessons as needed while you complete the activities.

IN THE REAL WORLD

You have learned so much about the continent of Europe. Imagine what our world would be like without this important continent. Imagine if our world did not have the incredible culture that we have thanks to Europeans. Imagine not having inventions like the telescope or eyeglasses without the presence of people who came from Europe. What do you feel are the reasons that make Europe such a significant place in the world? Discuss your thoughts with your instructor.

REVIEW

Maps of Europe

You learned that geopolitical, topographic, and tourist maps each tell a different story about the continent of Europe. Geopolitical maps change a lot over time. Think about how different maps of Europe today are different from previous geopolitical maps of Europe in the 1800s. Remember, a topographic map shows the elevation and shape of Earth's surface. Topographic maps do not change nearly as often as geopolitical maps do.

You also learned about major cities throughout Europe, such as Moscow, Paris, and London. You explored different geographic factors found all across the continent of Europe that influence where people live. Some geographic factors you read about were channels, canals, marshes, plains, foothills, and plateaus. You learned about geographic connections between continents, including large bodies of water like the Mediterranean Sea and canals.

Geopolitical Map of Europe

Topographic Map of Europe

TAKE A CLOSER LOOK

Human settlements were different in different regions throughout Europe. The environment influenced the settlements. It may seem like human settlements near mountains would be difficult, but the geographic feature of mountains found throughout Europe was an advantage for humans because it provided protection from invaders and rich soil for agriculture.

WRITE

Explain when you would use a geopolitical map, a topographic map, and a tourist map.

....
....
....
....
....
....
....
....

REVIEW

Europe's Physical Geography

Europe's physical geography is diverse, with vast mountains, plains, glaciers, and ocean coasts. Europe's many natural resources include natural gas, fish, water, and timber. Trade has helped make natural resources available to countries that lacked them in Europe. Europe's natural resources have affected the development of various European civilizations. Britain's forests were depleted by the war efforts during World War I and due to converting forests to farmland. People in Europe work in innovative ways to reduce negative environmental impacts through hydropower and geothermal power.

Physical processes, such as volcanic eruptions, glaciation, erosion, and plate tectonic movement, contribute to the availability and abundance of natural resources. While physical processes such as volcanic eruptions can seem like they would have only negative impacts, they help increase the availability of natural resources by improving soil quality.

Human migration can be voluntary or involuntary, and the Protestant Reformation played a key role in migration throughout Europe. Migration is not always involuntary. Some people choose willingly to migrate. This is voluntary migration. There were also other reasons that caused Europeans to migrate, such as cultural attitudes, political unrest, economic downturns, and natural disasters.

Migrations and migrants made positive impacts on the areas in Europe to which they moved. They contributed to art, architecture, communications, and science and impacted not only Europe but also the entire world. Migrants made Europe the major destination that it is today, as many travelers go to Europe to experience the vast presence of significant and diverse culture that the continent has to offer. Remember, the Louvre Museum in Paris, France, is the most visited museum in the world.

Europe and Asia are the only continents connected by a huge landmass. In fact, these two continents combined are referred to as Eurasia. Ask your instructor to help you find a picture of this on the internet. Then look at how the two continents are together. See how the two continents are together.

WRITE Describe at least two ways the geography of Europe benefits the European people.

....
....
....
....
....
....
....
....
....
....

PRACTICE

Four's a Crowd

Circle the word that does not belong.	Explain why that word does not belong.
Moscow, Paris, Boston, London	
channels, plains, canals, marshes	
vast mountains, plains, glaciers, vast deserts	
fish, natural gas, oil, minerals	
hydropower, geothermal power, volcanoes, innovative	
art, architecture, communications, landscape	
voluntary, migration, tourists, involuntary	
cultural attitudes, political unrest, economic downturns, natural disasters	

TAKE A CLOSER LOOK

A root word is a base part of a word without a prefix or a suffix. Let's look at some examples of root words used in this chapter.

- **attract:** the root word for attraction
- **geo and graph:** the root words for geographic
- **settle:** the root word for settlement
- **urban:** the root word for urbanization
- **reform:** the root word for reformation
- **threat:** the root word for threatened

When you see a big word you may not know, try to break it down to its root word. Then you can figure out the meaning of the root and the full word.

PRACTICE

Cause and Effect

Cause and effect is the relationship that exists between events or things. Cause is the reason something occurs. Effect is the result of something occurring. In the table below, you are given either a cause or effect. Fill in the missing information to complete the table.

CAUSE	EFFECT
....	Boundaries to countries on a map change.
Timber, an important natural resource in Europe, was used for WWI in the United Kingdom.	....

CAUSE	EFFECT
The physical process of erosion occurs often in Europe.	....
....	By humans settling near this geographic feature, they were offered protection from invaders and rich, fertile soil for growing food.

CAUSE	EFFECT
Some Europeans refused to convert to Catholicism.	....
....	Art, communications, architecture, and transportation improved in Europe.

PRACTICE

Positives and Negatives

In almost every scenario in life, you can find a positive and negative consequence. For each given topic, provide a positive consequence and a negative consequence.

TOPIC: There are many different geographic features in Europe.	
Positives	**Negatives**

TOPIC: Natural resources are being used often by Europeans.	
Positives	**Negatives**

TOPIC: Migration occurred throughout Europe.	
Positives	**Negatives**

REVIEW

Think about what you've learned about in this chapter. Circle how you feel:

4 – I know this chapter really well. I could teach it to someone.

3 – I know this chapter pretty well.

2 – I am still learning this chapter. I am not sure about some things.

1 – I am confused. I have a lot of questions about what I've learned.

Talk to your instructor about your answers. When you're ready, ask your instructor for the Show What You Know activity for the chapter.

Discover! Social Studies

5B

Table of Contents

Chapter 5: North America

Chapter 6: South America

Chapter 7: Oceania

Chapter 5
North America

Bonjour! It's me, Pierre!

While I took Chang to see the sights in Paris, Monsieur Jean was looking for a new home for our friend. In an average year, 90 million tourists come to France. Fait amusant: That is more than any country in the world! There is a lot to see, and I wanted Chang to have the best time ever.

Chang tried to take in all the sights. But I could tell he was sad. It is not easy to be without a home. We all need that security, you know?

Chang and I were sitting at one of the famous cafes on the left bank of the Seine River. Suddenly, Monsieur Jean ran up to the cafe. His hair was all wild. He said, "Chang, did you like Belize? Well, aside from the Jaguar?"

Chang said sadly, "Yes. Too bad those scary felines live there." Monsieur Jean smiled and waved a map in his arms. "Worry not, dear Chang! We can go to the swamps of Florida. The climate is similar to Belize. But there are no Jaguars in North America!"

Chang and I jumped up and hugged Monsieur Jean. We had packed our bags and got our passports before you could say allons-y!

A few hours later, our plane headed into Miami International Airport. Finally, we could see the swamplands from the aircraft. Maybe we had finally found a home for Chang?

As we ran off the plane, I yelled, "Viens avec moi!"

What Will I Learn?

This chapter focuses on North America. It looks at the geographic and cultural aspects unique to the continent.

Lessons at a Glance

Lesson 44

The Stories in Maps of North America

By the end of this lesson, you will be able to:

- identify different types of maps of North America

- determine a story each map tells

- compare and contrast the major cities in North America and the cities in your state or country

Academic Vocabulary

Read the following vocabulary words and definitions. Look through the lesson. Can you find each vocabulary word? Underline the vocabulary word in your lesson. Write the page number of where you found each word in the blanks.

- **geopolitical maps:** maps that show boundaries of countries, states, cities, and counties (page _____)

- **landform:** a natural feature of the surface of the Earth (page _____)

- **topographic maps:** a map that shows the elevation and the shape of Earth's surface (page _____)

Think about your city. What landforms can you see? Mountains? Lakes? In the space below, draw a map of your city only using the landforms. Share your map with your instructor.

EXPLORE

Maps tell us the stories of where we live. They can tell us where there are rolling hills, tall mountains, or even deep oceans. Think about where you live. What could a map of your area look like if it only showed its landforms?

Find a map of your town, state, or country that shows landforms like the one below. If you can't find a map to use, use the map of North America below. What do you notice about the map? What do you wonder? Write two to three sentences answering these questions.

READ

Topography in North America

When we think of maps, we often think of the kind that tells us where a place is. But did you know that a map can tell us so much more than just location? A **topographical map** shows the shape of the land. When we look at this map of the United States, we can see there are many landforms. A **landform** is a natural feature of the Earth. In the United States, we can see the western part of the country is mountainous. You know this because the map in that area is brown and gets darker as the elevation gets higher. Brown indicates a rising elevation, while green indicates a lower elevation. The center of the country is filled with vast plains, stretching from north to south. You know this because of the large green area on the map. This region is often referred to as the Great Plains region.

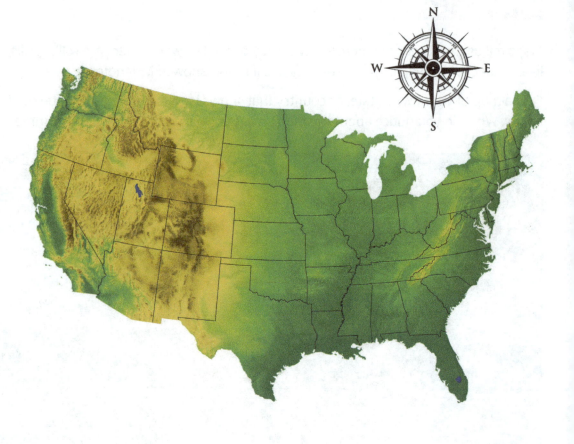

WRITE

What story does this map tell about the United States? Think about what information you can learn from it.

....

....

....

....

....

....

....

....

READ

North American Cities

North America is home to some of the largest cities in the world. Mexico City is the capital of Mexico, the second biggest city in the Americas and the 11th largest city in the world. It has one of the largest city plazas in the world, which contains the Mexico City Metropolitan Cathedral and the Presidential Palace. If you visit Mexico City, you can still see ruins from the Mesoamerican empires, including pyramids.

New York City has more people than any other city in North America. You can visit the Statue of Liberty or see a play on Broadway while visiting New York City. It is also home to the United Nations, an organization of countries that agreed to work together to prevent and end wars.

Also in North America is Toronto, Ontario, Canada. Toronto is the capital of Ontario and is the largest city in Canada. It is home to a diverse population with more than 200 ethnic groups being represented. When you visit Toronto, you could see the CN Tower—the tallest free-standing structure in the Western Hemisphere.

CN Tower, Toronto, Canada

WRITE

Now that you have learned a little about some of the biggest cities in North America, how does your hometown compare? Compare your hometown to one of the cities on this page. Write one way they are alike and one way they are different.

One way they are alike is ....
....

One way they are different is ....
....

Zocala Square in Mexico City

READ

Geopolitical Maps

Using a geopolitical map allows you to access the history of an area. A **geopolitical map** defines the size of a country by its political power. It shows divisions within an area, such as showing the borders of countries and states. This map shows the countries of North America and divisions within those countries, like states. Borders of countries can be defined not only by physical features like mountains and rivers but also by results of wars or agreements between countries or groups of people.

REVIEW

In this lesson, you learned:

- There are different types of maps of North America, including topographical and geopolitical maps.

- Each type of map can provide us with new and different information about the continent that tells a story.

- There are similarities and differences between cities, such as size, language, and important landmarks.

Think About It
What do you think influences where people live in North America?

WRITE

What story can you tell about North America from looking at the geopolitical map?

....
....
....
....
....
....
....

SHOW WHAT YOU KNOW

Choose the correct answer for each question.

1. What type of map is this?

   A. Topographical Map

   B. Geopolitical Map

   C. City Map

2. What type of map is this?

   A. Topographical Map

   B. Geopolitical Map

   C. City Map

3. What story does the map in question 2 tell you about the western part of the United States?

   ....

   ....

4. What is one way the cities of Toronto and New York City are the same?

   A. They are both located in the United States.

   B. They both have important landmarks like towers and statues.

   C. They both have a presidential palace.

5. What is one way a town or city in your state or country is like one of the cities in North America from this lesson? What is one way that it is different?

   ....

   ....

TAKE A CLOSER LOOK

Country Study

You will have the chance to create a country study for each continent this year. Decide on a North American country of interest to study more closely. You could keep either a digital or paper notebook to save your work.

As you go through the upcoming lessons about North America, you will examine your country and its connection to the subject of the lesson. For this lesson, complete the following activities:

- Find multiple maps of your country. Write about the story you think those maps are telling.

- Create a map for your country. Write the story your map tells about your country.

Lesson 45

Geographic Features of North America

By the end of this lesson, you will be able to:

- analyze geographic factors that influence where people live and how people came to settle North America
- develop spatial understanding of the location of geographic features in North America to those studied in previous chapters
- identify geographic connections between the continents

Academic Vocabulary

Read the following vocabulary words and definitions. Look through the lesson. Can you find each vocabulary word? Underline the vocabulary word in your lesson. Write the page number of where you found each word in the blanks.

- **Indigenous people:** the first people to live in an area (page _____)
- **isthmus:** a narrow strip of land with sea on either side (page _____)

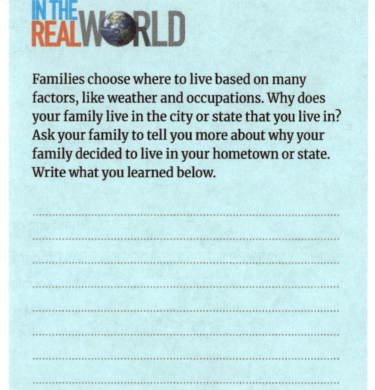

IN THE REAL WORLD

Families choose where to live based on many factors, like weather and occupations. Why does your family live in the city or state that you live in? Ask your family to tell you more about why your family decided to live in your hometown or state. Write what you learned below.

....

....

....

....

....

....

....

....

....

EXPLORE

Imagine you have set sail for a new land that promises hope and freedom. After weeks of difficult travel across the high seas, you catch a glimpse of this new land in the distance. Finally, the end of your journey is near. As you are filled with relief at the thought of touching dry land, you also begin to worry about the challenges that will lie ahead of you. You begin to question the weather, the resources you might have, and what you will do when you arrive. Suddenly, your ship bumps into the dock. You have reached the new land! You disembark with your belongings held tightly to your chest. What will you do now? What will you need to survive and thrive in this new place? Write your ideas on the lines below.

TAKE A CLOSER LOOK

Look at this picture. This family has just arrived in a new land. How would they get food? How should they find a place to live? How should they have planned this move? Talk about your answers with your instructor.

READ

Settling in North America

The **Indigenous people** in North America chose to live in different areas for many reasons, including geographic features like rivers, lakes, and the ocean, as well as forests, prairies, plains, and deserts. These geographic features provided them with food and resources to build their homes.

One geographic feature was a *boreal forest*. A boreal forest is a type of forest in Canada that grows in cold temperatures. Hunters and trappers survived by hunting caribou, reindeer, and other animals that lived there.

Other people settled in the grassland prairies, areas of land with grasses and a few pine trees. These are found in Canada, the United States, and Mexico. The grassland prairies had animals like buffalo to hunt, and they could grow crops like corn, beans, and peppers. They built houses out of the pine or other types of trees there.

The plains and areas near rivers or lakes provided fertile land to grow crops. Depending on the climate, the crops included corn, beans, wheat, squash, and berries.

In the United States and Mexico, the desert provided animals to hunt and vegetables and berries to gather. In the United States, the people built their homes out of stone or adobe. Adobe is a kind of clay. In Mexico, people used volcanic rocks, gold, copper, obsidian, and clay to make weapons and tools. Obsidian is a black and hard rock which is volcanic.

Those who lived near the Pacific or Atlantic Coast found food in the ocean. In the United States, they fished for shellfish, seals, salmon, and whales. In Canada, they built homes out of the red cedar trees that grew there. On the coast in Mexico, they used limestone and volcanic rock for building and to make tools and weapons.

IN THE REAL WORLD

The Strait of Gibraltar separates the Iberian Peninsula in Europe and Morocco in Africa. They are so close that there is only 8.1 miles between the two continents at this point. Ferries travel across the strait taking people quickly from one continent to the other.

Obsidian

READ

Geographic Connections

Some of Earth's continents are connected to one another. For example, Asia and North America are connected. At its narrowest point, Alaska and Russia are just 55 miles apart. They are separated by a body of shallow water known as the Bering Strait. However, a long time ago, the sea level dropped and a land bridge existed connecting the two land masses together. Today, the Bering Strait is a small, narrow and very cold waterway with strong currents that lead to the Bering Sea.

ONLINE CONNECTION

Do you know all of the geographic features in North America? Look online for an online game to play. There are many of them out there. To do that, search by typing in "North America geography online game." Then choose a game and practice.

Discuss with your instructor which geographic features you learned.

Another example of geographic connections to other continents is the Isthmus of Panama. An **isthmus** is a narrow piece of land that connects two large areas that would otherwise be separated by bodies of water. The Isthmus of Panama is a strip of land that separates North and South America. It also acts as a separation between the Caribbean Sea and the Pacific Ocean.

WRITE

What problems and benefits would there be for Alaska and Russia to be so close at the Bering Strait?

....

....

....

....

....

....

PRACTICE

You learned how the continent of North America is connected to both Asia and South America. Think about your studies of other continents. Do you recall the Strait of Gibraltar, the strait that separates Europe from Africa? How does the Strait of Gibraltar compare to the Bering Strait? How are the two similar and different? Use the Venn diagram below to compare the two.

STRAIT OF GIBRALTAR

BOTH

BERING STRAIT

REVIEW

In this lesson, you learned:

- Geographic factors influence where people live and how people came to settle North America.

- Regions of where Indigenous people settled in North America depended on resources.

- There are geographic connections between the continents.

Think About It
How do the geographic features of North America impact where people settle?

1. Which geographic feature connects North to South America?

    A. Ural Mountains

    B. Bering Strait

    C. Isthmus of Panama

    D. Gulf of Mexico

2. People settled in Canada's boreal forests because _____.

    A. they could make ships out of wood

    B. they could make tools out of volcanic rocks

    C. they could hunt and trap animals for food

    D. they could grow crops like squash and beans

3. People settled in the grasslands or prairies because _____.

    A. the land was very fertile

    B. they could make houses out of pine trees

    C. they could grow pineapples and green beans

    D. they could hunt caribou and reindeer for food

4. What geographic feature separates Asia from North America?

    A. the Atlantic Ocean

    B. the Bering Strait

    C. the Isthmus of Panama

    D. the Rocky Mountains

5. People settled near rivers because _____.

    A. there are volcanic rocks

    B. the land is fertile

    C. they can hunt reindeer

    D. salt is available there

6. People settled in Mexico's desert area because _____.

    A. they can hunt and trap bears

    B. they could eat salmon and shellfish

    C. they could grow vegetables and fruits there

    D. there is obsidian there to make weapons

7. People lived near the Pacific or Atlantic Coast because _____.

    A. there is obsidian there to make weapons

    B. they could hunt and trap bears

    C. they could eat salmon and shellfish

    D. they could grow vegetables and fruits there

Human Settlement in North America

By the end of this lesson, you will be able to:

- examine evidence of common patterns and features of human settlements
- compare and contrast human settlements of different regions in North America
- analyze how the environment influenced human settlements

Lesson Review

If you need to review factors that influence where people live, please go to the lesson titled "Geographic Features of North America."

Academic Vocabulary

Read the following vocabulary words and definitions. Look through the lesson. Can you find each vocabulary word? Underline the vocabulary word in your lesson. Write the page number of where you found each word in the blanks.

- **human settlement:** a place where people live (page _____)
- **megalopolis:** a densely populated region that encompasses several large cities (page _____)
- **nomad:** a person who moves from place to place and doesn't settle down for long periods of time (page _____)

CREATE

Human settlements, or communities where people live, come in all different sizes, shapes, and locations. On another piece of paper, draw your own settlement. It could be in a made-up country or on another planet. What places will you include? Grocery stores? Schools? Houses? Be creative! Give your community a name and label parts of your drawing to show and explain the different features to your instructor.

Imagine taking a train ride across America. What do you think you would see along the way? What different types of communities would you find? You may get to see so many different kinds of homes that people live in. They often choose their homes based on where they live and what they like to do.

Look at the homes below.

It's a real-life treehouse! And a home built out of a container!

Imagine you were told you could build any kind of house you wanted. What would you build? Where would you build it? Why do you think people choose to live in different types of homes and in different places?

....
....
....

To the left is another example of a unique home! This one was built on water! This gives a new meaning to the phrase "a house on the water."

READ

Common Patterns in Human Settlements

A **human settlement** is where people live. Before modern transportation, more than 80 percent of people lived in rural areas and had agricultural jobs, or jobs that supported farms. Large cities relied on boats to carry large amounts of goods, so the only big cities were on coasts near the ocean or on large rivers. This pattern existed all over the world until trains, cars and trucks, and airplanes changed everything. Now more than 80 percent of the population of Mexico, the United States, and Canada live in cities. Some of those patterns are settling around a certain industry, in areas with a good climate, near waterways, or near areas with good agriculture.

Where Do People Live?

Some old patterns of settlement are still happening. The three largest cities in the United States are New York, Chicago, and Los Angeles. All of these cities share one important common factor—they are all ports. They are all on large bodies of water, and they are also train and airplane hubs.

Mexico City, the largest human settlement in North America, is nowhere near the ocean or a large river. Why do 12 million people live there? The answer was the same in Aztec days. Mexico City has ample water to drink, a fertile valley to farm, and a pleasant climate.

Toronto, Ontario, Canada, is the capital city of Ontario. This major city of North America is home to over 6.3 million people.

Mexico City, Mexico, is the capital city of Mexico. This major city of North America is home to over 20 million people, and it is the largest city in North America.

Guadalajara, Mexico, is a major city of North America that is home to over 4 million people.

WRITE How do you think your area was settled? What features in your area make you think this?

READ

How Does the Environment Influence Settlements?

What would be important to you when choosing somewhere to live? You probably think of availability of food, seasonal weather, proximity to water sources, and ability to work and live in a community with others. Many years ago, humans lived as nomads. **Nomads** are people who move from place to place and who do not settle down for long periods of time. That means they moved from place to place over seasons and even years. They did this because humans were hunter-gatherers, meaning they would follow herds of animals to hunt for food and supplies. They would also move around as the weather and seasons changed, looking for edible plants and other sources of food.

Climate was an extremely important factor in human settlements because climate impacts agriculture, livestock, and overall well-being. It took some time, but humans began to learn how to cultivate the land by growing crops. And so, with a focus on agriculture and farming, living near the floodplains of rivers became desirable. Many of the first human settlements could be found along these rivers. Rivers allowed for boats to carry goods that could be traded. Trade was a vital part of how human settlements became wealthier and were able to develop.

WRITE

What environmental factors influence where people settle in North America?

....
....
....
....
....
....
....

ONLINE CONNECTION

Using a search engine, look for major cities in North America, such as Mexico City, Los Angeles, Toronto, or Vancouver. How do these major cities compare to that of the **megalopolis**, a densely populated region that encompasses several large cities, that exists between Boston and Washington, DC, in the United States? Use the following questions to help compare these cities:

1. **How** many people live in each city?
2. **What** is the land size of each city?
3. **What** historical buildings are in each city?
4. **What** year was each city established?
5. **What** sources of water are near the city, such as rivers, lakes, or oceans?

PRACTICE

North America is divided into eight regions. Read the chart to find out about each region. Complete the last column as you read. Use online resources for research with your instructor's help.

Region	Location	Characteristics Influencing Human Settlement	Do many people live in this region? What is the main reason?
1. Coastal Range	Along the Pacific Ocean, stretches from California to Canada	Dry in the south and rainy in the north; access to the Pacific for trade, fertile agricultural valleys, timber at higher elevations	
2. Basin and Range	West of the Rocky Mountains, east of the Coastal Ranges	High altitude; very little precipitation; some good grazing; agriculture difficult; mineral resources; some timber; no navigable rivers	
3. Rocky Mountains	West of the Great Plains, east of the Basin and Range	Rugged mountains from Alaska to Mexico; steep terrain, harsh winters, but mild summers; lots of access to rivers and lakes; small-scale agriculture; no navigable rivers	
4. Great Plains	West of the Mississippi Valley, east of the Rocky Mountains	Flatlands, grasslands, great for agriculture but prone to drought, harsh winters in the north and harsh summers in the south; some navigable rivers	
5. Interior Lowlands	West of the Appalachian Mountains	Rolling flatlands, many rivers, grassy hills, great for agriculture	
6. Canadian Shield	Area around the Hudson Bay	Hundreds of lakes carved by glaciers; many hills; harsh winters and short summers; poor agriculture	
7. Appalachian Mountains	From eastern Canada to western Alabama	Low, eroded mountains; difficult terrain; woodlands; access to water; coal resources	
8. Coastal Plain	Along the Atlantic Ocean and Gulf of Mexico	Many harbors; milder climate; easy access to rivers; large-scale agriculture	

REVIEW

In this lesson, you learned:

- Common patterns of human settlement in North America include settling near certain industries like fishing, mining, or farming, areas with good climates, areas good for agriculture, and areas with access to waterways.

- The eight different regions of North America have different features and human settlement patterns.

- Availability of water, climate, ability to grow crops, ability to raise livestock, and ability to trade influenced human settlement in North America.

Think About It

How does the physical geography of a region influence the development of settlements? Discuss your thoughts with your instructor.

Circle the correct answer.

1. Humans would often settle near areas with _____.

   A. rugged mountain ranges

   B. fertile soil for farming and raising livestock

   C. frequent droughts

   D. harsh winters

Please answer in complete sentences.

2. Why were the first human settlements along rivers?

   ....

   ....

   ....

   ....

3. How does the environment impact where humans settle?

   ....

   ....

   ....

   ....

Country Study
Let's continue to learn about the country that you selected to study closer. For this lesson, complete the following activity about your country:

· Find the common settlement regions of your country. What parts of the country do people settle in? What draws them to these regions?

Record your findings in your journal. Add pictures to your journal if you are able.

Lesson 47

Physical Geography of North America

By the end of this lesson, you will be able to:

- describe the physical geography of North America
- analyze the effects of other people's use of natural resources on the development of various Indigenous North American civilizations

Lesson Review

If you need to review where people settled in the past, please go to the lesson titled "Human Settlement in North America."

Academic Vocabulary

Read the following vocabulary words and definitions. Look through the lesson. Can you find each vocabulary word? Underline the vocabulary word in your lesson. Write the page number of where you found each word in the blanks.

- **arid:** dry; lacking water (page ____)
- **basin:** a dip in the Earth's surface (page ____)
- **geyser:** spring that periodically erupts columns of water and steam (page ____)
- **grasshouses:** dwellings made of woven prairie grass that covers a frame of wooden sticks (page ____)
- **reservoir:** a natural or human-made lake (page ____)
- **wattle and daub houses:** houses made of wood and covered with mud (page ____)
- **wigwam:** a tall, cone- or dome-shaped home made of birchbark (page ____)

CREATE

Gather materials from Earth around your home or yard. These can be things like sticks, grass, rocks, and anything else you might find lying on the ground. Examine what you gathered, and design a small model shelter using these materials. What might you use to connect your materials together? For example, mud can be used as glue. How well do you think your home will last over time?

Imagine waking up and stepping outside of your mud home, the sunshine piercing your freshly woken eyes through the tall trees. Your chapped lips remind you that you spilled the last of your fresh water yesterday. You are thirsty. Suddenly, you hear friends yelling in the distance. You had been working with them for days to dig a deep hole that would be used to retain water. You run to join them, hoping that they have seen a sign of water. It worked! All of your hard work has paid off, and there is now fresh water for you and your friends to drink. You run back to grab your bucket and rejoice in quenching your thirst with the refreshing water.

Why would this be something to be happy about? Why is having fresh water important? How is this scenario different from how you get water every day?

....
....
....
....
....

TAKE A CLOSER LOOK

Wells

For the Indigenous people of North America, access to water can be difficult. People and animals need water every day to survive. If water is hard to find in a region of North America, people can dig a well, a deep hole in the ground, to access water.

People still use wells today. If you or someone you know lives outside of a city, you might even know someone who uses well water!

READ

Physical Geography of North America

The Mississippi River flows through 10 states before draining into the Gulf of Mexico. It combines with the Missouri River and the Ohio River to form the longest river in North America.

The Great Lakes are five large lakes located along the border of the United States and Canada. The Great Lakes are named Lake Huron, Lake Ontario, Lake Michigan, Lake Erie, and Lake Superior. You can remember them using the mnemonic device *HOMES*, the first letter of each lake. Each lake has a separate **basin** (a dip in Earth's surface). They form a single connected body of freshwater.

Another geographical feature of North America is the mountainous west. This area stretches from northwest Canada down to Mexico and includes several mountain ranges.

North American Indigenous nations have lived in environments with geographical features and climates as varied as the **arid** (dry and lacking water) desert to the icy tundra. To build a strong civilization, people had to make the most out of the environment they inhabited. This meant working with the environment when building structures, learning to use natural resources in the most effective ways possible, and stewarding those resources so that they continue to be available for the future.

TAKE A CLOSER LOOK

Yellowstone National Park

The United States has 84 million square miles of national parks! These special places are designated for people to enjoy. They also preserve plants, animals, and geographic features for future generations. The world's first national park was Yellowstone National Park, dedicated in 1872. Yellowstone National Park is the home of Old Faithful, a **geyser**, or spring that erupts columns of water and steam.

Physical Geography of Mesoamerica

The Mayans and the Olmec are two of the best-known Indigenous civilizations in Mexico and Central America, the region known as Mesoamerica.

The Mayans were an advanced civilization, with cities joined by well-built roads. They dug underground **reservoirs**, or large lakes, to store fresh water. Mayans also discovered cocoa beans and how to prepare them to produce a bitter, yet delicious chocolate drink. Chocolate became so prized they used it as currency!

The Olmec made the most of their environment by sourcing food from the ocean and building in the mountains for protection. The Olmec crafted goods out of basalt and clay. They created long-distance trade routes, systems of writing and mathematics, and their calendar influenced future cultures. The Olmec are considered the "mother culture" of Mesoamerica.

Some Native American tribal nations took a nomadic hunter-gatherer approach, moving with the seasons to access resources. The Iroquois nation moved their homes through the year to get the most out of seasonal farming. Some tribal nations were stationary, such as the Pueblo, Cherokee, Chickasaw, Comanche, Creek, and Seminole nations.

ONLINE CONNECTION

Native American tribal nations had unique styles of homebuilding to use resources of any environment.

Grasshouses, sometimes called *wickiup*, were tall, conical homes made of woven prairie grass covering a frame of wooden sticks. Grass was also used for bedding, baskets, and mats.

Wattle and daub houses were common in the southeastern United States. They were made of wood and covered with mud, which was also used to make pottery.

Near the Great Lakes, birch bark was used to make **wigwams** (cone- or dome-shaped homes), canoes, baskets, and art.

READ

Impacts of European Settlement

As European exploration and settlement increased across North America, so did the number of people trying to make use of the same resources. Not only were there growing numbers of people using the same sources of water, food, and building materials, but European settlers were claiming lands that had previously been home for Indigenous tribal nations across North America.

Tribal nations that were even semi-nomadic became nomadic full time as they were driven away from the areas they traveled. Stationary tribal nations were forced to relocate or become nomadic. Sometimes these moves would take people away from the natural resources they relied on for survival and prosperity.

European settlers were generally monoculture farmers, meaning they planted one crop in a field at a time. This depletes the soil of nutrients, threatens the diversity of life in the environment, attracts pests, and requires more water. Over time, this can lead to environmental damage that can be long-lasting and even irreparable.

Indigenous tribal nations had to compete with increasing numbers of European settlers for resources, lost access to resources when settlers claimed their lands, and dealt with the consequences of environmental harm caused by the settlers.

REVIEW

In this lesson, you learned:

- The physical geography of North America is very diverse.
- Indigenous people of North America used natural resources such as water, rocks, mud, and grass to build their homes.
- European settlement led to changes in how natural resources and geographical features were used, significantly changing ways of life for Indigenous tribal nations of North America.

Think About It
When people settle in an environment, how do they change that environment?

SHOW WHAT YOU KNOW

Circle the correct answer for each question.

1. True or False   There is only one mountain range in western North America.

2. True or False   The Mississippi River dumps into the Pacific Ocean.

3. True or False   North America has many different types of geographical regions and features.

4. The Mayans created _____ to store freshwater.

Answer in complete sentences.

5. List two ways Indigenous tribal nations of North America used the natural resources of the regions they inhabited.

....

....

....

....

....

....

....

....

....

....

....

....

ONLINE CONNECTION

Perhaps no other American has loved the Mississippi River quite so famously as Mark Twain. He worked for a while as a steamboat captain on the river before finding success as an author. The Mississippi River is a focus of his memoir and an important symbol for freedom in his other works. Read a summary of and quotes from *Life on the Mississippi* to learn Twain's feelings for the river and the geographical changes he noted. Then research current rates of erosion in the Mississippi River Delta Basin in coastal Louisiana and possible solutions.

Lesson 48

Responding to Change: The Mississippi River

By the end of this lesson, you will be able to:

- identify ways people make changes and respond to changes to their environment
- analyze the reasons for the establishment of the Mississippi River and Tributaries Project and describe the Army Corps of Engineers' role in controlling Mississippi River flooding
- identify other ways that people in North America made changes to their environment
- illustrate examples of how they responded to changes in the environment

Lesson Review

If you need to review physical geography, please go to the lesson titled "Physical Geography of North America."

Academic Vocabulary

Read the following vocabulary words and definitions. Look through the lesson. Can you find each vocabulary word? Underline the vocabulary word in your lesson. Write the page number of where you found each word in the blanks.

- **deforestation:** the cutting down of large groups of trees or forests (page _____)
- **floodways:** channels built to take the floodwaters of a river (page _____)
- **infrastructure:** facilities that support modern human life, like water supply, housing, roads, schools, hospitals, bridges, and business and government buildings (page _____)
- **levees:** intentionally built embankments of land meant to prevent the overflow of water (page _____)
- **tributary:** a smaller river that empties into a larger one (page _____)

Every day our world changes! Ask your instructor to help you find photos of your hometown 10 to 20 years ago. These can often be found online or with the help of a local librarian. If you live near a university library, they often have special collections with these materials.

Explore the photos and see how your hometown and its environment has changed since those photos. Select two photos of the past, glue them to a separate piece of paper, and then draw what the areas currently look like. Discuss these changes with your instructor.

EXPLORE

Imagine you are a bird soaring over a large river. Through one eye, you see fish leaping out of the water beside a large steamboat. Through the other eye, you watch the current flow rapidly south. Your wings, becoming tired, settle by your side as you glide on your belly to the surface of the river. As you look ahead at the river, you notice the water is overflowing into the parks and onto the streets nearby. The grassy area you stopped at last time is now covered with water. You perch on the streetlight shown in the photo below and look around.

Looking at the photo, what do you think has happened to the large river in this area? How has it affected the surrounding area?

....

....

....

....

....

CREATE

Pretend you are the bird perched on the streetlight looking down on everything. What would this scene look like from above? What would be the same? What would be different? On another piece of paper, draw a picture of what you might see if you were the bird.

Mississippi River

Flooding is caused when a body of water overflows outside of its boundaries. People might try to prevent flooding, but, sometimes, even the best prevention methods can fail. The Mississippi River is a river that is known to flood.

As you know, the Mississippi River is an important river in North America. It has 250 different tributaries. A **tributary** is a smaller river that empties into a larger one. The Ohio and Missouri rivers are just two of the river's largest tributaries.

When a river floods, it can cover land to either side of the river for miles around. This can result in the loss of homes, farmland, and pastures. It can severely impact the infrastructure of the surrounding people. **Infrastructure** is facilities that support modern human life, like a water supply, housing, roads, schools, hospitals, bridges, businesses, and government buildings. People build **levees**, which are intentionally built embankments of land meant to prevent the overflow of water, to try to protect the infrastructure.

In 1879, Congress created the Mississippi River Commission to work on flood control, navigation, and environmental projects that affect the river. This Commission worked with the Army Corps of Engineers to create levees and dams to control the flood waters of the Mississippi River so they did not damage the surrounding areas. The Army Corps of Engineers is involved in keeping the nation of the United States secure while also reducing risks from natural disasters.

This photo shows flooding in the Mississippi River. The trees you see are normally in a field where plants grow and animals live. How might flood waters affect this environment? Discuss your ideas with your instructor.

The Great Flood of 1927

In the summer of 1926, unusually heavy rains began and continued on for months. The tributaries of the Mississippi River swelled to capacity, and some exceeded it. The flooding became known as the Great Flood and lasted well into 1927. The Mighty Mississippi swelled to 80 miles wide at some points. All of the levees broke, flooding over 26,000 square miles of land. Farmlands were saturated with water. Crops and homes were lost, with some areas seeing flood waters so high that the water reached over the rooftops. The flood destroyed many fruit and nut trees. Over 600,000 people were left homeless, without food, clothing, or work, and 250 people died. The water did not go down from April until August of 1927.

In response to the Great Flood of 1927, the Mississippi River and Tributaries Project was created by the 1928 Flood Control Act. This Act let the Army Corps of Engineers design and construct projects to control the floods of the Mississippi River and its tributaries. These included the world's longest system of levees as well as **floodways** (channels built to take the floodwaters of a river) to change the direction of the excessive flow from the river.

The floodways helped, but the Mississippi River has continued to flood. Thankfully, nothing as catastrophic as the Great Flood has happened since, but continued flooding does prevent new soils from depositing, which is needed to return the land to its previous fertile condition.

PRACTICE

The Great Flood of 1927 was the most destructive in the history of the United States. Put the following events in order using the numbers one through five, with one being the first to occur.

_____ Congress created the Mississippi River Commission to oversee funds for flood control.

_____ The world's longest system of levees was built along with floodways.

_____ The Native Americans warned the Europeans about the flooding of the Mississippi River.

_____ The Great Flood of 1927 occurred caused by heavy rains.

_____ The Mississippi River and Tributaries Project was authorized by the 1928 Flood Control Act.

READ

A Changing World

Levees and floodways have changed the Mississippi River. People often change their environment by building new roads and buildings, or using technology, like high-tech farming or drilling for oil. Sometimes these changes have environmental consequences.

One environmental change that has a far-reaching impact is deforestation—or the cutting down of large groups of trees or forests. **Deforestation** is used to get lumber or to clear land for agriculture or development. Clearing trees destabilizes ecosystems, which can lead to major consequences.

Deforestation increases air pollution and contributes to flooding. Old growth trees absorb more carbon from the atmosphere, and old growth tree roots absorb runoff water more deeply into the soil. Animals like rodents are being driven into areas dense with humans which can also lead to disease.

In Canada's Boreal Forest, the effects of deforestation are obvious. The Boreal Forest hosts many geographical features and is the natural habitat of the caribou. Caribou will not roam near industrially cleared or developed areas. The government monitors reports of deforestation using satellite and aerial imagery to track forest conditions. Almost two million acres of forest have been cleared.

WRITE

Deforestation changes the environment. What are the major impacts of deforestation?

....

....

....

REVIEW

In this lesson, you learned:

- Levees were added to the Mississippi River in an attempt to control flooding and change the outcome of the overflowing river.

- The Mississippi River and Tributaries Project was created to control Mississippi River flooding, and the Army Corps of Engineers controls and operates the levees so that the river flooding can be controlled.

- Deforestation in North America can be caused by agriculture, resource mining, or lumber yards, leading to the removal of animal habitats and animal food sources.

- The Canadian government is monitoring deforestation in its country.

Think About It

What kinds of changes can result when people remove certain resources from the environment?

Circle the correct answer.

1. True or False   People can change their physical environment by building shopping malls.

2. What did the Army Corps of Engineers do to control the flooding on the Mississippi River?

A. adopted a levees only policy

C. built levees and floodways

B. built taller bridges

D. widened the river

3. How does deforestation impact animal life? Select all that apply.

A. It removes animal habitats.

C. It gives them new places to live.

B. It prevents animal movement.

D. It can reduce their food supply.

4. How has the Canadian government responded to deforestation in its country?

A. They have applauded the workers.

B. They have provided additional funding for more industrial buildings to be built.

C. They are monitoring forest conditions via satellite or aerial imagery.

5. Agriculture is one cause of deforestation in Canada. What is another example?

....

....

....

6. Why was the Mississippi River and Tributaries Project established?

....

....

....

ONLINE CONNECTION

Water control requires a delicate balance of preventing catastrophic flooding and considering the whole ecosystem to keep the environment in balance. Sometimes, long term consequences aren't known until many, many years after projects have been implemented. Research the following water control structures and list the pros and cons they provide the region. Then, evaluate if these structures are successful and, if not, what you think should be done to improve them.

- Hoover Dam
- International Niagara Control Works
- Levee System of New Orleans

Physical Processes in North America

By the end of this lesson, you will be able to:

- identify examples of physical processes that contribute to the availability and abundance of a natural resource

- compare and contrast the availability and distribution of natural resources in North America across regions

Lesson Review

If you need to review landforms, please go to the lesson titled "Physical Geography of North America."

Academic Vocabulary

Read the following vocabulary words and definitions. Look through the lesson. Can you find each vocabulary word? Underline the vocabulary word in your lesson. Write the page number of where you found each word in the blanks.

- **coal mining:** the process of taking out coal from the ground (page _____)

- **flora:** native plant life occurring in an area (page _____)

- **physical process:** the natural force that changes Earth's physical features (page _____)

- **plate collision:** when two plates carrying continents collide and the continental crust breaks up and rocks pile up to form mountain ranges (page _____)

- **plate tectonics:** a scientific theory defining the large scale movements of the plates that make up Earth's crust and upper mantle (page _____)

IN THE REAL WORLD

When a volcano erupts, it leaves behind volcanic ash. The people who live near an eruption will often just sweep away the ash, but scientists have discovered that the ash isn't just trash. In fact, it can be used to produce a more environmentally friendly, and stronger, cement.

Cement has many uses in the world. On a separate piece of paper, think of things you have seen made of cement and draw them. Share your drawings with your instructor.

Imagine you are walking with your family, the warm breeze floating across your face as you stop to drink a sip of water. You look out and see a large field of trees, and you tell your family you should walk to it. They agree, and, as you get closer, you realize the trees are full of a whole bunch of apples. You quickly pick one off of the tree and bite into it. It's delicious and oh, so juicy!

Think about a time when you have picked fresh fruits or vegetables. Where did you have to go to find them? How did you prepare to pick them? On the lines below, describe your experience, including the size of the fields, the variety of plants, and the amount of plants in the surrounding area, as well as the taste of the just-picked fresh item. If you haven't gone before, what would you most like to go pick? Why did you pick that? What is special about that fruit or vegetable?

TAKE A CLOSER LOOK

Fruit Trees

Fruit trees live for a long time. The *Prunus* species of the plum, cherry, and peach trees are native to North America, along with some species of grapes. Most of these fruits are not the common ones found in the grocery store, but they are typically used in making jams and jellies.

....

....

....

Physical Processes

Things like fruit trees or volcanic ash are important natural resources that can be found in abundance in some areas of North America. Sometimes, **physical processes**, or natural forces that change Earth's physical features, can cause an area to be more likely to have natural resources.

Hawaii was formed by **plate tectonics**, a scientific theory defining the large-scale movements of the plates that make up Earth's crust and upper mantle, and volcanic activity in the Pacific Ocean. The volcanoes of Hawaii are referred to as gentle volcanoes because the lava flows freely. The fertile soil of Hawaii is made up of lava ash and soft, sandy stone. Because of the tropical climate and fertile soil, the growing season never ends. The growing season results in Hawaii being an excellent producer of sugarcane, pineapples, coffee, macadamia nuts, and exotic flowers. The coffee growing areas exist on all of the Hawaiian Islands with 900 farms on each and a total of 7,800 acres of coffee trees.

Other abundant materials in Hawaii are stone, cement, and sand and gravel, which are key materials for the construction of buildings. The production of cement requires lots of energy and high temperatures, which also creates a lot of bad emissions. Scientists have found that adding lava ash and rock makes harder cement in addition to making the process more environmentally friendly.

TAKE A CLOSER LOOK

Macadamia Nuts

Macadamia nuts were first planted in Hawaii in the 1800s, and they soon became popular. The nuts are grown in conditions unique to Hawaii due to the volcanic soil, tropical temperatures, and rainfall. Hawaii has more than 700 macadamia nut farms and eight processing plants.

Appalachian Mountains

The Appalachians Mountains are one of Earth's oldest mountain ranges. They extend two thousand miles from the Canadian province of Newfoundland all the way to central Alabama in the United States. They were formed years ago as **plate collisions**, which is when two plates carrying continents collide and the continental crust breaks up and rocks pile up to form mountain ranges.

The mountains are considered one of the most beautiful places to see **flora**, native plant life occurring in an area. They are full of thick forests where lumberjacks can cut down trees and use the lumber for furniture, homes, and ships. More than 98 percent of the forestland of the mountains is producing lumber to be used as hardwood nationwide.

In addition to lumber, coal mining is a large resource. **Coal mining** is the process of taking coal out of the ground. Coal is used as fuel to create electricity. Forty percent of the nation's coal is produced in the Appalachian Mountains, with ten major beds of coal producing over ten million tons a year.

ONLINE CONNECTION

Use a search engine to research how a physical process has affected your hometown or state. Type in the name of your area and a physical process. Remember there are many types of physical processes, like tectonic plate movement, erosion, and plate movements. What information did you find? Share this information with your instructor.

PRACTICE

List and describe one similarity and one difference in the types of physical processes that created Hawaii and the Appalachian Mountains.

	SIMILARITIES	DIFFERENCES
Hawaii		
Appalachian Mountains		

Regions in North America

North America can be divided into eight regions, each with its own availability of resources.

REGION	LOCATION	RESOURCES FOUND	AVAILABILITY
Coastal Plains	along the Atlantic Ocean and the Gulf of Mexico	oil, gas	Resources are plentiful but difficult to harvest. It takes large harvesting rigs and an involved process.
Canadian Shield	along the Hudson Bay, extending over eastern, central, and northwestern Canada	nickel, gold, silver, copper, cobalt	Resources are plentiful but difficult to extract. They are in the ground and require mining. This region is eighth in the world for the production of cobalt.
Rocky Mountains	western part of the United States and Canada	gold, silver, copper, lead	Resources are readily available. Nevada mines five percent of the world's production of gold yearly.
Great Plains	central United States	coal, uranium, oil, gas, coalbed, methane	The total amount of natural gas produced is 24.5 trillion cubic feet with reserves estimated at 28 trillion cubic feet.
Coastal Range	mountains along the Pacific coast stretching from California to Canada	coal, copper, oil, gas, rocks, and sediment	This region produces 140,000 tons of copper.
Interior Lowlands	west of the Appalachian mountains and east of the Great Plains	crude oil, coal, natural gas	In Texas, 30 petroleum refineries process 5.8 million barrels of crude oil daily.
Basin and Range	southwestern part of the United States and Mexico	mineral sediments from saltwater evaporation	The El Boleo mine contains 265 metric tons of copper, cobalt, zinc, and manganese, with reserves of up to 70 metric tons.

In this lesson, you learned:

- Plate tectonics created Hawaii, where you can find volcanic ash that makes cement stronger. Plate collisions created the Appalachian Mountains, where you can find lumber for hardwood and coal.

- North America has eight regions, each with their own distribution of resources.

Think About It

What are the key natural resources in North America?

Circle the correct answer.

1. What physical process contributed to the development of resources in the Appalachian Mountains?

   A. volcanic activity

   B. erosion

   C. plate collision

2. What North American region produces five percent of the gold in the world?

   A. Canadian Shield

   B. Basin and Range

   C. Rocky Mountains

3. What is the physical process that led to the development of Hawaii?

   ....

   ....

   ....

   ....

4. Describe how the resources of the Great Plains differ from those found on the Canadian Shield.

   ....

   ....

   ....

   ....

Using an online search engine, research the following about a country of your choosing:

1. What regions is your country divided into?

2. What physical processes have affected your country and led to the availability of natural resources?

Lesson 50

Natural Resources in North America

By the end of this lesson, you will be able to:

- identify key natural resources found in North America
- describe how the use, distribution, and importance of natural resources can affect different groups
- identify the impact of trade on the availability of natural resources

Lesson Review

If you need to review physical processes, please go to the lesson titled "Physical Processes in North America."

Academic Vocabulary

Read the following vocabulary words and definitions. Look through the lesson. Can you find each vocabulary word? Underline the vocabulary word in your lesson. Write the page number of where you found each word in the blanks.

- **corrosion:** the deterioration or breaking down of a metal (page ____)
- **irrigation:** the process of bringing water to places where it does not usually flow (page ____)
- **nonrenewable resources:** resources that cannot be replaced after they are used, like minerals (page ____)
- **oil refineries:** an industrial plant that transforms or refines crude oil (page ____)
- **renewable resources:** resources that can be used and replaced naturally, like trees (page ____)

IN THE REAL WORLD

Water is one of the most precious resources on Earth. It is necessary to sustain life, and only 1.2 percent of Earth's water is drinkable. This resource must be cared for to ensure future generations can enjoy it.

Water is not used only for drinking and bathing. Waterways are used to transport people and goods. Water is also used for recreation, like swimming and water skiing, and to get food through fishing.

How do you use water every day? Could you survive without it? Discuss these questions with your instructor.

Imagine you are digging in your backyard or favorite park. You meant to only dig a small hole, but your shovel slides in and out of the dirt with ease, and you find that your hole is larger than you expected. Pausing for a moment to wipe the sweat off of your brow and stretch your back, you drive your shovel back into the dirt. This time, however, it bounces back, stinging your hands. Bending down, you use your hands to dig and uncover what looks like a rock. What could it be? Write your ideas on the lines below. Share your ideas with your instructor.

....

....

....

TAKE A CLOSER LOOK

There are national parks in the United States where people can mine their own gems!

You can find emeralds at Emerald Hollow Mine in Hiddenite, North Carolina.

You can find sapphires like this one at Cherokee Ruby and Sapphire Mine in Franklin, North Carolina.

You chip away at the shiny part of the rock and bring it inside to clean it. As you clean it, you realize what you have is more than just an ordinary rock. It's a diamond! How did a beautiful diamond, like the ones you've seen in a store, get into the hole you were digging? Did someone lose it? Or is there more in the hole you dug? You grab your shovel to find out!

What would you think in this situation? Share your thoughts with your instructor.

READ

Natural Resources

Natural resources are useful substances found in nature. These include things like light, air, water, plants, animals, and minerals, including diamonds! **Renewable resources** are resources that can be used and replaced naturally, like trees. **Nonrenewable resources** are resources that cannot be replaced after they are used, like minerals. Let's look at natural resources in North America.

The main mineral resources in North America are coal, bauxite (used to make aluminum), iron, copper, and nickel (used to make steel). More precious metals, like gold and silver, are also part of North America's natural resources. In addition to minerals, oil and natural gas are also important natural resources and major energy sources for North America. In the past, the United States was the world's largest oil producer and the third-largest coal producer, with the biggest coal reserves.

North America produces a lot of agriculture, including grains and vegetables. A lot of agricultural areas have good climates and fertile soil for growing crops. Even dry areas have become better for growing because of **irrigation**, which is the process of bringing water to places where it does not usually flow. North America produces most of the world's corn, meat, cotton, soybeans, and wheat.

Look at this potato field on Prince Edward Island in Canada, where over 86,000 acres of potatoes are grown each year and shipped to over 20 countries around the world. Prince Edward Island produces the most potatoes for Canada even though it is the smallest province in the country.

WRITE

What are some reasons that North America is able to produce a lot of the world's food?

....

....

Discover! SOCIAL STUDIES • GRADE 5 • LESSON 50

READ

Using Natural Resources

Some natural resources found and used in North America include coal, nickel, oil, silver, and grains. Coal is a nonrenewable resource used as fuel to generate electric power in the United States. The heat produced by burning coal is used to make high-pressure steam to turn a turbine, which then produces electricity. Nickel is a nonrenewable resource resistant to **corrosion**, the breakdown of metal. It is used to make stainless steel, so you would find nickel in products like faucets, forks and knives, and batteries. Crude oil is a nonrenewable resource that comes from petroleum. Oil is used as a fuel and in many things, like cosmetics, medicine, paint, and plastics. Crude oil is made usable at **oil refineries**, an industrial plant that transforms or refines crude oil. Silver is a nonrenewable resource used for making jewelry and silverware. It is also used to make mirrors as it is the best-known reflector of visible light. Because of its many unique properties, it has more uses than gold. Television screens, microwaves, and even computer keyboards all have some amount of silver in them. Silver is durable and lasts for a long time. A type of grain known as wheat is a renewable resource most commonly used to make flour. People, in turn, use flour to make bread, pasta, cookies, and cakes. Grains can also be found in livestock feed, cooking oils, and some cosmetics.

ONLINE CONNECTION

Agricultural farming is important in North America. Use a search engine to learn more about the types of crops grown in North America. Can you also find where, specifically, these crops are grown? Write three crops and where they are grown on the lines below.

....

....

....

....

....

....

WRITE

How would you define renewable and nonrenewable resources? What are some of their characteristics? Write your answers on the lines below.

....

....

....

....

READ

Distributing Natural Resources

Natural resource availability varies from location to location based on climate and soil quality. For example, pineapples grow best in tropical environments, and they would not grow in northern climates with harsh winters or dry air. Leaf lettuce can get scorched by too much heat and direct sunlight. Without technology like greenhouses, human-made UV lights, and global transportation, people would only have access to resources available in their areas.

Flood control and water management efforts impact people who live near shared waterways. Dams increase droughts and flooding by diverting water away from rivers where it would naturally flow. Deforestation also contributes to drought and flooding by removing old-growth root systems that channel water into the soil. This limits people's access to the resources needed for food, textiles, and construction.

Trade and Natural Resources

Trade makes it possible for people outside of tropical areas to enjoy fruits like pineapples and bananas. But supplying resources to places they do not naturally occur can strain the environment and deplete nonrenewable resources. For example, the Bering Strait in Alaska contains Alaskan King Crabs. If people want to buy King Crab legs, it strains the King Crab population. Fishermen could overfish crabs to have enough to sell. Then fewer crabs reproduce to keep the population going.

REVIEW

In this lesson, you learned:

- Key natural resources in North America are grains and vegetables, coal, nickel, oil, and silver.

- Using and distributing natural resources can affect groups in different ways.

- Trade can put a strain on the availability of a resource. Nonrenewable resources cannot be replaced, and renewable resources can be used to the point of destabilizing their population or ecosystem.

Think About It
What causes people to migrate from one place to another?

Circle the correct answer.

1. Coal is an important natural resource because it can be
   used _____.

   A. to make silverware   **C.** as gasoline

   B. to generate electricity

2. Why would it be more difficult for someone in a cold, dry climate to
   have bananas?

   A. People in cold climates are always allergic to bananas.

   B. Bananas freeze into banana sicles if it's too cold.

   C. Bananas grow in tropical climates.

3. How are resources made available where they do not occur naturally?

   A. trade

   B. wanting them badly enough

   C. all resources are available everywhere

4. What depends on an area's available resources?

   A. energy   **C.** food

   B. tools   **D.** all of the above

5. True or False   Grains are mostly used to make jewelry.

6. True or False   Trade has no impact on renewable resources.

7. True or False   Different natural resources are available in different
   areas. Without advances in technology and
   transportation, people would be limited to the resources
   in their immediate area.

Look up what hardiness zone you live in. Then research which fruits and vegetables grow best in the zone you live in. What are the best times of year to plant these fruits and vegetables? How long do they take to grow? How many plants of each type would you need to plant for your entire family to have enough of each plant for the entire season?

Draw a garden and write a plan for how you would grow the best foods for your zone for your whole family.

8. What are some of the natural resources found in
   North America?

   ....

   ....

   ....

   ....

9. How have humans affected the availability of natural resources?

   ....

   ....

   ....

   ....

Migration in North America

By the end of this lesson, you will be able to:

- describe the factors influencing human migration
- compare and contrast the factors leading to various mass migrations movements in North America
- identify the factors that led to the migration of people from one region in North America
- examine the influences and contributions of the migrants to the new region

Lesson Review

If you need to review the effects of natural resource use, please go to the lesson titled "Natural Resources in North America."

Academic Vocabulary

Read the following vocabulary word and definition. Look through the lesson. Can you find the vocabulary word? Underline the vocabulary word in your lesson. Write the page number of where you found the word in the blank.

- **human migration:** the movement of people from one place in the world to another (page _____)

Have you ever seen birds migrating with the changing seasons? Some birds move as the seasons change to find more temperate climates. They move from north to south in order to escape winter. They fly to a warmer place that has more food sources, then return north before spring in time to lay their eggs.

What birds are common where you live? Research their migratory patterns by checking out books from a library or researching online. Draw a map that shows their patterns of movement and share your work with your instructor.

In North America, people who spend the winter in warmer southern climates are called *snowbirds*!

EXPLORE

"Let's go," Mom says. "Do we have to?" I ask. Mom puts her arm around my shoulder, embracing me for a moment. "Yes, it's time." It would be a long journey: a car trip, an airplane, and a train, but the move across the country was necessary. Dad's job received notice a few months ago that we would be relocating three thousand miles away from the only place I'd ever called home. My emotions were mixed, but I was excited to live somewhere new, for my dad's new opportunity, and new opportunities of my own.. You see, my favorite thing to do at home was to grow sunflowers and sell the seeds to construction workers nearby. Now we were moving somewhere warmer, with more sunshine. Would I be able to have my business in my new hometown?

IN THE REAL WORLD

When people move somewhere new, their experiences are unique. To gain access to what it's like to arrive in a new place, sometimes it helps to read about other people's stories, either in fictional accounts or in true stories.

Check out your local library to see if you can find examples of stories where someone had to move to a new place. Librarians have terrific recommendations if you don't know where to look!

Moving for a job is one reason people might move. What are other reasons people might move? List two below.

....

....

READ

Human Migration

Human migration is the movement of people from one place to another. People migrate for many different reasons. Sometimes these reasons are economic, meaning they are moving to find work or to look for a new type of work. Sometimes these reasons are social, meaning they are moving somewhere for a better quality of life or to be closer to family and friends. Sometimes they are moving because of environmental reasons. There might be natural disasters like floods or hurricanes that have destroyed where they once lived. Some people may also choose to migrate for political reasons, to escape a war, or because they are being treated unfairly for their religious beliefs.

PRACTICE

Factors of Migration

Complete the chart below to describe each type of human migration in your own words.

Type of Migration	Description
economic migration	
social migration	
environmental migration	
political migration	

The Bracero Program

People from all around the world began migrating to what is now the United States over 400 years ago. Some people moved upon hearing of the promise of better land and resources.

In late 1942, Mexico and the United States signed a treaty. Many young men from America had been sent off to fight in World War II, leading to a shortage of US workers. The treaty established the Bracero Program, which asked Mexican workers to come work in the United States. Under this program, Mexican workers entered the United States temporarily. Most workers worked in agriculture and farming, with a few working on railroads or in other industries. Between 1942 and 1964, approximately 4.6 million Mexican workers came to the United States to work through this program.

In the 1980s, the president of the United States instituted a Hispanic Heritage Month. The most notable contribution has been the influence of the Spanish language. Today, Spanish is spoken in 41 million homes in the United States. It is the second most studied language in schools, surpassing French.

A Bracero worker

Picking belt (4188901958).jpg by OSU Special Collections & Archives is in the public domain

The Great Migration

From 1915 through the 1920s, many African Americans fled the South and moved North looking for better jobs and better lives. This time was called the Great Migration. Despite being free, African Americans in the South were subject to Jim Crow laws, which limited freedom and opportunities for African Americans and separated them from white people. African Americans faced violent attacks from certain groups of people, making their homes unsafe.

African Americans who migrated to the North brought new influences. Blues music was a type of music that spoke of longing for a better life, but it also celebrated finding joy and success. African Americans living in Harlem in New York City brought about the Harlem Renaissance, a period in which a talented and determined group of writers and other artists used music to express pride in being African American.

Louis Armstrong is a notable musician from the early 1900s.

READ

The Gold Rush

In 1848, gold was discovered in California by a man named James Marshall. He told his friend, and the two tried to keep it a secret. However, word soon spread and people from around the world flocked to California. Before the gold rush, there were only about 14,000 settlers in California. In 1848, 6,000 more people arrived, with 90,000 arriving just one year later. Each time gold was discovered, new towns called boomtowns were formed. San Francisco is just one of many boomtowns.

Once the gold ran out, boomtowns were abandoned, and people moved to find gold in a new place. San Francisco was a small boomtown of only 1,000 people when the Gold Rush began. It quickly climbed to over 30,000 residents a few years later. The Gold Rush led to California becoming the thirty-first state in 1850.

WRITE

Think about your family. If you moved somewhere new, what talents or knowledge would you bring with you? How would you share it with others?

....
....
....
....
....
....
....
....

PRACTICE

Different Movements, Similar Outcomes

Use the Venn diagram below to compare and contrast two of the migration movements that were mentioned in this lesson: The Bracero Program, The Great Migration, and The Gold Rush.

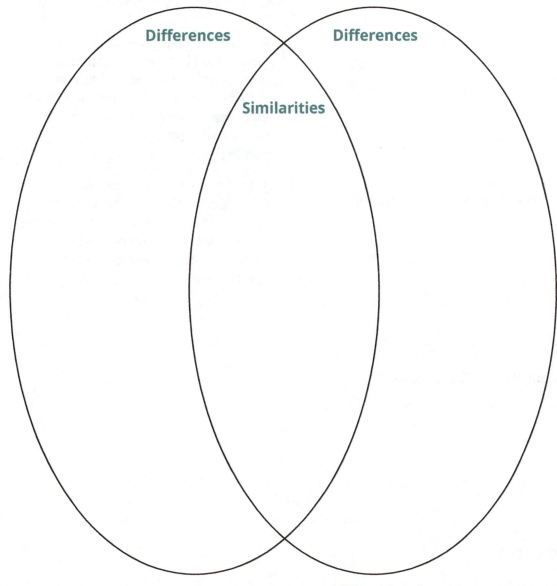

Differences

Differences

Similarities

REVIEW

In this lesson, you learned:

- Economic, social, political, and environmental factors influence human migration.

- These factors lead to various mass migrations movements in North America.

- There were factors that led to the migration of people from one region to another in North America.

- Migrants have influenced and contributed to new regions.

Think About It

How does a group of people establish a culture in a certain region or area?

Answer in complete sentences.

1. What factors influence human migration?

....

....

....

2. How do migrants contribute to the area in which they move?

....

....

....

3. How do the reasons people moved for the Bracero Program compare to the reasons people moved for the Gold Rush?

....

....

....

ONLINE CONNECTION

Research letters, stories, and information from one of the migration movements mentioned in this lesson to find out more about what it was like for people making that move. Find out what reasons people had for taking part in the movement.

Then, imagine you are a person taking part in that movement. Write a letter to a friend or family member explaining why you moved and what you are experiencing in your new home.

Circle the correct answer.

4. A family has just had their home devastated by a tornado, and they decide to move. Their decision to move is based on which migration factor?

A. economic

B. environmental

C. political

5. True or False   The Gold Rush is an example of migration.

6. True or False   There is more than one type of human migration.

Lesson 52

Cultural Features in North America

By the end of this lesson, you will be able to:

- identify the location of key cultural features and relate their significance
- relate how cultural features in a region influence population, the economy, government, and transportation

Lesson Review

If you need to review human migration, please go to the lesson titled "Migration in North America."

Academic Vocabulary

Read the following vocabulary words and definitions. Look through the lesson. Can you find each vocabulary word? Underline the vocabulary word in your lesson. Write the page number of where you found each word in the blanks.

- **architecture:** the artistic or scientific way of building (page ____)
- **artifacts:** objects of value made by humans, usually of cultural or historical interest (page ____)
- **social etiquette:** common, polite behavior in society (page ____)

IN THE REAL WORLD

You learned about culture and what it means. Culture includes art, food, music, and celebrations. Your culture is the reason you celebrate certain holidays, eat foods you eat, and listen to music you enjoy.

Think about a particular aspect of your culture that you really appreciate. This might be something that celebrates your heritage, like a dish from your ethnic background, a particular way of dressing, or celebrating something in your country.

Talk to your instructor about what you chose and why it is enjoyable or meaningful to you.

If an alien from outer space showed up on your doorstep tomorrow morning, what would you show them to teach them about your culture? What things best represent your culture in a way that would make a visitor from outer space understand what your people think is important and enjoy doing?

If you could take your visitor anywhere and do anything to show them what life is like in your culture, what would you do? Create a plan for a whole day of sightseeing, exploring, and trying as many parts of your culture that you think would help your visitor understand who you are and where you come from.

Countries, cities, parks, and restaurants are often made recognizable by something significant like landmarks, building styles, or artwork.

Chicago's Cloud Gate sculpture is often called "The Bean."

Casa Loma in Toronto, Ontario, is one of North America's true castles.

The Catedral Metropolitana in Mexico City is a must-see attraction in Mexico.

Cultural Features

You have learned about many types of cultural features. North America has many iconic cultural features known throughout the world that represent people and places.

CULTURAL FEATURE	EXAMPLE	SIGNIFICANCE
artifacts: objects of value made by humans usually of cultural or historical interest	Statue of Liberty, New York	Constructed in France and given as a gift of friendship to the United States, it is the greeting for thousands of immigrants who arrive in North America. It represents the United States as a land of freedom and opportunity.
symbol: things that stand for or represent something else	national flag of Canada	The red and white colors symbolize strength and pride throughout Canada. The maple leaf contains 11 points. The national flag was proclaimed on February 15, 1965. It symbolizes diversity, equality, and inclusion.
architecture: the artistic or scientific design of a building	Chapultepec Castle in Mexico City, Mexico	One of the only castles in North America, it was originally built to serve as a home for the commander-in-chief of the Spanish army. Currently, it is a tourist site for visitors.

TAKE A CLOSER LOOK

CN Tower in Toronto was completed in 1976 and stands 1,815 feet (553.21 meters) tall. It is a communication and observation tower originally built by Canadian National, a rail line. The Canadian Lands Company now owns it. For many years, it was the world's tallest freestanding structure and tallest tower. Now it is the world's ninth largest tower and is considered one of the Seven Wonders of the Modern World. It attracts 1.5 million visitors annually and employs over 150 people.

Behaviors in Culture

CULTURAL FEATURE TYPE	NORTH AMERICAN EXAMPLE		SIGNIFICANCE OF FEATURE
traditions: holidays, ceremonies, or festivals that represent a group's beliefs often passed down through generations	a wedding ceremony in Mexico		In a Mexican wedding, two people sponsor the bride and groom. These people often pay for part of the wedding, give the couple a Bible, read during the ceremony, and host the bridal party.
practices: behaviors or routines that people participate in	baseball field in the United States		Baseball is a popular sport in North America. Attending games on "Opening Day," the first game of the baseball season, is a regular practice.
language: what people speak in an area	a road sign in Canada written in both English and French		North America has over 150 different languages. Mexico's official language is Spanish. Canada's official languages are French and English. The United States does not have an official language.
dress: what people choose to wear	traditional clothing worn in Mexico		Traditional Mexican clothing includes a *huipil*, a sleeveless tunic worn with a skirt. It is worn based on people's beliefs, marital status, and the region in which they live.
social etiquette: common, polite behavior in society	greeting people in America		American greetings are often informal. Some people shake hands and say "hello." Americans ask, "How are you?" but the expected answer is "fine" or "good."
art: work that tells the story or feelings of a culture	a scenic picture of Canada		The Group of Seven were artists inspired by the wilderness and scenery of Canada.

Impact of Cultural Features

Cultural features can have major effects on population, economy, government, and transportation.

Cultural features are often a source of tourism. People flock to famous sites because of their popularity. When this happens, there is an economic impact. People who come to these locations are likely to spend money at local businesses nearby, resulting in jobs and financial stability for the area.

Strong economic opportunities attract people to live nearby. Where there are many people living, working, and visiting, effective transportation is needed. This can mean buses or trollies to get people to popular destinations and airports or ports to enable travel and shipping. Roads and bridges must also be built to safely handle the traffic load.

The seat of government is a cultural feature. Capitol buildings and places where important government business takes place create jobs for the people in the area and attract tourists. These places often feature attractive or interesting architecture and a lot of history.

Sometimes cultural features require special laws or rules to preserve historic buildings. Places that attract a lot of people and traffic often need special rules to manage the movement and safety of people in the area. Sometimes things like social etiquette, practices, traditions, and languages will have laws relating to them, like a country having an official language or celebrating national holidays.

In this lesson, you learned:

- Cities and countries have distinct cultural features, such as architecture and artifacts.
- Different cultures have different cultural behaviors, such as traditions, languages, dress, and art.
- Cultural features often impact the economy of a place by drawing tourists to visit.

Think About It
How does culture influence where people live and how they live today?

Identify one way that cultural features can impact each of the following things:

1. Population

....

2. Transportation

....

3. Economy

....

4. Government

....

5. Identify the feature and the location of the following cultural features and explain their significance.

CULTURAL FEATURE	FEATURE AND LOCATION	WHY IS IT IMPORTANT?

ONLINE CONNECTION

Look up the residence of the Canadian Prime Minister located at 24 Sussex Drive. Then look up the residence of the President of the United States at 1600 Pennsylvania Ave. After that, look up the Palacio Nacional, which is the official residence of the Mexican President. Consider the following questions while doing your research:

- Is the location of each residence significant?

- What do these residences look like? What kind of architecture do they feature?

- Who lives there? Is any other official business done there?

- Is there anything interesting about the history of each residence?

- How many people visit annually? How many people work there?

Lesson 53

Cultural Geography of North America

By the end of this lesson, you will be able to:

- investigate the cultural geography of North America
- explore broader influences of North American culture on individuals and civilizations around the world
- discover the lasting impact of North American culture on everyday aspects of modern day life

Lesson Review

If you need to review cultural features of North America, please go to the lesson titled "Cultural Features in North America."

Academic Vocabulary

Read the following vocabulary word and definition. Look through the lesson. Can you find each vocabulary word? Underline the vocabulary word in your lesson. Write the page number of where you found each word in the blank.

- **cultural geography:** the study of human connection to natural resources, the economy, religion, government, and the many other ways that humans interact with their world (page _____)

IN THE REAL WORLD

Here are some examples of things invented in North America: potato chips, light bulbs, cotton candy, sunglasses, chocolate chip cookies, personal computers, microwaves, and more! Think about what your life might be like without one of these. Look up a list of famous North American inventions, and determine which one would be the most difficult to live without today. Discuss your thoughts with your instructor.

Who is your favorite musical artist? Your favorite song? Do you have a favorite movie or TV show? Imagine you woke up tomorrow in a completely different part of the world. You are not familiar with your surroundings, and you do not speak the language. The fashion and food are very different from what you are used to.

As you explore the neighborhood you've found yourself in, you hear something familiar. The sound of your favorite song is drifting out of an open door. You walk closer to make sure your ears are not playing tricks on you. Not only is it your favorite song, but you smell your favorite food!

Would you be surprised to see these familiar parts of your culture in a very unfamiliar place? How would it make you feel?

....

....

TAKE A CLOSER LOOK

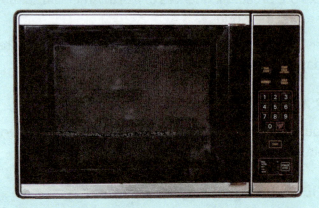

Microwave

Did you know the invention of the microwave was actually an accident? Percy Spencer, an American physicist, was experimenting with radio waves. He had a peanut butter candy bar in his pocket that melted during one of the experiments, which led him to realize that radio waves could cook food. He then invented the microwave oven! Microwaves can now be found in homes all around the world.

READ

North America's Cultural Influence

Cultural geography is the study of human connection to natural resources, the economy, religion, government, and the many other ways humans interact with their world. Examining homes in different regions shows how these ideas connect.

In most of Canada, building materials are in high supply, and the cost of lumber and stone is low. Buildings in Canada need to account for the cold climate. In Mexico, building materials are often in good supply. Mexican homes are generally built of concrete, stone, and tiles because of the warm climate.

The US Constitution established the legal relationship between the US government and its citizens. It has influenced world governments with ideas like amendment procedures and judicial review.

Media refers to methods of mass communication, like publication, broadcasting, and internet. North America created tools and methods of producing media, like computers and the internet, that have influenced the world. North America has created media like films, TV shows, news programs, and magazines that are popular all over the world.

Canada

Mexico

TAKE A CLOSER LOOK

North American Fashion

Can you imagine a closet without jeans and t-shirts? These items are found in closets around the world. Both jeans and t-shirts were invented in the United States. A person wearing a t-shirt, jeans, and braided leather huarache sandals from Mexico would be wearing North American inventions from head to toe!

North American fashion designers have become influential all over the world. They were not taken seriously, however, until 1973 when they won a friendly competition between French and American designers called The Battle of Versailles.

WRITE

Name and describe two ways that North America has influenced the world.

....

....

....

READ

North American Entertainment

The sport of baseball is one of North America's favorite pastimes. Baseball began to spread globally when teacher Horace Wilson introduced it in Tokyo, Japan. Japan established its first organized baseball team in the nineteenth century. Baseball still remains Japan's top sport.

Baseball also became popular in South America. North American oil workers in Venezuela would play baseball, which led to the Venezuelan Professional Baseball League. Venezuelan boys often grow up playing baseball, hoping to be scouted by Major League Baseball. Countries like the Dominican Republic, Puerto Rico, and Cuba have many aspiring players, and baseball is a major part of the national culture.

In the 1800s, artists and scientists developed new techniques and devices to advance photography, leading to the invention of motion pictures. It took years for films to be developed, with England and France leading the world. By the 1920s, Hollywood, in California,

became the dominant film industry worldwide. The longest-running film industry location in the world is Hollywood, California. Hollywood is also the largest revenue producer in the film industry worldwide. Films like *Casablanca*, *The Wizard of Oz*, and *E.T. the Extra-Terrestrial* are known as icons of American artistry and culture. Hollywood became so representative of the film industry worldwide that India's film industry became known as Bollywood.

TAKE A CLOSER LOOK

Fast Food

Quick-serve restaurants have become an icon of North American influence throughout the world. These restaurants have menus and processes that serve quick meals to busy consumers. McDonald's is a famous example. It is the largest restaurant company worldwide, with locations in 120 countries. You can get a burger with fries at any McDonald's location. McDonald's locations outside of the United States also offer menu items that reflect the culture of the country they are in. The menu includes pineapple pies in Thailand and a chicken pita sandwich in Morocco.

PRACTICE

Identify how North America has had a lasting impact on everyday life.

INFLUENCE	HOW HAS THIS INFLUENCE MADE AN IMPACT ON EVERYDAY LIFE?
fashion	
sports	
film	
fast food	

REVIEW

In this lesson, you learned:

- Humans shape their environment through their use of resources, media, government, and entertainment.
- North America has influenced the world through their forms of government, media, fashion, sports, film, and food.

Think About It
Can you think of any other ways North American culture has spread and influenced other cultures around the world?

Circle the correct answer.

1. True or False   Bollywood came before Hollywood.

2. True or False   Huaraches originated in Mexico.

3. True or False   Blue jeans and t-shirts were not originally from North America.

4. True or False   Yelling into a loudspeaker is an example of media.

5. True or False   *Casablanca* and *E.T. the Extra-Terrestrial* are iconic North American films.

6. How has McDonald's made a lasting impact on the world?

   A. It provides free hamburgers to everyone on Wednesdays.

   B. It is the largest restaurant company in the world.

   C. It provides delicious french fries.

7. How has baseball made a difference in the world?

   A. School uniforms are modeled after baseball uniforms all over the world.

   B. It made popcorn famous in Australia and New Zealand.

   C. It has become a popular sport for spectators and young athletes in many other countries.

8. How has the Constitution of the United States influenced other countries worldwide?

   ....

   ....

   ....

9. How can the home building style of an area represent cultural geography?

   ....

   ....

   ....

ONLINE CONNECTION

Research other fast food restaurants that originated in North America and have spread to other countries. Examine the menus they offer in each country where they operate. Create a slideshow presentation comparing and contrasting the different menu offerings from place to place.

Chapter 5 Review

By the end of this lesson, you will:

- review the information from the lessons in Chapter 5, "North America."

Lesson Review

Throughout the chapter, we have learned the following big ideas:

- You can use topographic and geopolitical maps to tell the story of North America. (Lesson 44)

- Indigenous people live throughout North America and use the resources they have access to. (Lesson 45)

- North America has different types of settlements, and people chose to settle in certain North American regions for various reasons. (Lesson 46)

- North America has important physical features, like rivers and lakes. (Lesson 47)

- The Great Flood of 1927 had a massive impact, and the Mississippi River and Tributaries Project was established by the Army Corps of Engineers to control flooding of the Mississippi River. (Lesson 48)

- Hawaii and the Appalachian Mountains were formed by physical processes, and various natural resources can be found in the eight regions of North America because of these physical processes. (Lesson 49)

- North America's natural resources include coal, nickel, oil, silver, and grains. (Lesson 50)

- Many factors cause people to move from one place to another, and migrants bring many ideas and talents to an area when they move to it. (Lesson 51)

- North America has many important cultural features, landmarks, and places of interest. (Lesson 52)

- North America's architecture, entertainment, and food have influence around the world. (Lesson 53)

Go back and review the lessons as needed while you complete the activities.

Talk to your instructor about the changes you have seen in your own hometown, such as changes in your area's physical features, natural resources, and cultural features. How have these changes impacted the people who live in your area?

REVIEW

North American Maps and Physical Features

You learned the stories maps tell in North America and how North America is connected to other continents. You learned that topographical maps show the landforms of regions and geopolitical maps tell the power of a region by identifying land borders.

topographic map   **geopolitical map**

The Indigenous people of Canada, Mexico, and the United States are very different. Here are some examples of groups from each country.

CANADA	MEXICO	UNITED STATES
Woodland	Mayan	Iroquois
Iroquois	Aztec	Chickasaw
Anishinaabe	Toltec	Diné (Navajo)
The Pacific Coast	Teotihuacan	Blackfeet

IN THE REAL WORLD

Plate tectonics formed Hawaii. Under the surface of the ocean, volcanoes are erupting and pushing the land upward. As this occurred, the islands of Hawaii formed. Additional volcanoes exist underwater, promoting the possibility of more islands forming.

Plate collisions formed the Appalachian Mountains. Two plates of rock are colliding and breaking up the continental crust. As this continues to happen and the rocks pile up, mountain ranges, like the Appalachians, form.

The Bering Strait connects continents. The Bering Strait separates North America and Asia by just 55 miles.

REVIEW

Natural Resources

Natural resources are found throughout North America. Grain is an example of a renewable resource found in North America. It is used as wheat in making flour, bread, and other baked goods. Coal is a non-renewable resource found in North America. It is used as fuel to generate electric power in the United States.

North American Cultural Features and Influence

CULTURAL FEATURE	INFLUENCE ON PEOPLE	INFLUENCE ON THE WORLD
Constitution	Citizens can understand the branches of government and their rights.	Other countries have used ideas from the US Constitution in their governments.
	Quick, consistent fast food provides people on the go with accessible and reliable options for dining.	North American fast food restaurants have become popular in other countries, offering their standard menu alongside items that fit the culture of each location.

 **WRITE** What other cultural features of North America have made an impact on the world?

....

....

....

Deforestation

Deforestation is the process of clearing trees for agricultural land or to provide lumber, which affects the environment. In Canada, endangered caribou will not cross any deforested areas.

PRACTICE

Vocabulary

As you learned about the continent of North America, you came across new vocabulary words. Think about the meaning of the following words and, in the space provided, define the vocabulary word using your own words.

VOCABULARY WORD	DEFINITION IN YOUR OWN WORDS
topographic map	
isthmus	
wigwam	
tributary	
plate tectonics	
plate collisions	
natural resources	
cultural features	
cultural geography	

Quick Tip
When you hear the word *culture*, you might think of things like the arts or the food that people eat. While those things are culture, *culture* is a much broader term that includes many other components with it. In these chapters, you heard *cultural geography* and *cultural features*. These might have been unclear to you if you thought of culture as only the study of things people like or do. Culture includes societies as a whole revealing the habits, customs, and capabilities of people.

PRACTICE

Cause and Effect

Cause and effect defines action and reaction. In the study of North America, you learned a lot about the causes of important events and the results, or effects, of those events. Below you will see some causes and some effects. Fill in the missing pieces with what you can remember from your learning.

EVENT OR FEATURE	CAUSE	EFFECT
Great Migration	Many African Americans in the South were faced with poor economic conditions and racial discrimination.	
Baseball		People in other countries decided to create professional baseball leagues and build stadiums so they could play baseball too. In Venezuela, young boys grow up dreaming of playing Major League Baseball.
The Great Flood of 1927		
The Coastal Region's Influence on Human Settlement		

TAKE A CLOSER LOOK

Migration

Human migration can be both voluntary and involuntary. Voluntary migration is when people choose to move based on their own needs or desires. Involuntary migration is when natural disasters or religious disagreements force people to move.

Two examples of migration for economic reasons were the Gold Rush, which occurred when gold was discovered in California, and the Bracero Program, which was implemented to provide work for Mexicans in the United States.

PRACTICE

Summarizing Information

Spend some time thinking about the two topics listed below and then create a summary explaining the details of the people or events. Remember, when you summarize you are writing in your own words and providing information about the major points of a topic.

As you reflect on the Indigenous people of North America, select a group to focus on. Provide a summary of the following:

- location of the group
- settlements of the group
- available resources to the group

....
....
....
....

As you reflect on the deforestation of areas like Canada's boreal forest, provide a summary explaining the following:

- defining deforestation
- impacts of deforestation upon the environment

....
....
....
....

WRITE

Think about your learning. What stands out to you in the lessons? What questions do you have? What do you wonder about? You can use this page to take notes, write out your responses, and then discuss them with your instructor.

South America

Bonjour, mon ami!

When we arrived at the swamps in Florida, they did not look like they did on the maps. Where the swamp should have been, there was a mini-mall. Humans had been drying up swampland for years in the United States. Now it was getting hard to find places for a friendly frog to live.

We did find unspoiled swampland in the Everglades. But we decided Chang should not stay there. What if they made that a mall too?

We didn't know what to do. But I remembered there was a part of America we had not visited.

I asked Monsieur Jean, "Are there any swamps in South America?" He looked at me and started muttering to himself. "Of course! Of course! What was I thinking? They have the biggest tropical swampland in the world."

I looked at the map, and there it was: the Pantanal, with 42 million acres of swampland. The swamp is spread out across three countries—Brazil, Bolivia, and a small country called Paraguay.

The flight to Brazil from Miami was eight hours. First, we drove down to the Pantanal. As soon as we got there, Chang knew. This was the place.

The weather was hot, perfect for a frog. There were yummy bugs.

It was so perfect down there that I was jealous Chang would get to live there. So we all did our happy dance.

But after we were done celebrating, I got sad. Does this mean our fun trip was over?

What Will I Learn?

This chapter focuses on the region of Oceania. It examines the geography and culture of the smallest continent.

Lessons at a Glance

Lesson 55

The Stories in Maps of South America

By the end of this lesson, you will be able to:

- examine different maps of South America
- determine what story each map tells
- compare and contrast the major cities in South America and the cities in your state/country

Academic Vocabulary

Read the following vocabulary words and definitions. Look through the lesson. Can you find each vocabulary word? Underline the vocabulary word in your lesson. Write the page number of where you found each word in the blanks.

- **cartographer:** people who draw and produce maps (page ___)

- **geopolitical map:** maps that show boundaries of countries, states, cities, and counties (page ___)

- **topographic map:** a map that shows the elevation and the shape of Earth's surface (page ___)

- **tourist map:** a map that shows destinations that are popular for tourists, helps tourists determine various destinations to visit, and assists with planning daily activities in a particular place (page ___)

CREATE

Our world is filled with places to explore. To explore, we need accurate maps. Cartographers are people who draw and produce maps. Do you think this would be a fun job?

Imagine you have been hired as a cartographer. Your first assignment is to draw a map of an area you are very familiar with. Examples are your bedroom, house, apartment building, backyard, or neighborhood. Create a map that labels important areas. Use the map to explain to your instructor how you would use the map to get from place to place.

EXPLORE

Isn't it fun going somewhere new and exploring? Have you ever been to a new city, state, or country? When visiting a new place, you have to decide what attractions or destinations are worth visiting. Then, you figure out how to get to those attractions. There may be a beautiful mountain range or waterfalls that you don't want to miss seeing.

Think of the last time you visited a new place. Write the name of where this city, town, state, or country was. Use the space below to draw pictures or use words to describe what you and your family did in this new city and how you figured out what you should go visit. Draw pictures or use words to explain what tools helped you reach your destinations.

....

....

....

Tourist maps help when we visit a new place.

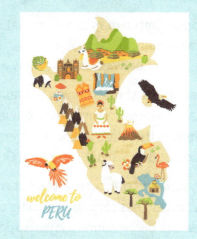

Peru

Rio de Janeiro, Brazil

Maps of South America

Have you ever used a map? If so, you already know that they provide a lot of different information. In fact, there are actually different types of maps. Let's take a look at topographic, geopolitical, and tourist maps of South America.

A **topographic map** is a map that shows the elevation and the shape of Earth's surface. A topographic map of South America is shown here. The brown areas on the map indicate a much higher level of elevation such as a mountain range or mountain ranges. The green areas indicate a very low level of elevation. The yellow areas are lower elevation than the brown, but a higher elevation than the green.

A **geopolitical map** shows boundaries of countries, states, cities, and counties. Geopolitical maps can actually change quite frequently over time because wars or other political events may cause boundaries to change. Below is a geopolitical map of South America. Can you count how many countries there are in South America? South America has 14 countries: Argentina, Bolivia, Brazil, Chile, Colombia, Ecuador, Falkland Islands (owned by the United Kingdom), French Guiana (owned by France), Guyana, Paraguay, Peru, Suriname, Uruguay, and Venezuela.

Another kind of map is a **tourist map**. A tourist map shows destinations that are popular for tourists, helps tourists determine various destinations to visit, and assists with planning daily activities in a particular place. Can you see anything that would be interesting on this map to visit? If so, circle the destinations that are appealing to you.

Every Map Tells a Story

Each map type described tells a different story. It is important to understand the stories maps tell so you know which map to use for different circumstances. Let's find out what kind of story each map of South America tells.

MAP TYPE	MAP EXAMPLES	STORIES THE MAPS TELL
topographic maps of South America		These topographic maps tell a story of the elevations in South America. There is an increased elevation on the West Coast and it extends from the north to the south border. There are also differences in elevation, though less, on the eastern border. This mountain range is not as long as the east coast mountain range. The second map is a topographic map of Peru, a country in South America. It is located on the west coast. The lighter brown color shows higher elevation than the green. Try circling on the map where you see the elevation increasing.
geopolitical maps of South America		The first geopolitical map shows all of the 14 countries and their borders in South America. It tells a story of the land that calls itself a country, showing its boundaries and the locations of each capital city. The second geopolitical map shows the cities of Brazil, which is the largest country in South America.
tourist maps of South America		The first map shows areas that may be of interest to tourists throughout South America. The second map shows a version of a tourist map for the country of Argentina. Both of these maps would help a tourist think about what they might want to see in the area. Another tourist map may be used to show roads and routes to reach the destinations of interest. On both maps, circle areas that interest you.

South American Cities

Now, let's find out about the three most populated cities in South America. As you are reading about each city, think about how they are the same or different from the city in which you live.

CITY	CHARACTERISTICS
Sao Paulo, Brazil	• over 21 million people live here • capital city of Brazil • filled with many skyscrapers • known as the Land of Drizzle because the weather has frequent and unpredictable rainfall • has the highest number of Japanese people outside of Japan, due to the two countries enacting a treaty that would relieve some of the poverty in rural Japan and Brazil's need for people to own and work on coffee plantations
Buenos Aires, Argentina	• about 15 million people live here • second most visited city in Latin America • filled with European architecture • produces and exports large amounts of agricultural products like grains (wheat, barley, rice), sugarcane, and citrus • referred to as the Paris of South America due to its wide, cobblestone, tree-lined streets, architecture, and open-air cafes • major port town and important for trade • capital and largest city in Argentina
Rio de Janeiro, Brazil	• over 13 million people live here • one of the most visited cities in the southern hemisphere • a major port for trade due to its location next to the South Atlantic Ocean • has many popular beaches • culture very centered around music • set between mountains and the sea

REVIEW

In this lesson, you learned:

• Topographic, geopolitical, and tourist maps of South America show different information about the continent.

• A topographic map shows the elevation of South America. A geopolitical map shows the country or city boundaries of South America. A tourist map shows destinations to visit.

• The three major cities in South America based on population are Sao Paulo, Brazil, Buenos Aires, Argentina, and Rio de Janeiro, Brazil.

Think About It
If you were visiting South America, which scenarios would require you to use each one of these types of maps?

Each of the maps below shows one of the 14 countries located in South America. Label each map type as either geopolitical, tourist, or topographic.

1. This map of Ecuador is a _____ map.

2. This map of Argentina is a _____ map.

3. This map of Bolivia is a _____ map.

Country Study
Decide on a South American country of interest to study more closely. You could keep either a digital or paper notebook to save your work. You will have the chance to create a country study for each continent this year. As you go through the coming lessons about South America, you will examine your country and its connection to the subject of the lesson. Find multiple maps of your country. Write about the story you think those maps are telling.

4. What story does a topographic map of South America tell? Select all that apply.

A. This map tells tourists how to get from place to place.

B. This map tells us where there may be a lower elevation.

C. This map tells where different boundaries are for cities and/or states.

D. This map tells us where the highest mountains are located.

5. What story does a tourist map of South America tell?

A. This map tells a person important destinations to visit and how to get from place to place.

B. This map tells us where there may be an increase in elevation or lower elevation.

C. This map tells different boundaries for cities and/or states.

6. If you wanted to visit all of the different countries in South America, but you didn't know how many countries were on the continent, which map type would you need?

A. geopolitical map

B. topographic map

C. tourist map

Lesson 56

Geographic Factors and Human Settlement in South America

By the end of this lesson, you will be able to:

- analyze geographic factors that influence where people live and how people came to settle South America
- develop spatial understanding of the location of geographic features in South America compared with those studied in previous chapters
- identify geographic connections between the continents

Lesson Review

If you need to review maps of South America, please go to the lesson titled "Maps of South America."

Academic Vocabulary

Read the following vocabulary words and definitions. Look through the lesson. Can you find each vocabulary word? Underline the vocabulary word in your lesson. Write the page number of where you found each word in the blanks.

- **canal:** a human-made waterway that allows for the passage of boats or ships (page _____)
- **human settlement:** a place where people live (page _____)

CREATE

Mountains, lakes, deserts, rivers, and oceans cover the landscape of almost all the continents on our planet. You probably have at least one of these landforms near you. Imagine what our world would be like without mountains, lakes, deserts, rivers, or oceans. Choose one of these geographic features. Write a short story about how life would be different if we did not have it.

EXPL🧭RE

Every place on Earth has its own unique landscape. Landforms like mountains, canyons, plains, marshes, rivers, and waterfalls exist all over the world. Nowhere has the exact same landscape as another place on Earth. What makes where you live unique? Take a moment to visualize the area without any buildings or human-made changes to the environment.

What do you think attracted people to the area where you live originally? What was it about the landscape and the environment that made it a good place to settle?

Select an area of the landscape near you, and draw a picture showing what your chosen area looks like in each of the four seasons.

Lake Titicaca

Lakes are a geographic feature that can be found on all continents. Lake Titicaca is the largest lake in South America. It is located in the Andes Mountains on the border of Peru and Bolivia. Lake Titicaca is 3,200 square miles large, making it close to twice the size of Delaware!

It is also one of the highest-elevated lakes in the world. Many Indigenous people, like the Incas, lived around this lake and used it for a fresh water supply. The water is famously still and bright, and provides a home for rare animals like giant frogs. Find the lake on the map.

READ

Geographic Connection to Other Continents

Continents are connected to one another by geographic features. Remember, geographic features are naturally created or human-made features of Earth's surface. The geographic feature that connects the continent of South America to Central America is a canal. A **canal** is a human-made waterway that allows for the passage of boats or ships. The canal connecting South and Central America is called the Panama Canal, and it was completed in 1904.

Oceans connect South America to other continents in the world. The Atlantic Ocean connects South America to Africa and Europe. The Pacific Ocean connects South America to Asia and Australia.

How People Settled in South America

Indigenous peoples have lived in South America for many years. The map (right) illustrates how Indigenous people arrived in South America. They traveled south from Central America.

From there, Indigenous people started to settle in many parts of South America. There are hundreds of Indigenous groups in South America. The map (far right) shows where many Indigenous tribes and nations settled in South America.

DOMINANT POPULATION
- Mestizo
- Native American

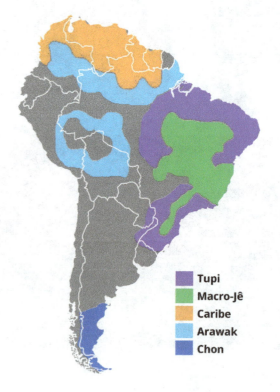

- Tupi
- Macro-Jê
- Caribe
- Arawak
- Chon

READ

Geographic Factors of South America

Mountains, rivers, deserts, and rainforests are the dominant geographic features on the continent of South America. The Andes Mountains are located on the west coast of South America. This collection of mountain ranges spans seven countries. The many volcanoes provide fertile soil. Glaciers provide sources of water in the Andes Mountains. The Andes extend down the entire coast.

The Amazon River system is another main geographic feature in South America. The Amazon River is the greatest river on the entire continent. It is stocked full of fish. It is about 4,000 miles long and crosses nine South American countries. The Amazon River is slightly shorter than the Nile River in Africa.

Rainforests are another geographic feature of the South American landscape. Rainforests are places that receive at least 80 inches of rain per year and have many trees. The Amazon rainforest is the largest rainforest in the world.

Another significant geographic feature in South America are deserts. One continuous desert exists along the Pacific Coast of South America. It stretches from Peru to Chile. South America has 14 different deserts. The largest desert is in Argentina and is called the Eastern Patagonia Desert.

TAKE A CLOSER LOOK

Have you ever gone swimming in a river? One man swam the entire length of the Amazon River! It took 66 days from the time he started swimming until he reached the end. He swam about 60 miles per day!

At one point, the Amazon River flowed backward. Researchers have found an entire coral reef system there. Not a single bridge has been built to cross the Amazon.

WRITE

If you were an early human settler, which geographic feature would you choose to settle near and why?

....

....

....

....

PRACTICE

Human Settlement in South America

Human settlement is a place where people live. The chart below explains patterns of human settlement that have occurred throughout South America.

Geographic Feature	Influences on Human Settlement
 **Andes Mountains**	This area was inhabited by the Incan Empire. Agriculture thrived in this area making it easy for human settlement. Humans could easily grow corn, potatoes, and beans. The Indigenous people also engaged in ceramics and weaving. There was a constant source of water for humans and agriculture.
Amazon River and the surrounding rainforest	The river provided an excellent source for travel, trade, fishing, and fertile soils. Cattle ranching, mining, tiber, and other forestry projects were easy to carry out in this area. Going deeper into the rainforest provided protection for human settlement. Indigenous peoples produced pottery and used clearing techniques to distribute useful species of animals.
 **Deserts**	Humans settled in this harsh environment. The Atacama Desert is located on the coast. Early human settlers could fish. The Chinchorro culture developed in this area, where it was easy for them to practice mummification. The desert has freshwater sources. Clay was easy to produce and used to make whole towns. In the present day, much of the area lacks human settlement.

REVIEW

In this lesson, you learned:

- Geographic factors influence where people live in South America.

- People came by first moving in a southern direction from Central America.

- Geographic features in South America include the Andes Mountains, the Amazon River, and rainforests.

- The Panama Canal connects to Central and North America. The Atlantic Ocean connects to Africa and Europe. The Pacific Ocean connects to Asia and Australia.

Think About It
How did people in South America use the natural resources of their environment to make the most of the areas they settled?

Circle the correct answer.

1. What is the geographic connection between South America to Central and North America?

   A. Andes Mountains

   B. Panama Canal

   C. Atacama Desert

   D. Atlantic Ocean

2. How did the Andes Mountains serve as a good place for human settlement? Hint: There are two answers.

   A. Agriculture was successful.

   B. The forest provided protection.

   C. There was a great amount of water available.

   D. The mountains provided an easy method of mummification.

3. True or False   Humans could not settle in the desert in South America.

Write the answer to the following questions.

4. How did people come to settle South America?

   ....

   ....

   ....

   ....

5. Explain how the Amazon River system is significant in human settlement for South Americans.

   ....

   ....

   ....

   ....

ONLINE CONNECTION

Research one of the geographic features listed in this lesson to discover how it has changed over time and what state that feature is in today. Who lives near your chosen geographic feature today? How do they interact with the land? Is the feature facing any environmental threats?

Create a slideshow presentation that discusses the history of your chosen geographic feature as well as its current condition.

Human Settlement in South America

By the end of this lesson, you will be able to:

- examine evidence of common patterns and features of human settlements
- compare and contrast human settlements of different regions in South America
- analyze how the environment influenced the settlements

Lesson Review

If you need to review geographic features in South America, please go to the lesson titled "Geographic Factors in South America."

Academic Vocabulary

Read the following vocabulary words and definitions. Look through the lesson. Can you find each vocabulary word? Underline the vocabulary word in your lesson. Write the page number of where you found each word in the blanks.

- **monsoons:** a seasonal wind that lasts for several months (page ____)
- **polar zone:** a lack of warm summers; cool summers and very cold winters, which results in treeless tundra, glaciers, or a permanent or semi-permanent layer of ice (page ____)
- **temperate zone:** mild, moderate temperature that is neither hot nor cold (page ____)
- **tropical climate:** a region near the equator with high levels of humidity and year-round warm temperatures (page ____)

Imagine you're on a ship that wrecked on a desert island in the Pacific. The boat is full of items that might be useful, but it is sinking. You have to get as many tools and necessary items as possible before the boat is submerged. You have time to grab six items necessary for survival:

- maps of the Pacific Ocean
- coffee maker
- cans of beans
- emergency blanket
- small mirror
- writing utensils
- seat cushions
- dresses
- hats
- matches
- aluminum foil
- radio
- bag of carrots
- sneakers

What six items would you choose? Why?

....

....

....

....

....

EXPLRE

Have you ever gone camping? Maybe you went camping at the beach, near a lake, in the mountains, or even in your backyard. You probably brought items with you to help you make it through the night comfortably. Even if you haven't been camping, you can probably think of things that would be important to have with you.

Imagine living in the mountains. Would this be an easy way of life? What would be some things you could use in the environment to help you live a comfortable life?

Now imagine living near the coast of an ocean. Would this be an easy way of life? What would be some things you could use in the environment to help you live a comfortable life?

Complete the Venn diagram. Compare living near the coast to living near a mountain. Make sure you include items that you would find in each area in order for you and your family to live a comfortable life.

Living near the coast　　　　　　**Living near a mountain**

Both

Patterns of Human Settlements

There are a wide variety of human settlement patterns in South America. You have already learned that the Indigenous people settled near key geographic features such as the Andes Mountains and the Amazon rainforest.

In the Andes Mountains in Peru, houses are built to protect humans from earthquakes and the cold climate. Traditional houses in this area are made of *quincha*, which is a wood or reed structure covered in mud and plaster.

In the Amazon rainforest, houses are built using materials from the rainforest, like wood and grasses. Houses are built on stilts or rafts to protect from the natural rising and falling of the river level.

Indigenous people were the first to settle in South America. They arrived from North and Central America and made their way to different parts of the country. Many Indigenous tribes settled South America, including the Inca, Chimú, Wichí, Mapuche, and Quechua.

Europeans, including Portuguese, Spanish, Italian, French, German, and British people, crossed the Atlantic Ocean to colonize parts of South America. Enslaved Africans were brought to South America to settle parts of the continent for the Europeans. They were mostly enslaved in the northern part of South America and Brazil to tend crops for the Europeans to sell. People from Asia also came to South America to work and settle parts of Peru, Brazil, and Guyana.

TAKE A CLOSER LOOK

South America is the fifth-most populated continent in the world. The city with the highest population in South America is São Paulo, Brazil. The patterns of greatest settlement in the present day are:

- the ancient Indigenous areas of the Andes
- the plantation areas settled by enslaved laborers
- areas of European immigration in southern Brazil, Uruguay, and Argentina

Homes in Peru

Homes in the Amazon rainforest

Regional Human Settlement

South America is split into four different regions: southern South America (green), eastern South America (yellow), western South America (blue), and northern South America (red). Let's find out some characteristics of, and how people settled in each of these regions.

Region	Countries	Characteristics
Southern South America (green)	Chile, Argentina, Paraguay, Uruguay	• Andes Mountains, lakes, fjords, and glaciers in the west and deserts in the east • inhabited by Indigenous people who were hunter-gatherers and practiced agriculture • colonized by Spain
Eastern South America (yellow)	Brazil	• includes flatlands, plains, mountains, and hills • some of the most fertile lands of the Amazon • settled by hunter-gatherers • great area for skilled farmers and fishermen • Paraguay River system provided a water source • around half of the continent's population is here today
Western South America (blue)	Bolivia, Columbia, Ecuador, Peru, Venezuela	• dominated by the Andes Mountains, which are high volcanic mountains • includes parts of the Amazon rainforest • the Inca established roads and major cities • Arawak, Guaicaipuro, and Tamanaco settled this region • colonized by Spain
Northern South America (red)	Guyana, Suriname, French Guiana	• called the Wild Coast • includes many river valleys • originally settled by the Arawak • colonized by the Dutch, French, British, and Portuguese • enslaved workers worked sugar plantations • mix of Europeans, Africans, and Native people live in this region today

READ

Environment and Settlements

Climate varies drastically by region in South America, influencing human settlement patterns. If the climate is cold, humans will have to prepare to stay warm. In dry climates, humans must figure out how to supply water for themselves, agriculture, and animals. High rainfall can be hard on homes and crops. South America experiences all of these challenges in different regions.

The **temperate zone** has a mild, moderate temperature that is neither hot nor cold. The region rarely suffers from heat because it is far from the equator. There is strong, constant wind and high humidity.

A **tropical climate** means it is a region near the equator with high levels of humidity and year-round warm temperatures. Tropical climates experience **monsoons**, which are a seasonal wind that lasts for several months. There is an equilateral climate, which means hot temperatures all year and high monthly precipitation.

The **polar zone** has no warm summers. It has cool summers and very cold winters. These conditions result in treeless tundra, glaciers, or a permanent or semi-permanent layer of ice.

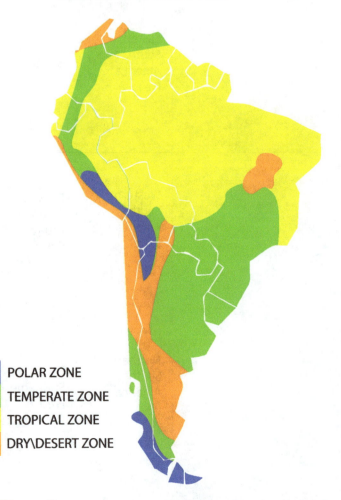

SOUTH AMERICA CLIMATE ZONES

- POLAR ZONE
- TEMPERATE ZONE
- TROPICAL ZONE
- DRY\DESERT ZONE

REVIEW

In this lesson, you learned:

- Common patterns and features of human settlements show that many settled in the Andes Mountains and the Amazon rainforest.

- Today, most South Americans live in eastern South America, Brazil, western South America, and the Andes Mountains.

- The environmental climate had influence over the settlements, but South Americans overcame many of those challenges and understood how to use the land to their benefit.

Think About It
Which region of South America would you choose to live in and why?

SHOW WHAT YOU KNOW

1. Two areas that were common for human settlement in South America were the
   _____ and the _____.

   A. Amazon rainforest

   B. deserts of South America

   C. Andes Mountains

   D. Galapagos Islands

2. The Indigenous peoples known as the _____
   had a major presence in this area and established roads and major cities.

3. True or False   Europeans had no role in the settlement of South America.

4. Describe some challenges the climate presented for human settlers in
   South America.

   ....
   ....
   ....
   ....
   ....
   ....
   ....
   ....
   ....

ONLINE CONNECTION

Search online for virtual field trips of either the Amazon River or Amazon rainforest. Watch the virtual field trip once to simply view it. Then rewatch it and take notes on your thoughts and observations. Afterward, create a 3D work of art based on what you have learned. You can create a diorama, sculpture, mobile, model, or anything you like to represent your impressions and learning of this incredible geographical region. Share your 3D artwork with your instructor.

Lesson 58

Physical Geography and Natural Resources of South America

By the end of this lesson, you will be able to:

- investigate the physical geography of South America
- analyze the influence of the effects of people's relationship to natural resources on the development of various Indigenous South American civilizations

Lesson Review

If you need to review common settlement patterns of humans in South America, please go to the lesson titled "Human Settlement in South America."

Academic Vocabulary

Read the following vocabulary words and definitions. Look through the lesson. Can you find each vocabulary word? Underline the vocabulary word in your lesson. Write the page number of where you found each word in the blanks.

- **coastal plains:** an area of low, flat land near the ocean (page _____)
- **highlands:** areas of high or mountainous land (page _____)

CREATE

Speculative historical fiction is a type of writing that imagines worlds beyond our own that are based in the past. You get to try your hand at this type of creative writing! Look at this historic site where an ancient civilization once lived in South America. Write a short speculative historical fiction story about what you think occurred in this majestic place. Include who lived here and how they used this land.

Finding water isn't a mystery that we don't have answers to these days. We can get water from indoor plumbing or even buy bottles of drinking water at just about any store. But what about when people first settled in an area?

Look at the image above. What if the area you settled was up on top of one of the mesas or deep into the surrounding desert, and this stream was the nearest source of fresh water. What options would you have to collect water for drinking, bathing, and growing plants?

Brainstorm a few ideas and discuss them with your instructor.

TAKE A CLOSER LOOK

The Yanomami

The Yanomami tribe was a group of Indigenous people who developed a civilization twice the size of Switzerland in the Amazon Rainforest. They understood how to use the natural resources available to them to live sustainable lives. They built their circular homes, called yanos, using materials that were available to them from the trees. They hunted animals such as tapir (an animal similar to a pig), deer, and monkey in the rainforest. They fished using reed canoes and fishing rods made of reeds from plants in the rainforest.

Physical Geography of South America

The physical geography of a continent determines its natural resources. The physical geography of South America can be divided into three different regions: mountains and highlands, river basins, and coastal plains.

The mountains and highlands run in a north to south direction. This region is made up mostly of the Andes Mountains, which is the longest mountain range in the world, measuring 5,500 miles (8851.39 km) long. Many areas are volcanic and some contain glaciers. **Highlands** are areas of high or mountainous land. The highland areas are the Brazilian Highlands and the Guiana Highlands.

The river basin runs in an east to west direction. The Amazon River is part of the river basin. It makes up most of the river basin in South America. It is defined as a dense, tropical rainforest. Another portion of the river basin is a vast grassland area called Paraná. This area is warm, humid, and has tremendous biodiversity in plant and animal life.

The coastal plains run in a north to south direction. **Coastal plains** are an area of low, flat land near the ocean. This can be found on the northeastern coast of Brazil next to the Atlantic Ocean. The coastal plain is also on the western, Pacific coast of Peru and Chile. This area is very dry. The Atacama Desert is part of this area and is known as the driest place on Earth.

TAKE A CLOSER LOOK

The Uro

The Uro were an Indigenous people in South America. They lived, and some still live, in what is present-day Peru and Bolivia. They make their homes from woven totora reeds. Totora is a species of plant whose stem is used as a valuable resource. The reeds are a highly useful natural resource that is specific to the Lake Titicaca area. The reeds can be used to make woven baskets, as a food source, and to build the homes that you see here. Another Indigenous people that used the reeds were the Rapa Nui of Easter Island in South America.

READ

Natural Resources in South America

South America is filled with an abundance of natural resources. Let's find out what natural resources are available on the continent of South America and what countries they are found in. Then, list ways this resource is useful for humans.

NATURAL RESOURCE	LOCATION IN SOUTH AMERICA
water	South America is surrounded by water. The Pacific Ocean is on the west coast, and the Atlantic is on the east coast. It is also home to the Amazon River and eight freshwater lakes.
trees	Trees provide an important resource, timber. It is thought that there are over 300 billion trees and over 16,000 different species of trees in South America.
fish	There are many freshwater fish and saltwater fish in South America. In the Amazon River, there are 2,000 different species of fish.
fruits	The climate on this continent is perfect for growing fruit. The most abundant tropical fruits in South America are bananas. Brazil is the third-highest producer of fruit in the world.
clay	Clay is made out of rocks and water. The Andes Mountains and surrounding deserts are close to rivers and the ocean, creating an ideal location to be able to produce clay.

PRACTICE

Without each of the natural resources listed below, the development of Indigenous people's civilizations would have been very difficult. As you read about each resource, imagine how a lack of it would provide hardships for the Indigenous people of this continent.

NATURAL RESOURCE	HOW IT HELPED INDIGENOUS PEOPLE	WHAT WOULD LIFE HAVE BEEN LIKE WITHOUT THIS NATURAL RESOURCE?
Water	travel, trade, drinking source for humans, drinking source for animals, agriculture	
Trees	to make roofs and utensils, building canoes, homes, and weapons, such as bows and arrows	
Fish	food for humans, trade, bait to catch other animals, ceremonial traditions	
Fruits	food for humans, trade, seeds to produce more fruit	
Clay	homes, pottery, art	
Stone	building roads and whole cities	

Circle the correct answer.

1. Which one is not one of the three physical regions of South America?

   A. river basin region
   C. coastal range region

   B. mountains and highlands region
   D. coastal plains region

2. Which natural resource played a major role in the development of the Incas' civilization?

   A. fish
   C. stone

   B. water
   D. timber

3. True or False   The river basin region of South America is defined as a dense, tropical rainforest.

Answer the following questions in complete sentences.

4. What were some important natural resources found in South America?

   ....

   ....

   ....

5. How would Indigenous civilizations of South America be impacted if there was a lack of trees? Provide at least three examples.

   ....

   ....

   ....

ONLINE CONNECTION

Peru is the birthplace of one of the world's most beloved resources: potatoes! Peru grows over 4,000 different species of potatoes in all shapes and colors. Research Peruvian potatoes to learn about the different types and nutritional qualities of at least three different varieties. Then create a slideshow presentation about what you have discovered. Next time you visit the grocery store or farmer's market, see what kind of unique potatoes you can find!

Adapting to Changes in the Environment in South America

By the end of this lesson, you will be able to:

- explain how people make and respond to changes in their environment in various ways
- identify the significance of the Inca road system
- examine other ways that people in South America made changes to their environment
- illustrate examples of how they responded to changes in the environment

Lesson Review

If you need to review how South Americans use the resources of their environment, please go to the lesson titled "Physical Geography and Natural Resources of South America."

Academic Vocabulary

Read the following vocabulary words and definitions. Look through the lesson. Can you find each vocabulary word? Underline the vocabulary word in your lesson. Write the page number of where you found each word in the blanks.

- **fan delta:** triangle-shaped deposits that form in the freshwater bodies of water at the base of landforms like mountains (page ____)
- **sediment:** bits of rock, dirt, and sand that settle to the bottom of water (page ____)
- **subduction zone:** a mountain formation in which a heavier tectonic plate moves underneath a lighter one (page ____)

Environmental factors change physical features. Gather some sand, mud, clay, or gravel. Use as many of these materials as you like. Use these materials to create different landforms, like mountains, plains, lakes, and rivers. Use your breath or a fan to create wind, from gentle to forceful. Observe how the wind affects your landscape. Use spray bottles, pitchers, or a hose to observe the flow and movement of water and how it affects your landscape. How do you think the environment changes over time? Share your ideas with your instructor.

How familiar are you with the system of roads in your community? Could you travel to the nearest grocery store, library, recreation center or park, or museum without a map or navigator?

Roads are very important for making travel more efficient, which means reaching the destination with the least amount of energy used. If the main roads you use to get to your favorite places were no longer there, do you know other routes you could use? Would they be more or less efficient than the roads you usually use?

Now imagine being an early settler in an area. It can be where you live now or somewhere else entirely. How would you go about setting up roads to help people get where they needed to go?

....

....

....

TAKE A CLOSER LOOK

Here are a few ways humans impact their environment:

- building and development
- deforestation
- desertification
- mining
- flood control
- water management

READ

South America's Environmental Changes

You learned how physical processes can change an environment. This is evident in South America in many ways. A subduction zone formed the Andes Mountains. A **subduction zone** occurs when a heavier tectonic plate moves underneath a lighter plate. In this case, an oceanic plate is moving under a continental plate, causing folds and faults to form these mountains. The Andes are the highest and broadest mountains to still be actively growing.

At the top of the Andes, many glaciers provide fresh water for people, plants, and animals. These glaciers have experienced widespread melting, which formed fan deltas. **Fan deltas** are triangle-shaped deposits that form in bodies of fresh water at the base of landforms like mountains. As the glaciers melt, water travels down the mountain and takes sediment with it. **Sediment** is bits of rock, dirt, and sand that settles to the bottom of water.

The Patagonian Desert, the world's eighth-largest desert, was formed by a rain shadow, which happens when a mountain range blocks rain and other moisture from an area of land, turning it into a desert. The Patagonian Desert is dry, harsh, and cold.

In ancient times, the Amazon River flowed from east to west. Scientists believe that, as the Andes Mountains formed, the river flowed west down the rising landscape, filling the fresh water lakes at its basin. Over time, erosion from the river's flow led to the lakes filling with sediment, raising the lake bottom higher and creating wetlands. Eventually, this rise was enough to push back against the river's flow, sending it back in the opposite direction. Now it flows west to east!

Andes Mountains

Patagonian Desert

Amazon River

Discover! SOCIAL STUDIES • GRADE 5 • LESSON 59

READ

Human Changes to South America

As people settle, they adapt to their environment to thrive. Over time, they also change their environment to suit their needs. They dig wells and irrigate to have fresh water, develop ways to travel, and build homes and other structures.

In South America, the Inca made the most of a very abundant resource in the Andes Mountains: stone. They used stone tools to craft enough stone structures like homes, buildings, and temples to support a population of roughly 10 million that were resilient enough to last for hundreds of years in an area prone to earthquakes.

The Inca also used stones to build a system of roads throughout their empire. Their road system spanned 25,000 miles (40,000 kilometers), making it the largest and best organized system of roads on the planet at the time. These roads were used to transport goods and for official state business, military purposes, and communication. Common people were not allowed on them. There were stations along the road where runners called *chaskis* would wait for a message to arrive. Messages could travel up to 150 miles (240 kilometers) in a day! This helped the empire's outlying areas to stay connected to the central government.

ONLINE CONNECTION

Incan Records

Though the Inca didn't use written language, they did develop an innovative way of record-keeping. Using alpaca wool to weave rope, they would tie a collection of ropes and knots together in a form called a *khipu*. The knots were used for record-keeping about things like the transport of goods, census data, tax collecting data, calendars, and historical information.

An Incan Stone Civilization

An Incan Stone Trail

READ

Adapting to Changes

The physical geography and rich natural resources of South America still face the challenges of change today. Due to rising temperatures, glaciers are melting rapidly in the Andes. Between 2000 and 2016, the Andes lost one-third of their ice. This is roughly three inches (eight centimeters) per year. This means an increase in glacial water for drinking, bathing, and agriculture, but eventually that glacial water will dry up as the ice melts. The glaciers also provide economic opportunity due to tourism.

The melted water travels down the mountain to bodies of water, carrying eroded rocks, dirt, and sand from the mountain. If the melting continues at current rates, people will have to relocate to more accessible water and economic opportunities.

In the Amazon Rainforest, logging and deforestation for timber have led to soil erosion, crop loss, and cycles of flooding and drought. As the region destabilizes, desertification becomes more likely. In the past 30 years, 15 percent of the Amazon Rainforest has been lost to deforestation. The Amazon Rainforest is considered the lungs of the planet, offsetting carbon and maintaining a stable biome for diverse plant and animal life.

Scientists, educators, and conservation groups are working to equip areas with firefighting equipment and to promote sustainable forestry and fire-free development in the area.

REVIEW

In this lesson, you learned:

- South America's physical geography has changed due to environmental factors, like erosion, glacial melting, desertification, and the flow of fresh water.

- As humans settle, they change the environment to suit their needs.

- The Inca had a highly developed society and used available resources to build structures and 25,000 miles (40,000 kilometers) of roads to support millions of people in the Andes.

- Environmental factors and human development continue to change South America's physical geography.

Think About It

How might South Americans respond to changes in their environment in the years to come?

Discover! SOCIAL STUDIES • GRADE 5 • LESSON 59

SHOW WHAT YOU KNOW

Place the following events in order from 1 (first) to 4 (last).

1. _____ Sediment caused the basin bottom to rise.

2. _____ Water flowed down the rising landscape into the basin.

3. _____ The Andes Mountains formed in a subduction zone.

4. _____ The wetlands rose enough to push back against the river.

Fill in each black with the correct answer.

5. The Inca built a system of _____ that spanned 25,000 miles (40,000 kilometers).

6. Roads were used for official state business, transport of goods, military purposes, and _____.

7. Messages could travel up to 150 miles (240 kilometers) in a day thanks to runners called _____.

8. _____ were not allowed to use the roadways.

9. This system enabled outlying areas to stay connected to the centralized _____, maintaining the strength of the empire.

ONLINE CONNECTION

Incan Communications and Records
Research Inca khipu further to find out more about this fascinating method of communicating and keeping records. Once you have learned more about how this tool was used, search for videos on how to tie a khipu and practice making your own!

Answer the following questions in complete sentences.

10. Describe one way in which changes to freshwater access led humans to change either their environment or how they lived.

....

....

....

....

11. How are people responding to deforestation in the Amazon?

....

....

....

....

Natural Resources in South America

By the end of this lesson, you will be able to:

- identify the physical processes that contribute to the availability and abundance of a natural resource
- compare and contrast the availability and distribution of natural resources in South America across regions

Lesson Review

If you need to review the geography of South America, please go to the lesson titled "Maps of South America."

Academic Vocabulary

Read the following vocabulary words and definitions. Look through the lesson. Can you find each vocabulary word? Underline the vocabulary word in your lesson. Write the page number of where you found each word in the blanks.

- **abundance:** a large amount of something (page ____)
- **climatic processes:** interactions in nature that relate to the climate (page ____)
- **decomposition:** the break-down of dead plants and animals into smaller material (page ____)
- **export:** a good that is sold and sent to other countries (page ____)
- **fossil fuel:** a nonrenewable resource made from decomposed plants and animals; these fuels are burned for energy (page ____)
- **geological features:** naturally created or human-made features of Earth's surface (page ____)
- **geologic processes:** the process involving how Earth or its surface is changed (page ____)
- **hydrologic cycle:** how water moves on the planet (page ____)

What do you remember about the water cycle? Remember the water cycle, or hydrologic cycle, explains how water naturally moves from place to place on earth. Create a diagram or a drawing showing what you remember about this natural process. Show your instructor your diagram and review this process together.

- **natural processes:** a series of steps or interactions in nature that create or change something (page ____)
- **natural resource:** any useful substance that can be found in nature (page ____)
- **nonrenewable:** cannot be reproduced or replenished (page ____)
- **ore deposits:** large quantities of a particular mineral (page ____)
- **renewable:** can be reproduced or replenished when needed (page ____)
- **terrain:** physical features (page ____)

EXPLORE

Brazil provides people across the globe with an important natural resource, wood. **Natural resources** are materials found in nature that can be used. Wood is a natural resource because trees grow in nature. Wood, or lumber, is used to build numerous products such as homes and furniture. Why does this country have an **abundance**, or an excess, of wood?

Brazil contains large rainforest environments. Rainforests grow here due to natural processes. A **natural process** is a series of steps or interactions in nature that create or change something. Every natural resource is the result of natural processes. The water cycle is an example of one natural process.

Can you think of another natural process? Discuss your thinking with your instructor.

TAKE A CLOSER LOOK

Satellite images are photographs taken from space. They allow us to see Earth and locations on Earth from far away. We can see mountains, forests, snow on high peaks, and even bodies of water.

South America's terrain, or physical features, are different depending on where you look. What physical features do you see when you look at this satellite image of South America? Can you find the Amazon Rainforest? What does this photograph tell you about the types of natural resources that might be found on the continent? Discuss your thinking with your instructor.

READ

The Earth Makes Natural Resources

The wood found in rainforests is the result of several natural processes. In the **hydrologic cycle**, or water cycle, water from oceans and lakes evaporates into the atmosphere as it is heated by energy from the sun. This water condenses as it rises and comes into contact with cooler air. It then falls back to Earth through precipitation, or rainwater. Rain runs into the soil, rivers, and lakes, providing fresh water for plants and animals.

The precipitation that rainforests receive is due to **climatic processes**. These are interactions in nature that relate to the climate. Rainforests have tropical climates. Found along Earth's equator, their temperatures are consistently warm, and water evaporates quickly in the heat. The warm air can also hold more water than cold air, creating high levels of humidity. The humidity, heavy rainfall, and heat provide conditions necessary for rainforests' many species of plants and animals to thrive.

Geologic processes involve the creation of Earth's mountains, rocks, minerals, and soil, or **geological features**. Rainforests contain large systems of rivers that, along with rainwater and flooding, erode, or break down rock. These forests therefore have few rocks. The soil is sandy and lacks nutrients.

Wood, metal, rock, oil, bamboo, clay, and water are just some of the natural resources people find, collect, and use. Each of these resources is found in certain locations due to natural processes.

WRITE

How are natural resources created?

....

....

....

....

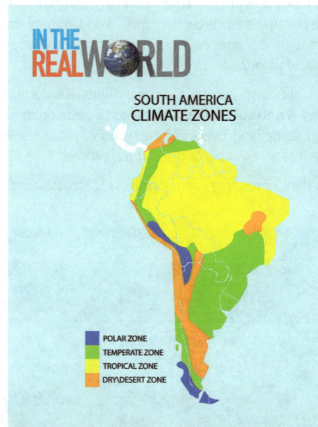

IN THE REAL WORLD

SOUTH AMERICA CLIMATE ZONES

- ■ POLAR ZONE
- ■ TEMPERATE ZONE
- ■ TROPICAL ZONE
- ■ DRY\DESERT ZONE

Regions of South America

Countries in South America that lie near the equator have tropical climates while areas closer to the southern polar region endure colder temperatures. Some countries have tall mountains, such as the Andes Mountain range that runs through the western part of the continent. Other regions have low, level plains. With varied physical features and climates, natural processes have resulted in the growth or settlement of different resources in each region of South America.

South America's Natural Resources

South America is rich in natural resources, but these resources are not distributed evenly across the continent. The Amazon Rainforest is located in northern Brazil and in parts of Colombia, Peru, and Bolivia. This region's plentiful natural resources include fresh water, lumber, gold, and iron. Tropical fruits and vegetables such as avocado, banana, pineapple, coffee, and papaya grow easily.

Argentina, Brazil, and Uruguay contain land called the Pampas. Here you can find grasslands with rich soil good for farming. With nutrient rich soil as a natural resource, this area is ideal for growing crops such as corn and wheat. Ranchers also raise livestock such as cattle.

Chile and Peru have extremely large coastlines that border the Pacific. The ocean waters here are rich in fish. Many of the fish caught are turned into fish meal, which is used to feed farm animals and create nutrient rich fertilizer.

Ore deposits are large quantities of a particular mineral. Brazil has one of the largest supplies of iron ore in the world. This metal is extracted from mines and becomes an **export**, or a good that is sold and sent to other countries. The Andes Mountain Region in Peru and Chile contains a large portion of the earth's copper ore. And the hot, dry desert region of the Atacama Desert has mineral deposits as well.

Natural resources on this continent are spread out unevenly. Each region has a unique combination of resources used by the population.

DECOMPOSITION

The Amazon Rainforest grows in sandy soil that contains few nutrients. How can so many species of plants and animals thrive in an environment with soil that is not rich in nutrients? The answer lies in another important natural process. When plants and animals die, they decompose on the forest floor. This process of **decomposition**, or the break-down of dead plants and animals into smaller material, provides nutrients for the top layer of soil. Remember that every natural resource is the result of natural processes!

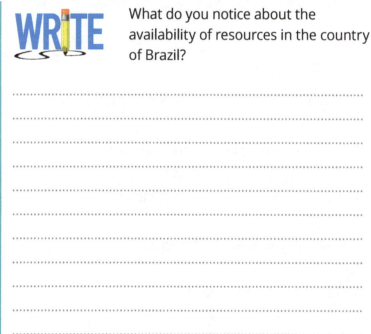

WRITE What do you notice about the availability of resources in the country of Brazil?

PRACTICE

Write the natural resources found in each region of South America on the lines below.

1. Resources found in the Amazon Rainforest

....

2. Resources found in the Pampas region

....

3. Resources found in the Andes Mountains

....

4. Resource found in Coastal regions

....

5. Other resources found in Brazil

....

6. A resource found in Venezuela

....

REVIEW

In this lesson, you learned:

- Natural processes result in the creation of natural resources.

- Each region of South America has natural resources that can be used by the people living in the region.

- The Amazon Rainforest's unique climate and physical features have led to the availability of resources such as fresh water, fruits, lumber, and metals.

- The Pampas region has rich soil, flat land, and a temperate climate that have led to successful agriculture.

- Brazil has a wealth of natural resources including fresh water, gold, iron, petroleum, and agricultural products.

Think About It
How do you think the resources in a particular region affect the people living there?

Choose the correct answer for each question.

1. Natural resources are the result of _____.

    A. humans making products

    B. humans living in a region

    C. natural processes

    D. factories and businesses

2. How are the resources of the Pampas region different from those found in the Amazon region?

    A. The Pampas region contains petroleum while the Amazon has plenty of rich soil.

    B. The Pampas region has rich soil while the Amazon has plenty of lumber.

    C. The Pampas region is known for fishing in rivers and lakes while the Amazon is known for growing corn and wheat.

    D. The Pampas region is known for growing wheat while the Amazon contains large amounts of coal.

3. _____ is a nonrenewable natural resource found in Peru and Chile.

Answer the following question with complete sentences.

4. Describe how climate affects the natural resources found in a region.

....

....

....

....

ONLINE CONNECTION

A food or energy web is another type of natural process. Food webs explain or show how the plants and animals in an ecosystem depend on each other to survive. Select an ecosystem you would like to study. Create a food web for the ecosystem you choose. What natural resources are a product of or depend upon this food web?

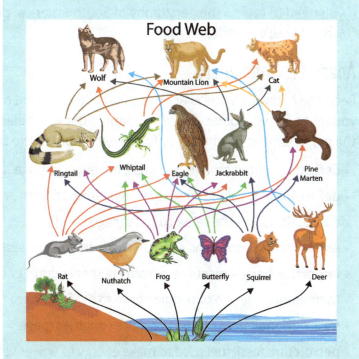

Food Web

Lesson 61

Importance of Natural Resources in South America

By the end of this lesson, you will be able to:

- identify key natural resources found in South America
- describe how the use, distribution, and importance of natural resources can affect different groups
- identify the impact of trade on the availability of natural resources

Lesson Review

If you need to review the geography of South America, please go to the lesson titled "Maps of South America."

Academic Vocabulary

Read the following vocabulary words and definitions. Look through the lesson. Can you find each vocabulary word? Underline the vocabulary word in your lesson. Write the page number of where you found each word in the blanks.

- **deficit:** an amount that is too small, not enough (page ____)
- **deforested:** forest or trees have been removed from an area (page ____)
- **domestic:** within the same country (page ____)
- **export:** to sell goods and send them to other countries (page ____)
- **import:** to bring a resource in from another country or continent (page ____)
- **Indigenous:** a group of people native to the land (page ____)
- **international:** between two or more countries (page ____)
- **petroleum:** fossil fuel used to make energy to power vehicles (page ____)
- **populations:** particular sections, groups, or types of people or animals living in an area or country (page ____)

Cut white paper into three by three inch squares. Make two identical cards showing each of South America's important resources. Leave one side of each card blank. Draw a pictures of:

- oranges
- bananas
- coffee
- corn
- wheat

- water
- metal
- wood
- fish
- oil

Once your cards are made, shuffle them. Invite someone to play with you. Turn your cards face down on a flat surface. Turn over two cards. If the cards match, or have the same picture, you keep them and have earned a point. If the cards do not match, turn the cards face down again, leaving them in the same places. Alternate flipping cards with the other player.

- **surplus:** an abundance or excess (page ____)
- **trade:** the action of exchanging something for something else (page ____)

EXPLORE

What is your favorite fruit? Apples, oranges, mangos? How many do you think you could eat in one day? One, two, or maybe three would be plenty. Now imagine you have three fruit trees filled with your favorite fruit in your backyard. What are you going to do with all this fruit? There is way too much to eat yourself.

With so much fruit, you have some decisions to make. You could give fruit away to your neighbors, friends, or family. You could make jelly or jam and preserve your extra fruit in jars. If you feel like making some money, you could sell your extra fruit!

Sometimes countries have extra natural resources that they don't need. They sell their extra resources to other countries who do need them. With so many natural resources, it's not surprising that South America sells a lot of resources to other countries.

What resources do you think South America sells to other countries? Why do you think South America has too many of these particular resources?

South America is able to grow a lot of coffee, especially the countries of Brazil and Colombia! Coffee is sold to countries around the world. If your parents enjoy a cup of coffee in the morning, there is a good chance that the coffee was grown in Brazil or Colombia. You can even check the package to see where the coffee was grown!

Coffee beans growing on a plant look very different from those you see in a store. They must be dried, roasted, and ground before they can be used to make a coffee drink.

READ

Agriculture in South America

Farming in tropical regions of South America provides many natural resources for the people. Coffee, bananas, oranges, and cashews are grown in countries such as Brazil, Ecuador, Colombia, Peru, and Chile. With a **surplus** of these goods, or more than the population needs, they can be **exported** to other nations. This means the goods are sold and sent to other countries. This **trade**, or exchange of goods between groups of people, helps build the nation's wealth.

Southern Brazil and Argentina, which have mild climates, grow products such as wheat and corn in the Pampas region. Cattle are also raised in this area. With a large surplus, Argentina and Brazil can export beef and corn to other nations.

The majority of the Amazon Rainforest is found in Brazil. The Amazon Rainforest's trees provide wood that timber companies sell both internationally and domestically. If a product is sold **internationally**, it is sold to another nation. If a product is sold **domestically**, it is sold to citizens in the country where it is made or grown.

While many countries grow a surplus of agricultural products, some countries have a deficit. A **deficit** means the country must import goods to support its population. It does not grow enough. To **import** means to buy and bring in goods from another country. The nations of Venezuela, Guyana, and French Guyana have a deficit of agricultural resources. They must import goods for the population.

How does agriculture differ across the continent of South America?

Trading in South America
What does trade between countries look like? Most goods sent to other continents must travel by boat.

Many of Brazil's surplus goods are shipped from Guanabara Bay in Rio de Janeiro. They travel to faraway places in shipping containers that keep the resources safe and dry.

READ

The Effects of Trade in South America

The harvesting, sale, and use of natural resources affects South America's **populations**, or groups of people, differently. It also affects the ecosystems where these resources are produced.

Citizens may benefit from the money earned from the trade of lumber, but there are groups of people who do not benefit. The Amazon Rainforest is home to many **Indigenous** people of Brazil. As large pieces of the Amazon are **deforested**, or cut down, these native people are further displaced and forced to move.

Portions of the Amazon Rainforest are also being destroyed to make room for new farms and ranches. Farmers and ranchers eager to sell more beef, coffee, and oranges across the globe, burn acres of rainforest for their farms. Cows graze and tropical fruit groves flourish in the tropical climate where forest was once found. This growth benefits farmers who wish to make profit. However, it negatively affects native people and the rainforest ecosystem. Farmers and the lumber industry are making popular resources more available, but in doing so, they are destroying rainforests and forcing Indigenous populations of people to relocate.

Brazil's iron ore and Chile's copper ore are both valuable trade exports. Used in the creation of steel structures such as buildings and the making of machinery, iron and copper ore brings money to these countries. Workers from other regions migrate to work in the mines of Chile and Brazil, leaving their communities behind.

WRITE

How has trade impacted the people of South America? How has trade affected the availability of natural resources?

....
....
....

TAKE A CLOSER LOOK

Amazon Rainforest

Brazil can afford to export goods such as beef, corn, coffee, bananas, and cashews. Each year more Amazon Rainforest is cut down or burned to make way for more farms. Many Indigenous tribes are forced off their land.

Hundreds of Indigenous tribes still live in the Amazon and do not trade their natural resources. They hunt, gather, and plant only what they will need to survive. They want to preserve their lands and avoid destroying their Amazon home.

What do you think should happen to the Amazon Rainforest? Should deforestation continue, or should native peoples and the forest itself be left in peace?

READ

Petroleum

Petroleum, the valuable fossil fuel used to make energy to power vehicles, is a natural resource that has caused great population shifts in South America. Venezuela, Ecuador, Peru, Brazil, and Colombia all drill substantial amounts of oil. Indigenous populations and farmers have migrated to petroleum rich areas for jobs with better pay.

The many natural resources present in South America provide a wealth of goods available for trade. However, groups and cultures have been forced to change as a demand for certain natural resources has increased. As groups of people make resources more available for trading, there is a shift in where people work.

PRACTICE

Fill in the blank spaces below with a cause or effect from the lesson.

Cause	Effect
	Coffee, bananas, and iron are traded with other nations.
There is a high demand for beef.	
	Indigenous tribes are forced off their lands.
Large quantities of trees grow in the Amazon.	
	Farmers and workers may move into cities or near mines.

REVIEW

In this lesson, you learned:

- Petroleum, coffee, bananas, iron, copper, and lumber are key natural resources in South America.
- Resources can be exported or imported depending on their availability.
- Groups relocate to find work on farms or in mines.
- Some communities, especially Indigenous people, are negatively impacted when a country harvests natural resources in natural environments.

Think About It

How can countries seek to improve their economies while protecting the environment and native people?

Which of South America's important resources do you use or consume? Do you eat bananas, travel by car, or have wooden furniture? Perhaps you eat cashews, oranges, or pineapples. Select one resource from South America and research how it is grown, harvested, and shipped to your country. Use what you learn to create a slideshow or sequence illustrating this resource's journey.

1. Use the map above to answer this question. Lumber, iron, and tropical fruits are natural resources found in which area?

   A. Amazon Rainforest   **D.** Paraguay

   B. South Pacific Ocean   **E.** Chile

   C. Venezuela

2. True or False   Nations can export natural resources when they have a surplus.

3. _____ people are sometimes forced to move when natural resources are grown, harvested, and used.

4. Nations with a _____ do not have enough resources for their population.

5. Why do some people or groups choose to relocate to new regions in South America?

....

....

....

....

....

....

....

....

Lesson 62
Human Migration

By the end of this lesson, you will be able to:

- extend understanding that human migration is influenced by many factors and that people migrate for voluntary and involuntary reasons

- compare and contrast the factors contributing to various mass migrations to Brazil

- identify the factors that led to the migration of people from one region in South America

- examine the influences and contributions of the migrants to the new region

Lesson Review

If you need to review when and why people first came to South America, please go to the lesson titled "Human Settlement in South America."

Academic Vocabulary

Read the following vocabulary words and definitions. Look through the lesson. Can you find each vocabulary word? Underline the vocabulary word in your lesson. Write the page number of where you found each word in the blanks.

- **immigrants:** people who have moved to a new land (page _____)

- **involuntarily:** forced, not done freely (page _____)

- **labor:** manual workers; physical work (page _____)

- **mass migration:** many, many people moved around the same time for similar reasons (page _____)

- **migrate:** to move from one area to another, sometimes in search of resources (page _____)

- **oppression:** when rights are ignored or taken away (page _____)

- **poverty:** poor conditions without enough money or resources (page _____)

PLAY.

You are immigrating, or moving, to a new country! Line up one of the ends of a paper clip with the dot in the center of the circle. Stick the point of a pencil in the end of the paper clip so that the clip will spin around the pencil when flicked. Spin the paper clip to see where it lands.

Where did your paper clip land? Research this South American country. What language do the people speak? What foods do the people eat? Will you live in a city or rural area? What resources are plentiful?

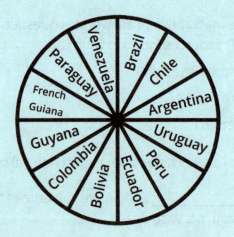

- **subsistence farmers:** family farmers who harvest just enough crops to feed themselves (page _____)

- **voluntarily:** not forced, done freely (page _____)

People move to new cities, states, and countries every day. They **migrate**. Many people move for a new job or to go to a new school. Some people want to experience a different culture and language. These are voluntary reasons for moving. Someone moves **voluntarily** when they choose to leave their home.

What will you need for your new life in South America? Think about the climate and geographical features of the land. Draw pictures of the items you will pack in your suitcase.

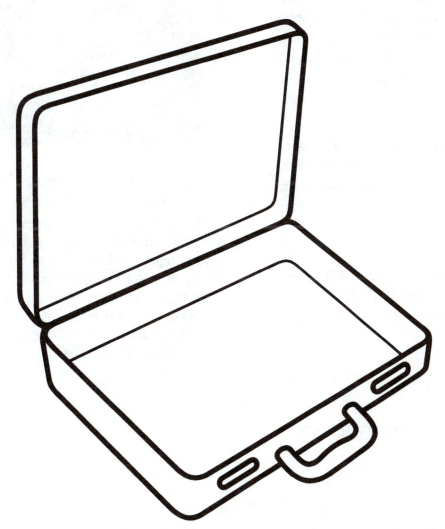

Immigration

Immigration can help people improve their quality of life. Many people move voluntarily, but some individuals immigrate to a new country or region involuntarily. This means they are forced to leave. During times of war, violence, enslavement, or oppression, citizens involuntarily leave their countries. Citizens are oppressed when their rights are ignored or taken away. Natural disasters such as hurricanes, earthquakes, drought, or famine are another cause of involuntary migration.

Immigrants in Brazil

Immigrants, or people who have moved to a new land, have moved to Brazil from all over the world. Brazil's immigrants have provided new skills, cultures, and labor to the country. **Labor**, or workers, help produce many products, farm land, and build businesses.

Colonial Era

In the 1500s, Spanish, Portuguese, and French explorers and colonists sailed to South America. They introduced new languages, religion, and cultures to the Indigenous people. They also brought disease and violence as they claimed the land for themselves. These first immigrants soon brought slaves from Africa to provide free labor. Many explorers and colonists voluntarily moved to South America. Unfortunately, slaves were forced **involuntarily** to move to a new home.

Industrial Era

In 1890, the population in Asia and Europe was growing fast. A **mass migration** to Brazil began. This means many, many people moved around the same time for similar reasons. Immigrants from both Europe and Asia wanted to take advantage of South America's small population and wealth of natural resources.

Post World War II

Following World War II, the United States took control of Okinawa, an island in Japan. More than 50,000 Japanese citizens from Okinawa immigrated to Brazil between 1953 and 1973. Many immigrants from the Middle East also migrated to Brazil. These men and women sought religious freedom as members of the Muslim, Christian, and Jewish faiths.

TAKE A CLOSER LOOK

Natural Disasters Cause Involuntary Immigration
In 2010, almost 100,000 immigrants arrived in Brazil following a large earthquake in Haiti. The Brazilian government gave these immigrants refugee status. A refugee is a person forced to leave their country involuntarily due to a natural disaster, war, or persecution.

WRITE

What is the difference between voluntary and involuntary immigration?

....

....

....

Migration Within South America

Not only have immigrants from other continents traveled to Brazil, but citizens of other South American countries have also relocated. Brazil has the largest economy in South America. Many South Americans from other nations have traveled to work in the oil, mining, lumber, or farming industry.

Many people living high in the Andes Mountains of Venezuela, Ecuador, and Bolivia live in **poverty**, or poor conditions without enough money or resources. These Andean communities face difficult decisions about their future. In their rugged mountain homes, these farmers raise potatoes, coffee, tobacco, and cotton. However, many farms do not bring in a surplus that can be used for trade. These areas also suffer from a lack of basic services that are available in cities. Health care and internet services are hard to come by. Transportation on dangerous mountain roads also impacts life and the ability to move easily between towns and cities.

These **subsistence farmers**, or farmers who grow only enough to survive, face an important choice in today's world. They must decide whether to remain in their home or to **migrate** to another region. Some of these farmers decide to relocate to the Amazon region in Brazil to work on another farm or in hopes of starting a new farm of their own. Others move to urban areas, cities where a variety of resources and services are available.

Indigenous Migration Within South America

Many of the farmers who choose to migrate from high in the Andes region and other regions across South America are Indigenous people, or native to the land. Their ancestors were not European settlers or colonists. These native people moving to larger cities such as São Paulo and Rio de Janeiro, have a great impact on the communities to which they move. They bring new languages, clothing, foods, and skills to these larger populations. These Indigenous people with greater access to education and services can create communities and organizations in their new homes, keeping their cultures alive. They can demand support from government institutions for Indigenous people's rights and aid for isolated and poor communities around the continent.

Immigration Out of Venezuela

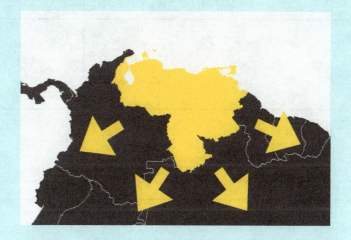

In 2014, a large wave of immigrants from Venezuela began entering Brazil. Food shortages leading to inflation, or high prices for goods, were causing hunger. Hunger was leading to violence. People became desperate to feed their families.

Do you feel this immigration is voluntary or involuntary? Discuss your thinking with your instructor.

PRACTICE

List three voluntary and three involuntary reasons people migrate.

Voluntary	Involuntary

WRITE

Why do people migrate to Brazil from other South American countries?

....

....

Why do people migrate from the Andes region to the Amazon region of Brazil?

....

....

....

1. What are voluntary reasons for migrating? Circle all correct answers.

   A. war

   B. famine

   C. natural disaster

   D. education

   E. jobs

2. How do immigrants help improve the communities to which they move?

   ....

   ....

   ....

   ....

   ....

   ....

3. True or False   Migrating to live close to family or friends would be considered involuntary migration.

Japanese Immigration

The Liberdade district of São Paulo, Brazil is home to many Japanese immigrants and their families. Visitors can experience Japanese culture here as they listen to the language, eat traditional foods, and admire architecture and decorations. This immigrant community is a valuable part of Brazil's diverse population. Thinking about what you have learned from the lesson, what part of Japan do you think most immigrants living in this district are from?

4. Circle the South American country where hunger and violence caused an involuntary mass migration that began in 2014.

Cultural Features of South America

By the end of this lesson, you will be able to:

- identify cultural features found in South America
- describe how cultural features in a region of South America influence factors of daily life, such as the economy, government, or transportation

Lesson Review

If you need to review the impacts of human movement in South America, please go to the lesson titled "Human Migration."

Academic Vocabulary

Read the following vocabulary word and definition. Look through the lesson. Can you find the vocabulary word? Underline the vocabulary word in your lesson. Write the page number of where you found the word in the blank.

- **cultural features:** unique traditions or aspects of a culture such as language, religion, and dress (page _____)

TAKE A CLOSER LOOK

The Indigenous peoples of South America contributed a lot to world history. Though some of the traditions and customs of the ancient Incas have been lost to time, there is still a lot we do know about the ways ancient Incas lived, worked, and played. Many descendants of the Incas living today keep the culture alive!

Investigate what daily life and culture was like for the ancient Incas and write a paragraph about a day in their life. Include two or three cultural features (or unique traditions or aspects of culture such as language, religion, and dress).

EXPLORE

So far, you have studied the geography of Africa, Asia, Europe, Central America and the Caribbean, and North America. Take a moment now to think back to what you learned about each area's landforms, patterns of human settlement, geographical features, and physical processes.

How did these things influence the cultural features of each region?

....

....

Now predict how you think the landforms, patterns of human settlement, geographical features, and physical processes of South America influence the cultural features of the continent. What do you think some of the cultural features of South America might be?

....

....

....

IN THE REAL WORLD

South American culture is rich with global influence, especially by advanced ancient civilizations. European colonization, enslaved Africans brought to South America, and immigration from Europe and Asia also influenced South America. All these people brought their traditions and customs to South America with them, creating a unique blend of cultures. Like the traditional weaving pictured below, each tradition and custom brought to South America works together to combine into beautiful cloth.

READ

Cultural Expression

Cultural features are the unique aspects of a culture, such as language, religion, and dress. When people express their culture, they keep their culture alive, strengthen their connection to the past, and build unity with the other members of the culture.

The Treaty of Tordesillas divided the world between Spain and Portugal, two global superpowers in the fifteenth century. Spain claimed almost all of South America except for eastern Brazil. Though this agreement was over 600 years ago, Portuguese is still the official language of Brazil, even though most of South America speaks Spanish.

Most people in South America are Roman Catholic. No South American countries have an official religion except Peru, which supports Catholicism. Indigenous religions are still practiced in areas with high Amerindian populations, especially Bolivia and Peru. Other world religions are also practiced in smaller numbers.

Dress depends on available resources and climate. In the Amazon, people wear feathered or quill headdresses, jewelry, face paint, and tattoos. In Ecuador and Colombia, cotton tunics and tube or wrap skirts are popular. In cold climates, people wear coats, hats, and footwear made of fur. The weaving style and stitches of textiles, shapes of clothing patterns, jewelry, details, and hat style reflect ethnic heritage.

King Fahd Islamic Cultural Center in Buenos Aires, Argentina.

WRITE

How do you think the presence of so many cultures for so many years has influenced the religious tolerance of South America?

....

....

....

....

Quyllurit'i festival parade in Peru, an ancient Inca celebration.

Monuments and Destinations

South America has many popular cultural destinations. The iconic, world-famous Christ the Redeemer statue in Rio de Janeiro, Brazil, attracts two million people each year to the national park it is located in. The long staircase allows foot traffic to the top.

The Rapa Nui people carved the mysterious Moai statues of Easter Island, off the coast of Chile, as early as AD 1250.

In 1960, artist Carlos Páez Vilaró built the Casapueblo, a Greek-inspired home in Punta del Este, Uruguay. It is now a resort with a hotel, restaurant, museum, and gallery.

In the middle of urban Lima, Peru, the ruins of Huaca Pucllana from a pre-Incan society from AD 500 remain. They served as part of the irrigation system and have ceremonial importance.

Machu Picchu was once the famous seat of Incan government and society. South America has many famous government structures. Casa Rosada in Buenos Aires, Argentina, is the presidential residence and seat of the government. Former First Lady Eva Peron gave speeches from the balcony that would later inspire a Broadway musical!

Capitolio Nacional is the home of both houses of Congress in Bogotá, Colombia. The building features a mural by artist Santiago Martínez Delgado, considered the country's most important fresco.

The glass tower in Casa Grande del Pueblo, the new presidential residence, was built in 2018. In front is Palacio Quemado, the former presidential residence and now-museum. To the right is La Paz Cathedral in La Paz, Bolivia.

Palacio de Carondelet is the seat of the Ecuadorian government, located in Quito, Ecuador. Construction began in 1790, and the building also served as the seat of the Southern division of Gran Colombia.

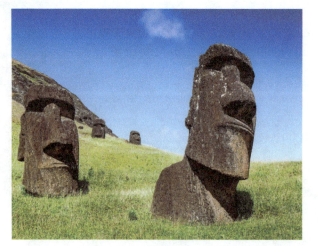

PRACTICE

Cultural features can impact daily life in many ways, including economy and government. Tourist destinations provide economic opportunities. Good economic opportunities attract new residents. Roads and public transit must accommodate the population. Laws keep people safe in busy areas, such as by creating pedestrian-only zones. Security might be necessary around certain monuments or government buildings. Governments decide whether to allow cultural expression. In Peru, for example, Amerindians publicly celebrate Incan religious traditions even though the government officially supports Catholicism.

Select two cultural features discussed in the lesson and explain how they have influenced one aspect of daily life.

CULTURAL FEATURE	INFLUENCE ON DAILY LIFE

REVIEW

In this lesson, you learned:

- South America's cultural features are as rich and varied as their geography and their history.

- Many different cultures interacting with each other through time have created a lot of blending and sharing of traditions and customs.

- Cultural features in South America include language, religion, dress, monuments, historical sites, and government buildings throughout the continent.

- Cultural features can influence daily life, like traffic, public safety, and even if or how cultural expression is allowed.

Think About It
What cultural feature of South America would you most like to experience, and why?

Match the cultural feature or landmark to its location.

1. _____ Christ the Redeemer

2. _____ feathered or quill headdresses

3. _____ Huaca Pucllana

4. _____ Casa Grande del Pueblo

5. _____ Portuguese language

6. _____ largest percentage of Hindus in the Western world

7. _____ Moai statues

8. _____ Palacio de Carondelet

9. _____ Casa Rosada

10. _____ Casapueblo

A. Quito, Ecuador

B. Punta del Este, Uruguay

C. Easter Island, Chile

D. Lima, Peru

E. Amazon

F. Buenos Aires, Argentina

G. Brazil

H. La Paz, Bolivia

I. Rio de Janeiro, Brazil

J. Suriname

ONLINE CONNECTION

Select a government district in the capital of one South American country to research. Find out the history of their government buildings, if they are located on a plaza or square of cultural importance, and explore the architecture of the buildings in the district. What does the design of these buildings say about or mean to the culture where they are located?

Use your research to create a slideshow presentation or poster to teach others about your chosen location. Share your work with your instructor.

Choose which type of impact each scenario below describes.

economic   transportation   population   government

11. making a law to close parks overnight for public safety _____

12. small businesses benefitting from tourists shopping nearby _____

13. deciding to build a new rail line to lessen traffic _____

14. great public transit, lots of housing, and good job opportunities _____

15. governments deciding how or if they will allow different types of cultural expression _____

16. requiring all new roads to be able to handle heavy traffic _____

South American Culture and Geography

By the end of this lesson, you will be able to:

- investigate the cultural geography of South America
- explore influences of South American culture on individuals and civilizations around the world
- discover the impact of South American culture on everyday aspects of life

Lesson Review

If you need to review cultural features of South America, please go to the lesson titled "Cultural Features of South America."

Academic Vocabulary

Read the following vocabulary words and definitions. Look through the lesson. Can you find each vocabulary word? Underline the vocabulary word in your lesson. Write the page number of where you found each word in the blanks.

- **cultural diplomacy:** the act of sharing culture with the world (page _____)
- **intergovernmental organization:** an agreement joining countries together as a group to promote and defend their common interests (page _____)

Do you ever use a ballpoint pen to write? Argentine journalist László József Bíró invented the ballpoint pen after noticing that printer's ink dried faster than quill ink. He developed an oil-based ink that would write smoothly and dry more quickly as it transferred from the ballpoint to the paper.

Look around your house for different kinds of ballpoint pens. See if you can take the parts of these pens apart and put them back together. Notice how each part works together. It is amazing how trying to solve a problem can lead to an invention used all over the world!

You have learned how the diverse backgrounds of people from all over the world who settled in South America began to blend and influence one another. You have also seen how culture influences outwardly as you've studied the cultural geography of other regions around the world.

The inventor László József Bíró lived in Argentina, but he was originally from Hungary. He and his brother moved to Argentina after fleeing the Nazis in 1943. In his new home, he was able to sell his patent to Marcel Bich, the owner of the BIC company that is known worldwide for their ballpoint pens.

When the Bíró brothers immigrated to Argentina, they brought aspects of their Hungarian and Jewish culture with them. When they sold the pen patent to the French BIC Company, cultural exchange continued back from Argentina to Europe.

You have learned that cultural exports are the things a culture shares with the world. But even though the ballpoint pen is a cultural export, it is people who share culture around the world. It is the natural sharing of culture between people of different lands that creates strong relationships and bonds throughout the world.

| Hungary | Argentina | France |

Can you think of ways cultural features have moved into your country and back out again? Have groups of people that have settled in your country made contributions to your culture that are now part of your country's cultural geography? Discuss your thoughts with your instructor.

READ

Cultural Geography

Cultural geography studies the way humans connect to things like natural resources, the economy, government, and religion in order to interact with the world. It asks, "How have humans connected to the world around them to create and shape their culture?" and "How have humans shared and spread their culture outwardly with the rest of the world?"

South America is a place where many cultures intersect. Even in areas like Peru where Catholicism is the official religion, Indigenous people are encouraged to celebrate the traditions of their heritage. When tourists come to see ancient Inca ceremonies, they go home and share their experience with others, spreading culture worldwide.

THE IMPACT

As people move throughout the world and interact with each other, they share and spread their cultures. This is called **cultural diplomacy**, and it creates interest, appreciation, and respect for other cultures. As this goodwill spreads, it helps to develop stronger relationships between countries and cultures in ways that traditional foreign policy and relations cannot.

For example, Rio de Janeiro hosts the world's largest carnival with 2 million visitors per day! Since 1723, this festival has included parades, music, street festivals, and beach parties. Many events feature performances by samba schools that play a style of music and do traditional dance, both called *samba*. This uniquely Brazilian music and dance genre has roots in cultural exchange between enslaved Africans and Brazilians during the early 19th century. It is considered one of Brazil's most important cultural phenomena.

Carnival Parade in Rio

WRITE

What is one difference cultural geography and cultural diplomacy make in the world?

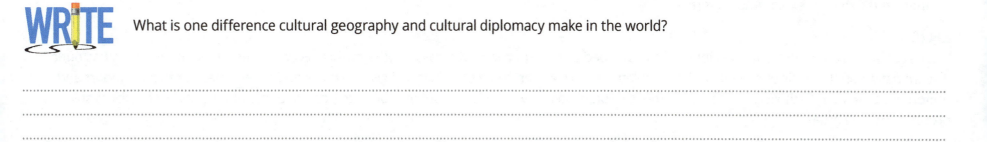

READ

Shaping South American Culture

There are many ways a culture can be shaped, so let's take a look at four main components that shape South American culture.

NATURAL RESOURCES

South America has tremendous resources, but their most valuable resource is the dense forest covering much of South America. They also have many valuable minerals like gold, silver, iron ore, and petroleum. South America is known for its agriculture and wool, but there is a lot of growth in manufactured goods like machinery, chemicals, and paper as exports.

ECONOMY

The economy of each country in South America varies based on their most valuable exports and industries. Several South American countries have experienced economic downturns recently, but have since recovered because of increases in public investment and private spending on goods and services.

The Amazon Rainforest stretches across large areas of South America.

GOVERNMENT

Today, every country in South America is a presidential republic except Suriname (which is a parliamentary republic). The countries of South America have been working in recent years to form an **intergovernmental organization**, or an agreement joining countries together as a group to promote and defend their common interests.

RELIGION

You have learned about the ways religions have developed or been introduced across South America. Every country in South America has outlawed discrimination on the basis of religion in their constitutions. However, some countries still give financial and other types of official support and preference to Roman Catholicism. People are free to worship as they choose without fear of state persecution, but religious inequality is still a problem in some areas.

READ

Cultural Exports and Exchange

Tourism and entertainment are also big contributors to South American culture, so let's take a close look at each.

TOURISM

South America's varied landscapes, climate, and geographic features attract tourists from all over the world. Tourists come to see what remains of ancient civilizations at Machu Picchu or Hualca Pucllana in Peru. Visitors also come to the Andes Mountains, Patagonia Desert, Amazon River, and Amazon Rainforest to see colorful rock formations, unique animal and plant species, glaciers, and waterfalls. People also love to see the important, interesting, and beautiful aspects of culture in towns and cities across South America.

ENTERTAINMENT

South America has produced many globally famous entertainers.

- Carmen Miranda was a Brazilian entertainer known for her singing and dancing—and her headdresses featured stacks of fruit on her head!

- Actor, comedian, producer, and playwright John Leguizamo is from Colombia and has won a special Tony Award and a Primetime Emmy for his contributions to the dramatic arts.

- Venezuelan-born Carolina Herrera, who is a famous fashion designer, has dressed many US First Ladies!

- Fashion journalist Nina Garcia from Colombia is the editor-in-chief of *Elle* magazine and has been a judge on the US TV show *Project Runway* since it began in 2004.

- Argentine footballer Leo Messi has won World Footballer of the Year six times.

- Pelé, from Brazil, won the World Cup three times and was even named Athlete of the Century by the International Olympic Committee in 1999.

REVIEW

In this lesson, you learned:

- Cultural diplomacy is exchanging cultural artifacts or sharing cultural features with others outside the culture, and it is an essential tool for building good relationships between countries.

- Many diverse groups of people have settled in South America, creating a rich cultural exchange.

- People are drawn to South America to experience the history, tradition, and beauty of its geographic formations and landmarks.

- South America has produced scientists, inventors, creatives, and athletes known worldwide for their extraordinary talents and global cultural contributions.

Think About It

What is the most interesting contribution to global culture produced by South America that you have learned about? Why?

WRITE

How do famous singers or sports stars promote cultural diplomacy around the world?

....

....

SHOW WHAT YOU KNOW

Use the words from the Word Bank to complete the sentences.

Word Bank: heart geography wood exports samba diplomacy Andes Mountains

1. Cultural _____ studies how humans connect to things like natural resources, the economy, government, and religion in order to interact with the wider world.

2. One of Brazil's most important cultural phenomena is a dance and music genre called _____ that is a blend of African and Brazilian elements.

3. Three main regions of South America's geographic features are the Amazon, the Patagonian Desert, and the _____, all of which attract nearly a million visitors annually.

4. South America's greatest natural resources are metals and minerals, agriculture, wool, and _____ from the continent's dense forests.

5. Cultural _____ are things shared between cultures.

6. Cultural _____ is the act of sharing or exchanging culture.

7. An Argentine doctor invented the first artificial _____.

Answer the following questions in complete sentences.

8. Why are cultural exchange and diplomacy important?

....

....

9. Name one factor you think has helped make South America's cultural geography so rich, and explain how it has helped.

....

....

Chapter 6 Review

By the end of this lesson, you will:

- review the information from the lessons in Chapter 6, "South America."

Lesson Review

Throughout the chapter, we have learned the following big ideas:

- Maps can tell stories about South America's land and its features. (Lesson 55)
- Landforms and geographic features impact where and how humans settled across South America. (Lesson 56)
- Human settlement is influenced by the environment and its changes. (Lesson 57)
- Indigenous peoples of South America built advanced societies that made use of available resources in ways that influenced humans that settled later. (Lesson 58)
- Environments change over time, both through natural processes and by human change. (Lesson 59)
- South America is rich with natural resources because of the vastly different environmental regions, like the Andes Mountains, Amazon River, and Amazon Rainforest. (Lesson 60)
- Timber from the dense forests across South America is one of the continent's greatest resources, along with metals, wool, petroleum, and agriculture. (Lesson 61)
- People migrate to other countries for voluntary and involuntary reasons. (Lesson 62)
- South America is made up of many different cultures, and human migration has led to a lot of cultural exchange influencing those cultures. (Lesson 63)
- Because South America has a long history of cultural exchange through human migration, complex cultures have developed throughout South America. (Lesson 64)

Go back and review the lessons as needed while you complete the activities.

CREATE

South America is a large, diverse continent full of different people, cultures, landforms, waterways, and many other geographic and cultural features that have influenced the world throughout history.

Using the big ideas from this chapter, create a visual representation of these ideas in the form of a quilt. You can draw, paint, mosaic, or use digital art programs to create your quilt. Just make sure to have one square for each big idea you include. Share your quilt with your instructor.

REVIEW

Maps

Maps tell different stories about the places they display. Topographical maps show things like land elevation and waterways, and geopolitical maps show borders and how continents relate in space to other continents. Look at the image to the right. What story does this map tell?

CONNECTION TO OTHER CONTINENTS

South America is only physically connected to one other continent, North America. The Isthmus of Panama connects North America to South America, bordering Colombia on the South American side.

GEOGRAPHIC FEATURES

South America has incredibly diverse landscapes and landforms throughout the continent. These features provide abundant resources that have provided benefits for people settling across the continent for many years.

Look at the regions below and give one example of a resource that could be found there.

Andes Mountains: _____

Patagonia Desert: _____

Amazon River: _____

Amazon Rainforest: _____

Indigenous Resources, Culture, and Influence

Many Indigenous tribes settled in South America. These peoples traveled from North America into South America. Collectively, Indigenous peoples of South America are typically referred to as Amerindian. The Incan civilization flourished between 1400 and 1533. This advanced empire had a centralized government that was able to stay connected to outlying regions through their road system, used only for official things like government business, military use, and communication.

South America is rich with resources that strengthen their economy to this day. Timber is their most abundant resource, but they also profit from metals like iron ore, copper, silver, and gold, as well as textiles, agriculture, petroleum, and manufactured products like machinery, chemicals, automobiles, and transport equipment.

South American cultures are diverse, having been influenced by Indigenous peoples, European colonizers, migrants, and enslaved Africans. Because the people of South America are so diverse, their cultural and religious expressions are too. South America is tolerant, but in some areas religious discrimination still occurs.

South American culture has influenced the world. Many people travel to South America to visit destinations like Machu Picchu in Peru, Christ the Redeemer in Rio, or Kaieteur Falls in the Amazon. South America has also given the world innovations like the ballpoint pen and artificial heart as well as contributions through athletics, music, art, and literature.

PRACTICE

Three's a Crowd

Circle the word in each group that does not belong.

1. temperate zone   fossil fuel   polar zone

2. geologic processes   climatic processes   cultural features

3. surplus   deficit   terrain

4. involuntary   renewable   nonrenewable

5. ore deposits   fossil fuels   abundance

6. tributaries   mass migration   hydrologic cycle

7. human settlement   subduction zone   immigration

8. population   import   export

9. voluntary   involuntary   Indigenous people

10. cultural features   subsistence farming   cultural diplomacy

REVIEW

It's a good idea to think about the different categories and types of words you have studied in this chapter. Think about the larger ideas groups of terms relate to, like:

- geology or physical processes
- climate
- water
- landforms
- population and human movement
- trade and economics
- cultural exchange and influence

PRACTICE

Cause and Effect

Match each cause statement that follows to its effect.

1. _____ A tectonic plate is subducted below another tectonic plate.

2. _____ A network of sophisticated roadways for official business is created.

3. _____ Alternative renewable energy sources like wind and solar were explored.

4. _____ Rivers carry sediment downstream.

5. _____ European colonizers brought enslaved Africans to South America.

6. _____ Peru gives preferential treatment to the Catholic church.

7. _____ Tourists have a cultural experience and share about it when they go home.

A. Indigenous people are still allowed to express their traditions because of the benefit it brings to the culture and economy.

B. Cultural diplomacy occurs and creates goodwill and strong relationships between countries and cultures all over the world.

C. The Andes Mountains formed.

D. Involuntary migration occurred and resulted in a significant cultural exchange.

E. Outlying regions of the Inca Empire were kept connected to the central government.

F. The need for nonrenewable energy sources like fossil fuels decreased.

G. Erosion occurs along shorelines upstream and deposits sediment downstream.

REVIEW

Remember that cultural exports are things that are exchanged between cultures. The act of sharing culture is known as cultural diplomacy. These activities have to do with cultural exchange, and it benefits the world in many ways—sometimes even by saving lives, like in the case of the artificial heart!

PRACTICE

Summarizing

Being able to summarize is an important academic skill. When you summarize, you retell what you have read or learned, but you only include the most important details and ideas from it.

Review the big ideas from each lesson in the chapter and think about the big ideas you have learned. List one sentence summarizing the main point of four lessons in this chapter.

Lesson ____: ....
....
....
....

Lesson ____: ....
....
....
....

Lesson ____: ....
....
....
....

Lesson ____: ....
....
....
....

Think about what you've learned about in this chapter. Circle how you feel:

4 – I know this chapter really well. I could teach it to someone.

3 – I know this chapter pretty well.

2 – I am still learning this chapter. I am not sure about some things.

1 – I am confused. I have a lot of questions about what I've learned.

Talk to your instructor about your answers. When you're ready, ask your instructor for the Show What You Know activity for the chapter.

WRITE

Think about your learning. What stands out to you in the lessons? What questions do you have? What do you wonder about? You can use this page to take notes, write out your responses, and then discuss them with your instructor.

Chapter 7
Oceania

Bonjour!

It had been a tough time for Chang. He was sad because his home had been destroyed. It is not easy to live when you have nowhere to go. I hope you appreciate your home! I appreciate mine a lot!

Finally, we found the perfect place for Chang to live. The Pantanal is the biggest swampland in the world. Chang would have lots of room to hop around. He could eat as many yummy flies as he wanted! Bon Appetit Chang!

But then I was sad. I didn't want our trip to end. Maybe it didn't have to! Want to hear what happened next?

Viens avec moi!

Fait amusant: During our trip, we had been to many continents. But Monsieur Jean reminded us that there was one we hadn't visited. "Antarctica?" Chang guessed. Jean replied, "That is just for penguins. I am talking about Oceania. If we go there, we can say we have been to every continent in the world."

I didn't need more convincing, and my friends didn't either. So we took the next flight to Australia. We chilled on the beach at the Gold Coast. Chang, Monsieur Jean, and I agreed to take a trip together every year.

But let's remember to protect nature. We have to make sure that frogs and other animals have places to live. It's so sad when we don't.

I hope you enjoyed taking this trip with us. We loved having you with us. Until next time, au revoir!

What Will I Learn?

This chapter focuses on the region of Oceania. It examines the geography and culture of the smallest continent.

Lessons at a Glance

The Stories in Maps of Oceania

By the end of this lesson, you will be able to:

- examine different maps of Oceania
- determine what story each map tells
- identify major cities in Oceania and locate them on a map
- compare and contrast the location of major cities in Oceania to the location of cities in your community with respect to nearby geographic features

Academic Vocabulary

Read the following vocabulary words and definitions. Look through the lesson. Can you find each vocabulary word? Underline the vocabulary word in your lesson. Write the page number of where you found each word in the blanks.

- **arid:** dry (page ____)
- **coral reef:** an ocean feature that is made up of millions of coral skeletons (page ____)
- **metropolis:** a large, busy city (page ____)
- **political map:** a map that shows the government borders for countries, states, and counties as well as locations of cities and capitals (page ____)
- **topographic map:** a map that shows the elevation and the shape of Earth's surface (page ____)

Looking at the Oceania region on the map, why do you think that the region has the word *ocean* in it?

In 1812, the geographer Conrad Malte-Brun coined the French term *oceanie*. This was most likely because the region, made up of islands, is connected together by the ocean. More specifically, the Pacific Ocean holds the Oceania region together.

Think about your state or region. Draw a quick outline of the area below. Next label areas of water such as a creek, lake, river, or ocean. Are there any land features unique to your area such as mountains or hills? If so, identify their approximate location on your sketch. In addition, include the name of your town and, if possible, any nearby towns or cities. What other landmarks would be significant to mark on the map?

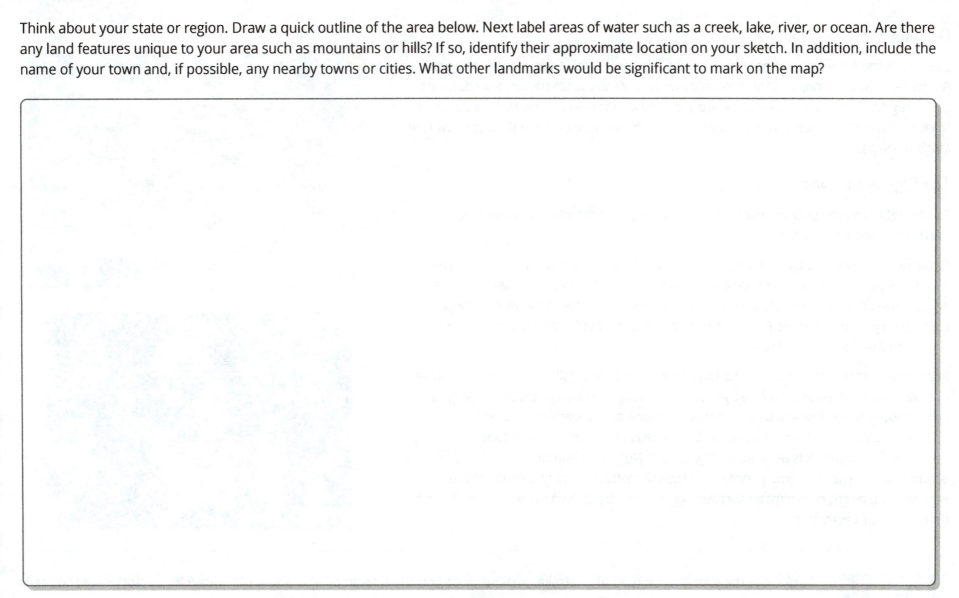

What other characteristics does your region have that make it unique? Is your area famous for a landmark, food, or water area? Why? Why do people come to your area? What is your favorite part of the area you live in?

Oceania

Oceania is the smallest continent on Earth by land area, with 14 countries including Australia, New Zealand, and Fiji. Australia and New Zealand are the largest countries in the region. The islands in Oceania are grouped into three regions: Melanesia, Micronesia, and Polynesia. You can learn about and explore Oceania through different kinds of maps.

The Stories in Maps of Oceania

To the right is a **topographic map**, or a map that shows the elevation and shape of Earth's surface, of Oceania.

Oceania is surrounded by vast amounts of water. This topographic map shows you variations of blue. The darker blue areas show where the water is deeper than the lighter blue areas. The waters surrounding Oceania are home to the world's largest coral reef system called the Great Barrier Reef. A **coral reef** is made of millions of coral skeletons that form rocky ocean features.

In addition to the water, you see the large landmass of Australia. If you look closely at the island of Australia, you will see green areas along the eastern coast. These green areas show you land where trees grow. As you look at the western area of Australia, you can see the majority of it is brown. This area is often called the Outback of Australia. The Outback is an **arid**, or dry, desert. Not many humans live there. Australia is often called "the land down under" because the whole country is south of the equator. You might notice many surrounding islands are shown in green. They have a dense area of vegetation.

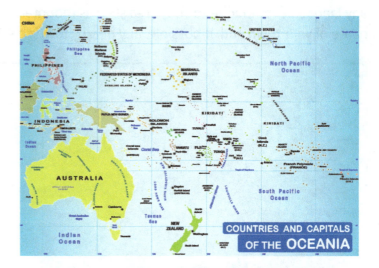

Looking at the topographic map of Australia, what story do you think could be told about the water? What story could you tell about the green areas of the map?

....

....

READ

Identifying Locations in Oceania

Below is a political map of Australia, a country on the continent of Oceania. This is the largest country in the Oceania region. It is also the biggest island on Earth. Australia is largely made up of desert, so most of the population lives in coastal towns and cities.

A **political map** shows the government borders for countries, states, and counties as well as locations of cities and capitals. This map of Australia identifies cities like Sydney, Canberra, and Brisbane.

ONLINE CONNECTION

Sydney Opera House

One of the most famous landmarks associated with Sydney, Australia, is the Sydney Opera House. The unique design makes it recognizable to people all over the world. The opera house has five theaters, two main halls, four restaurants, and a souvenir shop. During a Sydney Symphony Orchestra performance, the temperature must be kept at 72.5°F (22.5°C) to keep the instruments in tune. Use an online search engine to look at various pictures of this beautiful theater.

READ

Major Cities in Oceania

Major City	Features
 **Sydney, Australia**	■ Most populated city in all of Oceania ■ Located on the east coast of Australia ■ Surrounded by the world's largest natural harbor ■ More than 250 languages spoken here
 **Melbourne, Australia**	■ Second most populated city in Australia ■ A **metropolis**, or a large, busy city, on the natural bay of Port Phillip ■ Rates highly in education, entertainment, and health care ■ Distinct honor as the world's most livable city
 **Auckland, New Zealand**	■ Most populated city in New Zealand ■ Home to the largest Polynesian population in the world ■ Desirable fertile land ■ Settled on an isthmus, a narrow strip of land surrounded by sea on either side

REVIEW

In this lesson, you learned:

- Different kinds of maps tell different stories.
- A topographic map shows the landscape of Oceania, and a political map shows the cities, states, and countries of Oceania.
- Some of the major cities in Oceania include Sydney and Melbourne in Australia and Auckland in New Zealand.

Think About It

How do you think this region will be different from other continents you have learned about?

WRITE

How is your hometown similar or different to Oceania? What features are significant to your hometown?

....
....
....
....
....
....

PRACTICE

Circle these cities on the map on the left: Sydney, Canberra, and Brisbane. Notice how these cities are all located on the coast.

You can also see how the country is divided into six states. One of the states is Victoria. Circle the city of Melbourne in the state of Victoria.

The map on the right shows you the island country of New Zealand. It encompasses two land masses: the North Island and the South Island. Circle the region of Auckland on the map. Circle the region where the capital of New Zealand is located, Wellington.

1. Look at the map at right of Australia. What type of map is this?

   A. topographic

   B. political

   C. population

3. On this blank map of Australia, label the cities of Sydney and Melbourne.

2. When you look at this map of New Zealand, what "story" does it tell you?

   A. It tells the elevations of the land and bodies of water.

   B. It tells the cities, states, and surrounding countries.

   C. It tells how many people live in New Zealand.

4. My hometown or state is similar to the Oceania region because:

....
....
....
....
....

5. My hometown or state is different from the Oceania region because:

....
....
....
....
....
....

CREATE

Decide on an Oceanic country of interest to study more closely. You could keep either a digital or paper notebook to save your work.

As you go through the coming lessons about Oceania, you will examine your country and its connection to the subject of the lesson. For this lesson, complete the following activities:

· Find multiple maps of your country. Write about the story you think those maps are telling.

· Create a map for your country. Write the story your map tells about your country.

Geographic Features of Oceania

By the end of this lesson, you will be able to:

- analyze geographic factors that influence where people live in Oceania

- identify the significance of key geographic features of Oceania

- compare and contrast patterns of human settlements of different regions in Oceania and analyze how the environment influenced these settlements

Lesson Review

If you need to review maps of Oceania, please go to the lesson titled "The Stories in Maps of Oceania."

Academic Vocabulary

Read the following vocabulary words and definitions. Look through the lesson. Can you find each vocabulary word? Underline the vocabulary word in your lesson. Write the page number of where you found each word in the blanks.

- **biodiversity:** the variety of life that can be found on Earth or in a particular ecosystem (page _____)

- **desert:** a dry, arid place where it can be hard for people to live (page _____)

- **desert pavement:** areas of closely packed pebbles (page _____)

- **geographic features:** naturally created or man-made features of Earth's surface (page _____)

- **Indigenous people:** the first people to live in an area (page _____)

- **population density:** the number of people who live in a particular area (page _____)

Features in Your Hometown

People often choose where they live based on features that are important to them. For example, fishermen like to live close to the water so they can work or enjoy their favorite pastime.

Think about your hometown. What are your favorite features where you live? On a separate piece of paper, draw a picture of your favorite features in your hometown. Share your drawing with your instructor.

EXPLORE

Imagine that last night at the dinner table, your adventurous family decided on their next adventure—moving to a new place! The best part is that you get to help decide where to go! Think about the important features like climate, ease of access to shopping, recreational areas, and topography of the land that could impact what kind of work your family does.

List your must-have features for your new hometown below.

....
....
....

Oceania contains different geographical features that influence where people have settled and still live today. There are cities, mountain regions, islands, desert areas, and areas used for farming. Why might those geographical features make people choose to live in different parts of Oceania?

....
....
....

Choosing Where to Live

Look at the list below and think about what climate, topography, or areas these people would want to live near.

- Surfer
- Skier
- Farmer
- Marine biologist
- Inuits

READ

Geographic Features and Population

How do people choose where to live in Oceania? One of the greatest impacts on this decision are **geographic features**, or naturally-created or man-made features of Earth's surface.

Australia is rich in natural resources and fertile soil, but almost one-third of the country is covered in desert. A **desert** is a dry, arid place where it can be hard for people to live. The famous Outback contains the country's largest deserts, with extremely high temperatures, little water, and almost no plants. Not as many people live in desert areas because the conditions are harsh. Most Australian cities and farms are located in the Southwest and Southeast regions, where the climate is more comfortable, and the coast is nearby. Would you rather live in the desert or coastal areas of Australia?

The map shows you the population density of Australia. **Population density** is the number of people who live in a particular area.

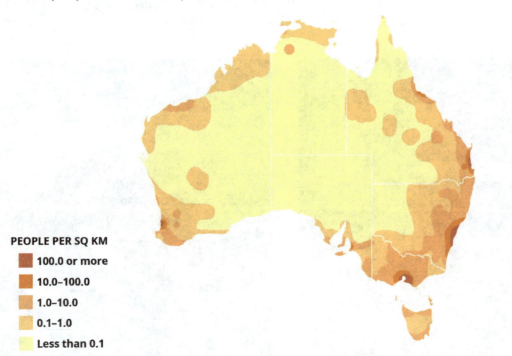

PEOPLE PER SQ KM

- 100.0 or more
- 10.0–100.0
- 1.0–10.0
- 0.1–1.0
- Less than 0.1

The Aborigines

The Indigenous people, or the first people to live in an area, of Australia have a specific name. They are called *Aborigines*. The Aborigines are composed of many distinct groups who originally inhabited the island of Australia. Aborigines value cultural rituals, face painting, ceremonies, and distinct music. They have lived on the continent for many years.

According to the population density map, where do most people live? Which geographical feature is present in the area with most of the people?

....

....

....

....

....

....

....

....

....

....

READ

Geographic Features

Diverse landscapes can be found in Oceania, particularly in Australia and New Zealand. The highest temperatures can reach 123° Fahrenheit (51° Celsius), and the lowest can reach -14° Fahrenheit (-26° Celsius). Read below to find out more about some of the key geographic features in Oceania.

GREAT DIVIDING RANGE

- also known as the "Eastern Highlands"
- largest mountain range in Australia, running along the entire east coast
- complex mountain range with plateaus, upland areas, flat areas, and low hills
- the difference in the height of the mountains affects Australia's climate, causing lots of rain where mountains are the steepest

GREAT BARRIER REEF

- the largest coral reef system and living structure in the world
- located in the Coral Sea, off the coast of northeast Australia
- contains over 900 islands and 2,900 individual coral reefs
- an amazing example of **biodiversity**, which is the variety of life that can be found on Earth, including plants, animals, fungi, and microorganisms

GREAT VICTORIA DESERT

- the largest desert in Australia, situated in the western and southern regions
- receives 8-10 inches (20-25 centimeters) of rainfall per year
- consists of sand dunes, small sandhills, grassland plains, salt lakes, and **desert pavement**, which are areas of closely packed pebbles

SOUTH ISLAND

- the largest landmass of New Zealand
- divided along its length by the Southern Alps, with the highest peak of Mount Cook
- the East Coast is home to the Canterbury Plains
- the West Coast is home to rough coastlines.

READ

Comparing the Settlement Regions of Oceania

Did you know the continent of Oceania is divided into four regions? Let's take a closer look at each one.

MICRONESIA

The major industries in Micronesia are fishing and agriculture. People settled near coasts and water channels to allow for boat access to the island. The climate here is tropical, with heavy year-round rainfall, especially in the east.

MELANESIA

Harvesting vegetables, fish, and spices provide jobs to locals living in Melanesia. People settled near coasts so they could sail their canoes. The climate here is tropical, as well as hot and humid.

POLYNESIA

People living in Polynesia farm fish, sweet potatoes, and coconuts. People settled near social groups, food sources, and places they could defend themselves well. The climate here is tropical, hot, and humid with cool winds.

AUSTRALASIA

People living in Australia mine for coal and diamonds as well as farm. Many farmers produce wool from their sheep. The people settled near the coast, where they had access to water and good soil for crops. The climate here is mild with abundant sunshine.

PRACTICE

Look at the picture. It is a picture of a group of houses in the Melanesia region. Write about what you think the people in this picture do during a typical day. Why do you think they decided to live here?

REVIEW

In this lesson, you learned:

- The vast deserts and mountains that exist inland lead most people to live on the coastlines in the countries of Oceania.

- The Great Victoria Desert, Great Barrier Reef, South Island, and the Great Dividing Range are key geographical features in Oceania.

- There are four regions in Oceania: Micronesia, Melanesia, Polynesia, and Australasia.

- People settled in Oceania's regions for access to mining, farming, a mild climate, fertile soil, and access to water areas.

Think About It
Which Oceania region would you choose to live in? Why?

Circle the correct answer.

1. Why do people generally settle on the coasts of Australia?

   A. the climate is more comfortable

   B. there are no roads to get to the west

   C. the only airports are located on the coasts

2. Which regions of Oceania are most alike? Circle all correct answers.

   A. Melanesia

   B. Micronesia

   C. Polynesia

   D. Australasia

3. How did the environment influence people to settle in Melanesia?

   A. the coasts provided places for them to sail their canoes

   B. the rocky terrain was good for farming

   C. coal mining meant jobs for people

Answer the following question in complete sentences.

4. Select one of the geographic features you learned about and write a brief description of it.

....

....

....

....

....

....

Country Study

Let's continue to learn about the country that you selected to study. For this lesson, complete the following activity about your country:

- Research the regions of settlement in your country. Where do most of the people live? Can you find a population map to include in your research?

- How many regions does your country have?

- What are the key geographic features of your country? Can you find pictures to represent these features?

Lesson 68

Physical Geography of Oceania

By the end of this lesson, you will be able to:

- investigate the physical geography of Oceania
- analyze the effects of the influence of people's relationship to natural resources on the development of various Oceanian civilizations

Lesson Review

If you need to review geographic features, please go to the lesson titled "Geographic Features of Oceania."

Academic Vocabulary

Read the following vocabulary words and definitions. Look through the lesson. Can you find each vocabulary word? Underline the vocabulary word in your lesson. Write the page number of where you found each word in the blanks.

- **archipelago:** a chain of islands (page ____)
- **atoll:** an island shaped like a ring with a base of coral (page ____)
- **continental island:** a land mass surrounded by water rising above a continental shelf (page ____)
- **lagoon:** the pool of water inside an atoll (page ____)
- **Pacific Ring of Fire:** a horseshoe-shaped series of volcanoes around the Pacific Ocean (page ____)
- **tectonic activity:** the movement of Earth's crust (page ____)
- **tectonic plates:** pieces of land that connect together and make up Earth's surface (page ____)
- **volcanic island:** an island formed from lava (page ____)

CREATE

Can you create a landscape?

1. Grab a sheet of aluminum foil that is a little larger than the bottom of your kitchen sink.

2. Crumble up the aluminum foil into a ball.

3. Straighten the aluminum foil out, but don't try to make it perfectly flat. It should have peaks and valleys.

4. Place the foil in the bottom of your sink and run a little water on it. Do you see silver mountains rising above the water? You just made an island like the islands of Oceania!

EXPLORE

Oceania is still being formed today. The Australian **tectonic plate** is moving north at a rate of 2.2 inches (5.6 centimeters) per year. The Pacific tectonic plate is moving northwest at a speed of 3 to 4 inches (7-11 centimeters) per year. Because of this movement, there is a gap in Earth's crust where islands are being created—and these are the islands of Oceania!

About 70 years ago, geographers were in a deep debate between calling the land Australia or Oceania. Before the 1950s, students learned that Australia was a continent by itself. Now, students are taught that Australia is just an island that is a part of the continent of Oceania. Do you think this was an argument worth having? On the lines below, make a prediction about which side you will be on at the end of this lesson.

Geographers divide Oceania into four regions based on plate tectonics, culture, and history. The four regions are Australasia, Melanesia, Micronesia, and Polynesia. *Australis* is Latin for "southern." *Nesoi* is Greek for "islands." A strict translation of the four regions (in order) would be "Southern Land," "Black Islands," "Small Islands," and "Many Islands." Scientific names are often based on Latin and Greek word roots.

PAPUA NEW GUINEA

SOLOMON ISLANDS

SAMOA

FIJI

VANUATU

TONGA

New Caledonia (France)

AUSTRALIA

NEW ZEALAND

Continental Islands

Oceania is mostly composed of four types of islands: continental, volcanic, limestone, and coral. Each type was formed due to different landforms above and below the ocean.

Australia, New Zealand, and New Guinea are the major continental islands. **Continental islands** are land masses surrounded by water rising above a continental shelf. Each of these islands has mountains, highlands, coastal plains, rivers, and lakes. The majority of Oceania's people live on continental islands.

Australia and New Zealand have subtropical climates because they are further from the equator. Australia's eastern mountain range shields the interior from the rains blown in from the Pacific Ocean, so it has a large desert covering the western parts of the landmass. Australia's northern and northeastern coasts are covered in fertile, flat plains. The east coast is made of foothills and coastal plains filled with a variety of forests including a rainforest.

New Guinea is close to the equator, so it has a tropical climate. The rainforest in New Guinea faces many of the same challenges as the Amazon. On the other hand, New Zealand has high, snowy mountains that are good for skiing and lumber as well as fertile sea coasts where most of the population lives.

The Indigenous peoples lived simply from the bounty of the land and sea. They cared little for the zinc, iron, gold, and opals the land might give them, but wood was another matter. Trees were hollowed out for boats, and Indigenous explorers crossed the seas. Using wood, humans spread across three million square miles of ocean.

READ

Fire and Water

Above the ocean, mountain ranges form chains, or a series of peaks and ridges. Imagine a mountain range under the sea. It would also have peaks and ridges in a chain. The tallest peaks and ridges would rise above the water. Some would come close to sea level but would not quite peek out. A chain of islands is called an **archipelago**. Early migrants moved east from Asia and Australia by hopping from one island to the next along the archipelagos they found. An island can only feed so many people, so finding a new island with clean water became part of Polynesian culture.

About 60 percent of Oceanic islands are the tops of ocean mountains and volcanoes. **Volcanic islands**, or islands formed from lava, are created when magma from deep in Earth escapes through holes or tears in Earth's crust. Once magma hits the air, it is called lava, which cools down to form new rock.

About 39 percent of Oceanic islands are volcanic, 17 percent are made from limestone mountains and ridges, and 7 percent are part volcanic and part limestone.

Oceania sits on the southeastern part of the Pacific Ring of Fire. The **Pacific Ring of Fire** is a band of 450 volcanoes that wrap around the Pacific Plate from New Zealand to Japan, Russia, Alaska, and the west coast of North and South America.

ONLINE CONNECTION

On page 2 of this lesson, you were asked to make a prediction whether Australia is a continent or Oceania is a continent. Now it's time to do some online research. Find out what the experts say and then choose your side.

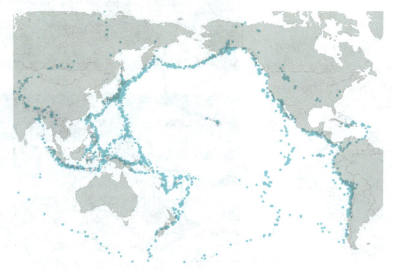

Pacific Ring of Fire

READ

Ridges and Reefs

Large coral reefs can be found throughout the Oceania region. Coral are animals that grow in shallow parts of the ocean and leave behind boney skeletons that form reefs. Coral looks like a bunch of plants, but it's not. Coral grows in shallow sea water at the edges of a landmass. The Pacific Ocean's undersea ridges and the areas around existing islands create fertile, sunlit areas for reefs to form.

Ocean currents will sometimes push sand up over the reef until it emerges from the sea to form an island. Sometimes the ocean floor itself will rise up due to some underlying **tectonic activity**. Either way, a little sand and a friendly current, wind, or bird will eventually bring plant seeds. Trees and plants secure the fragile sand and allow the island to attract more sand that adds to the island's area.

Some coral likes to grow in rings. When a ring of coral rises up to form an island, it is called an **atoll**. The water inside an atoll is called a **lagoon**, which are often rich fishing areas. Because coral islands are so low, some islands, like Tuvalu, are in danger of disappearing back into the sea, but islands with healthy reef systems like the Marshall Islands are actually growing in size.

These smaller islands had few resources except for fish. As humans moved east across these islands, they brought new crops and animals like taro and pigs.

A Lagoon Inside an Atoll

REVIEW

In this lesson, you learned:

- There are four regions that make up Oceania: Austalasia, Melanesia, Micronesia, and Polynesia.
- Oceania's islands formed from volcanoes, limestone, and reefs.
- The Indigenous people of Oceania brought new food resources with them as they migrated.

Think About It
Now that you have learned about Australia and Oceania, do you think Australia is a continent or just an island that is a part of the continent of Oceania?

Answer the questions below by filling in the blank or circling the correct answer.

1. _____islands offer the largest area of land for human habitation in Oceania.

2. What is a chain of islands called?

   A. an archipelago

   B. a ridge island

   C. a coral island

   D. a volcanic island

3. What natural resource allowed Indigenous people to migrate across the ocean?

   A. coal

   B. fish

   C. wood

   D. kiwi

4. If an island has a healthy _____, it may grow larger.

Write your answer on the lines below.

5. Describe how the Indigenous people used natural resources to thrive in Oceania.

....

....

....

....

....

....

....

Country Study

Research the names of countries in Oceania. There are 14 to choose from. Collect as many facts as you can about the way the Indigenous people of that country lived before European colonization.

- What did they eat?
- What did they grow?
- What materials did they use to build shelters?
- What was their religion like?
- What kind of clothes did they wear?
- Add any other questions you think are important.

Responding to Change

By the end of this lesson, you will be able to:

- extend understanding that people make and respond to changes to their environment in various ways
- analyze the effects that the introduction of agriculture had on newly settled regions
- examine other ways that people in Oceania made changes to their environment
- illustrate examples of how they responded to changes in the environment

Lesson Review

If you need to review physical geography, please go to the lesson titled "Physical Geography of Oceania."

Academic Vocabulary

Read the following vocabulary words and definitions. Look through the lesson. Can you find each vocabulary word? Underline the vocabulary word in your lesson. Write the page number of where you found each word in the blanks.

- **degradation:** breaking down and making less valuable (page _____)

- **erosion:** the wearing away of the land by forces such as water, wind, and ice (page _____)

- **mangroves:** trees or shrubs that grow in flooding areas and form dense and thick roots (page _____)

- **soil salinity:** the amount salt in the soil (page _____)

Reshaping the Landscape

People need water. The Australian government estimates that the population of southwest Queensland will almost double between 2020 and 2050, so the need for water in this dry part of Australia will also double. One solution is to build a dam to recreate a reservoir. A dam causes an intentional flood that creates a new lake. The land under the new lake once belonged to people and to an ecosystem.

Think about the pros (good things) and cons (bad things) that happen when humans change a landscape on purpose. Discuss your thoughts with your instructor.

Have you ever picked a dandelion and blown on it? The fuzzy seeds scatter on the wind. Some of the seeds will land on rocks. These won't grow. However, other seeds will land in a newly tilled garden. These seeds will quickly take root and grow. Lastly, some seeds will land in places where there is just enough soil to start growing, but in the end, they will wither and die before a new dandelion can grow and make new seeds.

Heraclitus, a Greek philosopher from the Golden Age, said, "The only constant in life is change." He didn't say change was good or bad. He said you can't stop change. The dandelion is a lesson in change.

Think of humans as seeds. Long ago, someone got in a boat made out of a tree trunk and sailed to the next island they could see. It was a nice island, so they went back and convinced their brothers and sisters to build boats so they could all migrate to the new island. In this way, the seeds of human change blew across the waters.

Was it okay for humans to move to that new island?

....
....
....
....
....
....
....
....

Development of New Zealand

Palmerston North, New Zealand (Palmy), was once a clearing of land in the forest occupied by small Māori communities. After more people colonized in that area, it depended on public works and sawmilling. Today, it has developed into the eighth largest city in New Zealand with museums, art galleries, and performing arts venues.

Change and Response

It is easy to see the changes in Palmerston, and it seems like a nice place for people to live. Step-by-step, people made changes to the environment. What happens when people skip the steps that keep a place Earth-friendly? A change that damages Earth can lead people to respond by defending Earth.

PAPUA NEW GUINEA

Papua New Guinea's mining industry is one of the most important employers in the country. While mining is important to the Papua New Guinea economy, it is also contributing to environmental **degradation**, or breaking down the environment and making it less valuable. For example, the Ok Tedi Mine—a copper and gold mine—produced tons of waste rocks and toxic runoff that flowed into the river system. It has destroyed the fishery system of the OK Tedi River as well as the agricultural plots near the river bank. Heavy rainfalls have caused the toxins to run off into the nearby rainforests and **mangroves**—or trees or shrubs that grow in flooding areas and form

dense and thick roots—leaving behind dead forest and no clean drinking water. The nearby community of the Yonggom people spoke up to the government for help and forced a change. The mine paid for a dredging operation, or the removal of residue and waste from the bottoms of water bodies. The mine also paid for other efforts to revitalize the destroyed areas around the mine.

WRITE Describe how the people of Papua New Guinea responded to the destruction of agricultural land and fisheries due to the Ok Tedi Mine.

....
....
....
....
....

READ

Effects of Agriculture

Clearing land for agriculture is not new, but it always has an impact on the environment. Sometimes, we do not see the cost of change until much later.

In New Zealand, the Māori people reduced New Zealand's forest cover by half using controlled forest fires in order to clear land for agriculture. Additionally, almost 40 species of birds became extinct because of this habitat destruction. One bird species in particular—the moa, which was a giant bird that the Māori would easily catch and feed large villages with—also became extinct.

In Australia, the constant clearing of land has made the soil more vulnerable to **erosion**, or the wearing away of the land, and decreased the agricultural value of the land. In addition, land clearing is the leading cause of **soil salinity**, or the buildup of salt in the soil. The salt greatly reduces the fertility of the land. To add to this, the removal of native plants has also increased the length and severity of droughts that Australia faces.

ONLINE CONNECTION

Use an online search engine to learn more about solar farms in Australia. Australia is currently seeking to build the world's largest solar farm. Research this topic and form an opinion about whether you agree or disagree with the large solar farm. On a separate piece of paper, write a paragraph explaining your opinion with reasons why from your research.

WRITE

The text lists several positive and negative effects of agriculture. Use the information above to complete the chart.

Region	Positive Effects	Negative Effects
New Zealand		
Australia		

READ

Environmental Stresses in Oceania

Over time, people have shaped and responded to change in Oceania. Here are some examples of problems and solutions in Oceania.

Group	Stress	Response to the Change
Polynesia	Overfishing by foreign nations has endangered fish species and the overall availability of fish to eat.	The creation of ocean preserves has supplied protected areas where fish reproduce. Fishing just outside the preserves has improved the quantity of fish caught and reliability of finding fish.
Australia	Australia's population growth requires a lot more power to run modern houses.	Solar farms: People are creating large-scale solar farms in Western Australia, as these have the potential to supply towns and cities with renewable electricity. Solar panels: More than a quarter of all Australian households have rooftop solar units.
New Zealand	New Zealand is also in need of modern electric power.	New Zealand's strong, westerly winds have led people to use windmills to generate electricity for the entire country.

Think about the environment where you live. Identify an environmental stress that is causing problems. What solutions do your climate, weather, and landforms offer? The answers could be very different in different places.

REVIEW

In this lesson, you learned:

- People change the environment and sometimes have to fix problems from those changes.
- People respond to the degradation of the environment.
- Agriculture affects the environment.
- The people of Oceania have found some positive solutions by using available natural resources like sun and wind and by protecting the places where fish reproduce.

Think About It
What other kinds of positive solutions or options are there for improving Oceania's environment? Why should more positive solutions be found and used?

....
....
....
....
....

1. How did agriculture affect the bird species in New Zealand?

   A. It made over 40 different species of birds go extinct.

   B. It increased the number and kinds of birds.

   C. Birds were not affected.

2. What did the Polynesians do in response to overfishing?

   A. They planted mangroves.

   B. They imported fish to eat.

   C. They created ocean preserves to protect fish breeding grounds.

3. In Australia, abundant _____ is being used to power homes and businesses.

4. In New Zealand, abundant _____ is being used to power homes and businesses.

5. According to Heraclitus, the only constant is _____.

6. Explain how mining in the Ok Tedi Mine affected the Yonggom people.

TAKE A CLOSER LOOK

Country Study

Let's continue to learn about the country you selected. For this lesson, complete the following activity about your country:

- Research how the people of your country have changed the land or sea.
  - What changes have people made?
  - How have these changes affected the people and environment?

Physical Processes of Oceania

By the end of this lesson, you will be able to:

- identify the physical processes that contribute to the availability and abundance of a natural resource
- compare and contrast the availability and distribution of natural resources in Oceania across regions

Lesson Review

If you need to review physical geography, please go to the lesson titled "Responding to Change in Oceania."

Academic Vocabulary

Read the following vocabulary words and definitions. Look through the lesson. Can you find each vocabulary word? Underline the vocabulary word in your lesson. Write the page number of where you found each word in the blanks.

- **erosion:** the wearing away of the land by forces such as water, wind, and ice (page _____)

- **natural resources:** any useful substance that can be found in nature (page _____)

- **physical process:** the natural force that changes Earth's physical features (page _____)

- **tectonic activity:** the movement of Earth's crust (page _____)

- **trade winds:** winds blowing almost constantly in one direction (page _____)

Scientists believe the coconut palms spread across the Pacific on ocean currents, the coconut floating from one island to the next. Ocean currents are a natural process.

The coconut itself can be eaten, made into milk or flour, or used as a source of water. The oil can be used for cooking and cleaning. The shells can be carved into bowls or artworks. The fibers from the husks can be used as rope. You can make a roof from the leaves, a broom from the twigs, fire from the wood, and medicine from the flowers.

EXPLORE

Imagine you are a seabird flying high over a beach in California. The wind beneath your wings takes you higher. Suddenly, a strong wind carries you out over the sea. Before you know it, you are miles from home and going farther west than ever before.

After traveling for days, you spot an island where you can land. The island is rocky, boring, and noisy! Other seabirds sit on the rocks, enjoying rest before looking for fresh fish to eat. Those birds left a big mess! As you land, a tiny seed that has been caught in your feathers for the entire trip falls out. Even as you leave, the seed has been covered by the new, rich soil of the volcanic island and is beginning to grow. Life persists.

The short-tailed albatross, the bar-tailed godwit, and the Pacific golden plover all migrate from the South Pacific to North America and back every year. Birds (and fish) are some of the greatest explorers on Earth.

How could migratory birds affect an ecosystem? Why is their influence important or useful for the development of new human civilizations? Discuss your ideas with your instructor or another adult.

Trade Winds

Earth has its own air-conditioning system, both in the sky and in the water. Warm equatorial air and water is pushed north or south toward the poles. The North Pole and South Pole return the warm air after cooling it off. This means sailors can depend on finding winds that cross the ocean at the same latitudes, both north and south. Sailors call these winds trade winds. Migrating birds call them convenient. The official definition of a trade wind is a wind blowing almost constantly in one direction.

Physical Processes

Oceania has many different kinds of **natural resources**, some from the land, some from under the land, and some from the sea. Where agriculture gives bountiful harvest, the land has been enriched by the **physical processes** of weather, erosion, and sometimes volcanic activity. Areas mined for metals, fossil fuels, and gems are much older than the newer volcanic islands.

Tectonic activity, one of the physical processes, pushes metals, minerals, and gems from Earth's lower mantle closer to the surface over time. Australia, New Guinea, and New Zealand, the continental islands, are places where gold, iron, silver, copper, and coal can be found in abundance. There is little mining in the other islands except for New Caledonia, which has 5 percent of the world's nickel.

Erosion is the process of breaking down rock by wind, water, or ice. The tropical weather brings a lot of rain and wind to erode the brittle volcanic rocks of Melanesia, Micronesia, and Polynesia. The frequent wind and rain is due to the **trade winds**. The result is patches of soil fertile enough for the inhabitants of an island to farm. Few of these islands grow enough food to export. The continental islands are another story. With their larger land mass, there are larger farming areas available. These islands are big enough to have rivers that flood and renew the soil from their sources in the mountains. Australia and New Zealand have plains where grain can be grown or cattle and sheep can graze.

Climate

Oceania spans three climate zones: tropical, subtropical, and temperate. The tropical zone has vegetation similar to the Amazon rainforest or the rainforests of Africa. The subtropical zone has deserts, forests, grassy plains, and sunny coasts similar to the southern half of the United States, northern Mexico, or the Mediterranean. Oceania's only temperate zone is found on the South Island of New Zealand where you can find deciduous trees, a warm summer, a mild spring and fall, and a cold winter (but not too cold).

Natural Resources

With 7.8 billion people on Earth, we sometimes think of natural resources as things that end up in a local store. In general, only Oceania's Australasia region has enough in abundance to export all over the world, while the rest of the people of Oceania only have enough land and labor to feed themselves. In the chart below, the three island regions have been grouped together under the name Pacific Islands, and Austalasia has been separated into its three major land masses.

Natural Resource	Region & Availability	Special Note
Forest Products	Australia: abundant (exports) New Zealand: abundant (exports) New Guinea: abundant (exports) Pacific Islands: subsistence	Australia has improved the sustainability of its wood exports by planting tree plantations and preserving natural forests.
Fishing	Australia: abundant (exports) New Zealand: abundant (exports) New Guinea: abundant (exports) Pacific Islands: subsistence	While there are plenty of fish near the Pacific Islands, other nations do most of the fishing. In general, there is not enough labor (people) or capital (money) for the small islands to compete with the big fishing fleets of Asia or the Americas.
Minerals & Metals	Australia: abundant (exports) New Zealand: abundant (exports) New Guinea: abundant (exports) Pacific Islands: subsistence	The world's largest opal was found in Australia. It weighs 7.5 pounds.
Farming & Ranching	Australia: abundant (exports) New Zealand: abundant (exports) New Guinea: abundant (exports) Pacific Islands: subsistence	In New Zealand, the sheep population outnumbers the human population 12 to 1. New Zealand wool is some of the most popular in the world.

PRACTICE

Geographers use maps to illustrate many things. Mark this map with the symbols in the key by following the clues in the following description.

Cattle for meat and dairy thrive on the tropical north coast. Wheat and other grains, seed-oil crops, and vegetables grow well in the Mediterranean climate of the southwest and southeast coast. Surrounding the desert in the middle of Australia, grasslands are great for raising sheep. Tree plantations get enough rain on the east coast.

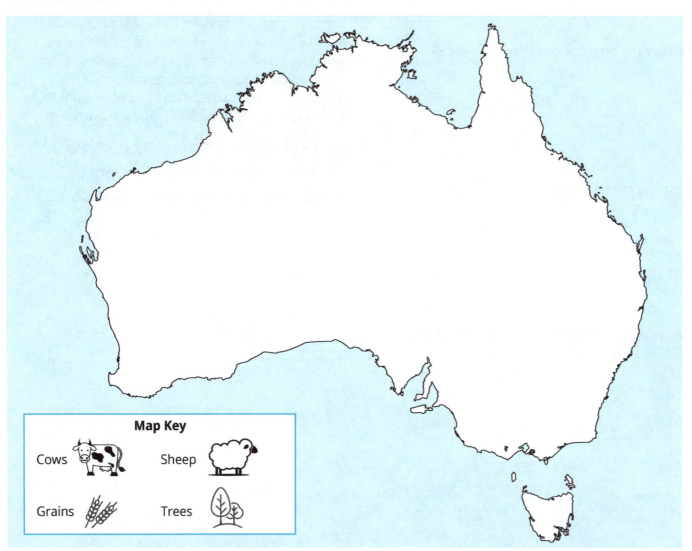

REVIEW

In this lesson, you learned:

- Natural processes such as tectonic activity, weather, and erosion are major contributors to Oceania's abundance.

- Australasia has resources to export, but most of the other islands have enough to thrive on local resources only.

Think About It

Would you like to live on an island that was hard to get to? Would you like to live in a place where you had to fish every day for meat and grow your own food? Would you like to live in a place where you knew everyone?

Circle the correct answer.

1. What physical process pushes metals to the surface of the mantle for mining?

   A. water erosion

   B. tectonic activity

   C. wind erosion

2. What physical process creates fertile soil yearly on a volcanic island? Select all that apply.

   A. water erosion

   B. tectonic activity

   C. wind erosion

3. What physical process or effect helped early sailors move around Oceania?

   A. trade winds

   B. monsoon winds

   C. tectonic activity

   D. erosion

4. Explain how the natural resources of Australasia differ from the resources of the Pacific Islands.

   ....

   ....

   ....

   ....

   ....

   ....

ONLINE CONNECTION

Use the internet to find out more about the weather on a Pacific Island. For example, the island nation of Palau gets an average of 120 to 160 inches of rain a year and has windy conditions from trade winds half the year. That would cause a lot of erosion! You could pick the island you are already researching.

· What island or island nation did you choose?

· How much rain does the island get annually?

· Did you find out anything about how windy it is?

Natural Resources in Oceania

By the end of this lesson, you will be able to:

- identify key natural resources found in Oceania
- describe how the use, distribution, and importance of natural resources can affect different groups
- identify the impact of trade on the availability of natural resources

Lesson Review

If you need to review physical processes, please go to the lesson titled "Physical Processes of Oceania."

Academic Vocabulary

Read the following vocabulary words and definitions. Look through the lesson. Can you find each vocabulary word? Underline the vocabulary word in your lesson. Write the page number of where you found each word in the blanks.

- **infrastructure:** facilities that support modern human life, like water supply, housing, roads, schools, hospitals, bridges, and business and government buildings (page ____)
- **trade:** the action of exchanging something for something else (page ____)

Sugar

Let's learn more about sugar! Search for an online video about how sugarcane is harvested. Make a list of all the things you can think of that contain sugar and how we use them today. Think about how foods, or items with sugar, might have been different in availability in the past compared to present day. Discuss your ideas with your instructor.

When you peer out of your window, what naturally occurring things do you see? Things that are naturally occurring are not made by humans. They may be things like trees, birds, grass, or flowers. Look at the images below, and then write how these items might be useful for your everyday life.

....

....

....

....

TAKE A CLOSER LOOK

Bananas

Trees do more than just provide us with things like paper or wood chips. Have you seen fruit growing on trees, or perhaps a nest that bird families call home? Below is a picture of a banana tree. Bananas, for example, have been an important fruit in the world of the Pacific Islanders since the Indigenous people have inhabited the land. Did you know bananas grow "upside down" from the way we typically see bananas when we buy them?

Key Natural Resources

Nature provides us beauty, food, and even the oxygen we need to breathe. The natural resources in Oceania are bountiful in some regions and can be scarce in others. Review the information below about some of the key natural resources in Oceania.

AUSTRALIA

- wheat, oil, seeds, and legumes
- wool from animals
- paper and wood chips
- commercial fishing (rocks, pearls, and abalone)

PAPUA NEW GUINEA

- sweet potatoes
- sugarcane
- dried coconut
- coffee
- cocoa
- rubber
- eucalyptus
- pine and rosewood
- commercial fishing (prawns, sea cucumber, tuna, and lobster)

NEW ZEALAND

- livestock like beef cattle, dairy cows, and sheep
- crossbred wool, which is a rougher and more textured material than traditional wool
- grapes
- commercial fishing (mussels, rock lobster, squid, and salmon)

PACIFIC ISLANDS

- bananas
- coconut
- kava, a plant whose roots are made into a drink
- sugarcane
- vanilla
- squash
- non-commercial fishing (salmon and tuna)

TAKE A CLOSER LOOK

Eucalyptus

Do you know what eucalyptus smells like? Eucalyptus trees are the most common type of tree in Australia. They cover 77 percent of all of Australia's forests. The majority of these trees are evergreen and retain their leaves all year long. The oil from these trees is often used in products to reduce cold symptoms and in creams for joint pain.

READ

Use and Distribution of Natural Resources

The uses and distribution of the natural resources in Oceania may be similar; however, the impact is different in each country.

NATURAL RESOURCE	USE	DISTRIBUTION
Fish	Fish is a meal source for the local people and for commercial fisheries to export to other countries.	Australia, New Zealand, Papua New Guinea, and the Pacific Islands have abundant fish resources.
Wood	Wood provides hardwood flooring, wood chips, paper, and wood for construction.	17 percent of Australia has forests, while New Zealand has 38 percent and Papua New Guinea has 63 percent. Some of the Pacific Islands contain up to 60 percent of forests.
Sugarcane	Sugarcane is used as a food additive and for making molasses. It is used to make vinegars, cleaning products, medication, and cosmetics.	Sugarcane is found in Papua New Guinea and some of the Pacific Islands.

INFRASTRUCTURES ACROSS OCEANIA

There are many natural resources throughout Oceania. However, the ability to use the resources to support the economy is not equal. Australia and New Zealand have commercial fishing and wood plantations to help their economies. On the other hand, the Pacific Islands do not have these **infrastructures**, or facilities that support modern human life. The Pacific Islands lack water supplies, housing, roads, schools, hospitals, bridges, and business and government buildings in order to build commercial fisheries, wood plantations, or sugar mills.

ONLINE CONNECTION

Rubber trees grow all over the Amazon forest and are found in regions like Papua New Guinea. Use an online search engine to learn more about how rubber is harvested. Create a graphic, such as a timeline or visual organizer, showing the step-by-step process for harvesting these trees from start to finish. Share your graphic with your instructor.

WRITE

What are the key natural resources in the Pacific Islands?

....
....
....
....
....
....
....
....
....
....
....

READ

Trade

Trade is the action of exchanging something for something else. Trade is important because it allows for different products or services to reach various areas, such as other countries outside of the region. Some countries trade more readily and easily with one another. Natural resources such as wood can be in high demand for trade. When wood plantations are created to grow trees, they make more of that natural resource, which can then be traded with other countries. In other countries where plantations have not been built, the natural resources can become depleted quickly, which leaves that resource in low supply. The country then does not have any wood to trade with other countries.

The countries of Oceania trade fish with other countries like China, Japan, and even the United States. Countries want to trade their goods with other countries because it creates jobs and brings money to their country. It also allows the country to purchase goods that are not readily available to them. This is why people create environments for natural resources to expand in their country through wood plantations and commercial fisheries.

PRACTICE

Reflect on two of the natural resources you learned about. Describe the distribution of these resources in Oceania and how trade impacts these natural resources.

Wood: ....
....
....

Fish: ....
....
....

REVIEW

In this lesson, you learned:

- Wood, fish, fruits, and vegetables are key natural resources found in Oceania.

- Wood is used to make paper or building materials, and countries like New Zealand have been able to support wood plantations to create more availability of the natural resource.

- Trade with other countries is a valuable factor for the countries in Oceania.

Think About It
What do you think is one of the most important natural resources of Oceania?

SHOW WHAT YOU KNOW

Choose the correct answer for each question.

1. Which is a natural resource found in Papua New Guinea?

    A. rubber

    B. squid

    C. vanilla

2. How is wood used in Australia?

    A. to make new trees

    B. to make paper

    C. as firewood to keep homes warm

3. Some of the Pacific Islands do not have access to _____ to build commercial fisheries.

Answer the following questions in complete sentences.

4. How might trade impact the availability of natural resources in Oceania?

    ....

    ....

    ....

    ....

5. What may be the impact of over-producing food products or wood logs in New Zealand?

    ....

    ....

    ....

    ....

In Your Country

You have learned about some of the natural resources in Oceania. See if you can discover what natural resources exist in your country and how they are used.

1. What natural resources can be found in your country?

2. How does your country use and trade these natural resources?

Discuss your answers with your instructor.

Lesson 72

Human Migration in Oceania

By the end of this lesson, you will be able to:

- extend understanding that human migration is influenced by both known and unknown factors
- identify the factors that led to the immigration of people from one region in Oceania
- examine the factors that contributed to the Polynesian Migrations and analyze the evidence supporting each factor
- examine the contributions of migrants from one region in Oceania to another

Academic Vocabulary

Read the following vocabulary words and definitions. Look through the lesson. Can you find each vocabulary word? Underline the vocabulary word in your lesson. Write the page number of where you found each word in the blanks.

- **human migration:** the movement of a population of people from one location to another (page _____)
- **pull factors:** factors that attract people to a new place (page _____)
- **push factors:** factors that force people to leave their place of origin (page _____)

Convicts as Ancestors

From 1788 to 1868, prisoners were transported from Great Britain to Australia as punishment for their crimes. For them, life was difficult because they were forced to help build the colonies. When they weren't working, many were chained with shackles. Once they had completed their sentence, many of the prisoners settled in Australia.

Have you ever wondered how people first moved from place to place? Especially to remote islands? Imagine you are the first person to find a remote island. Do you think it would be scary or fun? How might you build a house? What would you sleep on? In the first column, make a list of tasks you think you would need to do once you arrive on the remote island. In the second column, make a list of natural resources that you would look for as food, building materials, and more.

Factors of Migration

Human migration is the movement of a population of people from one location to another. Some factors influence people's movement to certain areas while other factors drive people to leave their place of origin.

Pull factors are factors that attract people to a new place. Factors that could be classified as pull factors include better climate, better political stability, better social environment, better economic conditions and possibilities, and better healthcare and education systems.

However, **push factors** are factors that force people to leave their place of origin. Factors that could be classified as push factors include lack of employment, poverty, discrimination, lack of good healthcare and education systems, natural disasters, and political unrest (such as violence and wars).

MOVING WITHIN OCEANIA

People move to specific places and locations within Oceania because each place has something special to offer. Many people who move to New Zealand are in search of seasonal job opportunities, relief from population pressure, and political stability. Many people who move to Australia are in search of seasonal job opportunities, beautiful scenery, and a high quality of life. However, most people who move to these places move away from the Pacific Islands for a variety of reasons. Some reasons include rising sea levels, a decrease in habitable coastal areas, saltwater contamination of freshwater resources, an increase in ocean temperatures that affect their fishing industries, and a higher probability of natural disasters.

Reread the text above and underline keywords, like *jobs* and *population*. Choose three keywords and write a sentence about the factors that influence moving in Oceania.

Keyword - ....

....

Keyword - ....

....

Keyword - ....

....

READ

Polynesian Migration

One of the most mysterious immigrations for researchers has been the Polynesian Migrations. Researchers have often wondered how Polynesians migrated from their isolated islands to other locations in Oceania. After extensive research, they think they may have discovered it!

A team at Macquarie University in Sydney, Australia found there were several periods of time when the winds shifted and allowed for easier access to sailing from the central Pacific to New Zealand and Easter Island. They made this discovery by recreating wind patterns and sea level pressure conditions over time.

Additionally, researchers found wood fragments from a canoe on the New Zealand shoreline. There was a sea turtle etched into the wood on the canoe itself, an image not normally found in New Zealand art. Sea turtles are predominantly featured in Polynesian art. Another boat with similar features was found on the Society Islands.

As a result of these factors and historical evidence, researchers believe that early Polynesians built canoes to sail to new places when the winds changed to make sea travel possible.

Circle the location of Polynesia on this map.

Petroglyphs

Petroglyphs can provide clues about how people lived when they were carved. The symbols etched into the stone can be analyzed for their meaning. They can show us what the people of the time valued, what they may have eaten, or how they interacted with the world around them. What do you see in this Petroglyph picture?

WRITE

How were the Polynesians able to sail to islands far away?

READ

Migrant Contributions

New Zealand's indigenous people are known as the Maori. They arrived from the Polynesian islands and settled in New Zealand. They created their own tribes and developed order in their society. They are well known for their intricate wood-carved sculptures and woven baskets. They introduced vegetables from the Polynesian Islands, including the sweet potato. In addition, Maori prepared defense weapons to protect their people. These weapons were made from carved wood. Later, Maori had peaceful interactions with Europeans. The Maori and the Europeans traded extensively with each other, and some lived within each other's tribes.

Once the Pacific Islands were settled, Polynesians continued to move from island to island. On each island, people had to learn how to support themselves through fishing and farming. Many of the islands developed their own version or dialect of their original language. They were the first people group to use astronomy to navigate the ocean. The Pacific Islanders had a strong oral history through which the day-to-day ways of living were passed down and taught to the next generation. Each island and people group had an organizational structure to their group usually governed by chiefs.

A Maori Wood-Carved Statue

Polynesian Island Dancers

Make a list of three ways migrants in Oceania contributed to society.

1. ....
2. ....
3. ....

In this lesson, you learned:

- Human migration is influenced by both push and pull factors.

- Several factors, such as seasonal jobs or changes in the environment, led to the migration of people from one region to another in Oceania.

- The factors that contributed to the first Polynesian Migrations are unclear, but most likely wind factors and voyaging canoes played a role.

- Migrants made contributions by building colonies.

Think About It

Do you know if the ancestors in your family migrated from a different region? If they did, what contributions did they bring with them? If not, think about what kind of contribution you could make to a different cultural group or society.

SHOW WHAT YOU KNOW

Choose the correct answer for each question.

1. Which of the following is a push factor for human migration?

   A. A person is happy with their occupation.

   B. A person is dissatisfied with the education system.

   C. A person is satisfied with their local government.

2. Which of the following is a pull factor for human migration?

   A. A person wants to receive better healthcare.

   B. A person has a good job where they are currently living.

   C. A person likes their current social environment.

3. The movement of people from one location to another is
   called _____.

4. What two factors are thought to have contributed to Polynesian Migration?

   A. _____

   B. _____

Answer the following question in complete sentences.

5. What may motivate someone to move to Australia?

   ....

   ....

   ....

   ....

ONLINE CONNECTION

Long before the invention of GPS, clocks, instrumental panels, and compasses, the Pacific Islanders who sailed to discover the islands had different tools. They used the sun, stars, clues about how the waves formed, and other signs from animals in nature to decide how to navigate the ocean. Research online to find out how to navigate using the stars. Search with the key question, "How do I navigate using the stars?"

Cultural Features of Oceania

By the end of this lesson, you will be able to:

- identify cultural features found in Oceania
- describe how cultural features in a region of Oceania influence factors of daily life such as economy, government, or transportation

Academic Vocabulary

Read the following vocabulary words and definitions. Look through the lesson. Can you find each vocabulary word? Underline the vocabulary word in your lesson. Write the page number of where you found each word in the blanks.

- **architecture:** the artistic or scientific way of building (page _____)
- **artifacts:** objects of value made by humans, usually of cultural or historical interest (page _____)
- **cultural features:** unique traditions or aspects of a culture, such as language, religion, and dress (page _____)

IN THE REAL WORLD

Think of the ceremonies or holidays you and your family celebrate. Imagine the foods you eat, the clothes you wear, the people who attend, and the activities you do to celebrate. On a separate piece of paper, draw your favorite celebration or holiday, including the food, clothing, people, and activities.

EXPLORE

Imagine that you are being introduced to a new group of people. You have some knowledge of the group:

- They like to eat meat and fish.
- They like to dance using large movements.
- The hibiscus flower is the symbol of the group.
- They enjoy vibrant colors like lime green, fuchsia, and purple.

They have commissioned you to sew an outfit for them. Use the space below to draw the outfit you would make.

Traditional Dress in Fiji

Clothing in Fiji includes the national dress called the sulu. It is worn by both men and women. They can be elaborately decorated or plain. Sulus for men are often fitted as part of their suit for work or church, while sulus for women are often long, floral dresses.

Cultural Features

Cultural features include unique traditions or aspects of a culture, such as language, religion, and dress.

One type of cultural feature is **artifacts**, or objects of value made by humans, usually of cultural or historical interest. An example of artifacts is the moai statues in Polynesia. The moai statues are carved from volcanic ash and are believed to represent ancient Polynesian ancestors. The statues face away from the ocean and toward the villages as if to watch over the people.

Cultural features also include **architecture**, or the designing of a building using art and technique. One example of architecture is the Beehive in Wellington, New Zealand. Built in 1979, the Beehive building is closely linked with the New Zealand government. It contains offices of the prime minister and other ministers in New Zealand. It is the official meeting location for cabinet members of the government.

Art is a very popular and common type of cultural feature, as it tells the story or feelings of a culture. Aboriginal rock art in a gorge in Queensland, Australia, is a great example of art. Aboriginal people created many different forms of rock art. Some sites are where spiritual rituals were performed and are very important to them. During these rituals, the Aboriginal people created paintings and rock engravings. They also painted on the bark of eucalyptus trees. These left permanent features for generations to view.

The Moai statues

The Beehive

Aboriginal rock art

Choose one of the cultural features above and describe its significance.

....

....

....

....

READ

Influences of Cultural Features

Cultural features can influence the people of an area by affecting what people do or what happens in a place. They can give people reasons to visit new places. People might flock to Australia to see Aboriginal rock art or wood carvings or to purchase a *pareo*, a traditional garment. Let's see how cultural features can influence the population, economy, government, and transportation.

POPULATION

Cultural traditions impact the population of many Polynesian countries. In Fiji, life is traditionally shared between family members, and the interest of the family is more important than that of individuals. The households are multigenerational, meaning you will often find elders, parents, and grandchildren living under the same roof. Ultimately, people do not often move to other regions because they stay with their families in one location. This keeps the population stable in most of the smaller island countries.

ECONOMY

In Papua New Guinea, the arts offer people the potential to connect and inspire a new interest in their traditions. Since the arts often receive limited financial support from the national government, artists sell their work in tourist areas and festivals. This also allows them to connect with other community-based artists. The artists can work together to increase economic opportunities by doing things like creating art centers. Art centers provide support for materials and workshops, administrative support, and exhibitions.

WRITE

How do the arts influence the economy in Papua New Guinea?

....

....

....

....

....

....

....

READ

GOVERNMENT

The Parliament House is an architectural feature located in Australia's capital city, Canberra. It is the central hub for government in Canberra and hosts many of its largest and most important events. When it was designed in 1978, many people had opinions about the building. They wanted the building to give Australia an outward sign of national identity and prestige. This building became known as a sign of political maturity and unification within Australia.

TRANSPORTATION

Public transportation exists in New Zealand. It is common practice for New Zealanders to use the bus system. Most major cities like Christchurch, Auckland, and Wellington have public transportation systems based on buses. The bus system allows people to reach both the North and South Islands easily for work or pleasure.

The Parliament House in Canberra

Buses are a common source of transportation.

REVIEW

In this lesson, you learned:

- Some of the cultural features of Oceania include art, artifacts, and architecture.

- A few examples of cultural features of Oceania include; the Beehive in New Zealand, Aboriginal rock art in Queensland, Australia, and the moai statues on Easter Island.

- Cultural features can influence transportation by increasing travel, the government by representing the people's opinions, the economy by producing artwork, and the population by the traditional family structure.

Think About It
Does your country have any cultural features?

WRITE

Choose either *transportation* or *government* and describe how it has influenced the people of Australia and New Zealand.

....

....

....

Choose the correct answer for each question.

1. What is a key cultural feature located on Easter Island in the Polynesia region?

   A. aboriginal rock art   C. Beehive

   B. moai statues

2. How does the Parliament House in Australia show how architecture can influence the government and people?

   A. by demonstrating unification and political power

   B. by demonstrating that a large building is powerful

   C. by demonstrating that uniquely designed buildings are intriguing

Use the words from the Word Blank to complete the sentences.

Word Bank: festivals buses tradition rocks tourist areas
                eucalyptus tree bark

3. Aboriginal people created art on _____
   and _____.

4. The _____ of families living in multigenerational households influences the population of Fiji because families do not move away from each other.

5. A popular transportation mode in New Zealand are _____, which allow people to work and travel between the North and South Island.

6. Artists in Papua New Guinea use _____ and _____ to sell their works, which, in turn, supports the local economy.

Country Study
Let's continue to learn about the country you selected. For this lesson, look into the cultural features of your country and answer the following questions:

1. What cultural features exist in your country? Where are they located? Why are they important?

2. Select two cultural features and identify how they help the population, economy, or government.

Answer the following question in complete sentences.

7. Explain why Australian Aboriginal rock art is a significant cultural feature.

....

....

....

....

....

....

....

Cultural Geography of Oceania

By the end of this lesson, you will be able to:

- investigate the cultural geography of Oceania
- explore broader influences of Oceanian culture on individuals and civilizations around the world
- discover the lasting impact of Oceanian culture on everyday aspects of life

Lesson Review

If you need to review cultural features, please go to the lesson titled "Cultural Features in Oceania."

Academic Vocabulary

Read the following vocabulary words and definitions. Look through the lesson. Can you find each vocabulary word? Underline the vocabulary word in your lesson. Write the page number of where you found each word in the blanks.

- **cultural geography:** the study of human connection to natural resources, the economy, religion, government, and many other ways that humans interact with their world (page _____)
- **meringue:** a dessert made of egg whites and sugar (page _____)

Leis were originally worn by ancient Polynesians. Many people think of leis in connection with the state of Hawaii. This is because people native to Hawaii are of Polynesian descent and brought the tradition with them from the Pacific Islands to Hawaii. The lei is traditionally used to signify a greeting or to show a rank or royalty. Create an ancient lei using materials you already have or can easily find. Ancient leis were not just made of flowers but included items such as leaves, shells, seeds, nuts, feathers, and even bones and teeth of various animals.

EXPLORE

Think about what impact you have on people around you. Do you care for others in your family? Do you help your friends? Have you picked up trash so the world would be cleaner? These are all examples of how we impact the world around us. Our actions each day affect other people and can change the world we live in. Think of a time you did something to help someone else or a time you helped make something better. Draw a picture or write a few sentences about that time in the box below.

Electric Drills

You may have seen a family member or friend using an electric drill before. Electric drills are often used so that screws can be driven into a surface more quickly and easily. Electric drills were first introduced in Australia. At that time, they were large and used mainly for coal mining.

The people who live in Oceania have affected the world as well. Based on what you already know about Oceania, how do you think they have made an impact on others? Share your thoughts with your instructor.

Cultural Geography of Oceania

Cultural geography is the study of human connection to natural resources, the economy, religion, government, and many other ways that humans interact with their world. People shape their world by creating things like language, entertainment, art, and architecture.

RELIGION

The religious traditions of Oceania's Indigenous people primarily focused on the relationship of humans to nature. The Aboriginals believed in Dreamtime, a time they claim wandering spirits created the features of the land, plants, animals, and humans. They believed that all natural things have a spirit and are related.

ARTS

The Indigenous people of the South Pacific often used art, music, dance, and storytelling to distribute knowledge from one generation to another. The Māori in New Zealand developed skills in canoe making, basket making, tattooing, and wood carving. Today, the Māori meeting houses are still decorated with beautiful wood carvings.

ARCHITECTURE

The Sydney Opera House is an iconic building in Sydney, Australia. It is shaped like the sails of a boat. Millions of people visit the opera house each year. It has been made a World Heritage site, a special place that is to be protected for future enjoyment.

ENTERTAINMENT

Australia and New Zealand have recently produced many famous musicians, writers, and artists. This includes movie stars like Mel Gibson, Nicole Kidman, and Russell Crowe.

The Didgeridoo

The didgeridoo is a famous wind instrument that originated from the Aboriginal people of northern Australia. It was played in ceremonial celebrations. It is hand-carved from wood. Its popularity has grown and spread all over the world. It is now included in entertainment in other countries and different genres of music.

Influences Around the World

Oceania is a vast region made up of many cultures. These cultures have influenced populations worldwide.

WOOL

New Zealand wool is the cleanest and whitest wool produced in the world. It is highly sought after because New Zealand does not use harsh chemicals to treat its wool. The wool is used for carpeting, bedding, upholstery, yarn, and apparel. The fibers are some of the most durable in the world. New Zealand exports wool to over 50 different countries, including China, the United Kingdom, India, and Italy.

LORD OF THE RINGS

The beautiful scenery of the country of New Zealand has created the pristine backdrop for the famous *Lord of the Rings* and *Hobbit* movies. One of the most popular locations is Matamata, which was rebuilt and made into a permanent attraction for visitors. The movies are credited with increasing tourism numbers to the country.

PAVLOVA

Pavlova is a **meringue**, or a dessert made of egg whites and sugar. The dessert is named after a ballet dancer traveling between Australia and New Zealand. This dessert is very popular in both countries and across the world. It is often eaten on special occasions and served with cream and fruit.

Matamata

Pavlova

How have people through generations shaped the arts, food, or tourism in Oceania?

....
....
....
....
....

READ

Impacting Everyday Life

Oceania has also left a lasting impact on people's lives. Many important inventions were created in Oceania. Read about some of these inventions below.

BLACK BOX

The black box flight recorder was invented by an Australian scientist, Dr. David Warren. This device is indestructible and records the final moments of a crashed plane's last flight. This information may help prevent future airplane crashes. Although it is called the black box, it is bright orange so that it may be more easily spotted among the airplane's debris. Today all large US planes contain black boxes.

COCHLEAR IMPLANTS

A professor at Melbourne University in Australia was the first to invent the bionic ear. Bionic ears, also called cochlear implants, are inserted into the head of deaf or partially deaf people. The implant electronically stimulates the auditory nerve, giving people the ability to hear.

ULTRASOUND SCANNER

A group of Australian scientists discovered a way to differentiate ultrasound echoes bouncing off of soft tissue in the body and convert them into TV images. This discovery changed prenatal care by offering images of the unborn baby without the use of X-ray machines. Today ultrasounds are used to examine other organs in the body as well.

Black box

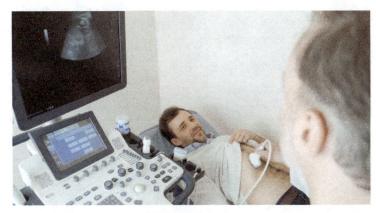

Ultrasound

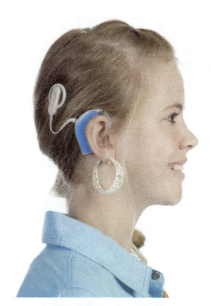

Cochlear implant

PRACTICE

Now that you have learned about many of Oceania's influences and inventions, explain how the following have made a lasting impact on the world.

1. wool

....

....

....

....

2. black box recorder

....

....

....

....

3. Sydney Opera House

....

....

....

....

REVIEW

In this lesson, you learned:

· People shape their world through art, architecture, religion, and entertainment.

· The use of wool, the pavlova dessert, and the *Lord of the Rings* movies have influenced people around the world.

· The black box, ultrasound scanner, and cochlear implants have had lasting impacts on the world.

Think About It
What do you think has been one of Oceania's greatest influences or inventions?

SHOW WHAT YOU KNOW

Choose the correct answer.

1. How did the filming of the *Lord of the Rings* movies influence other groups of people?

    A. It made them want to film their own movies.

    B. It made them want to visit the filming locations in New Zealand.

    C. It made them want to travel to Australia.

2. The _____ implants have made a lasting impact on the world by giving hearing to over 180,000 deaf or partially deaf people.

Answer the following questions.

3. Make a list of items derived from Oceania that have made a lasting impact on people in Oceania and other countries.

    ....

    ....

    ....

4. Look at the picture of the Sydney Opera House. Describe how the opera house has shaped the cultural geography of Australia.

    ....

    ....

    ....

ONLINE CONNECTION

Look into your country one more time. As you explore, look for the cultural geography within your country. Use the internet to search for cultural geography keywords and your country's name.

1. What influence does your country have worldwide?

2. What lasting impacts has your country made on everyday life?

Chapter 7 Review

By the end of this lesson, you will:

- review the information from the lessons in Chapter 7, "Oceania"

Lesson Review

Throughout the chapter, we have learned the following big ideas:

- Maps can tell many different stories. (Lesson 66)
- Geographic features influence where people live. (Lesson 67)
- Physical geography influences people's relationships with natural resources. (Lesson 68)
- People make changes to their environment. (Lesson 69)
- Physical processes can lead to the availability of resources. (Lesson 70)
- There are major natural resources in Oceania. (Lesson 71)
- The people of Oceania migrated from one area to another. (Lesson 72)
- Cultural features influence populations. (Lesson 73)
- Cultural geography exists in Oceania and makes a lasting impact worldwide. (Lesson 74)

Go back and review the lessons as needed while you complete the activities.

CREATE

Imagine you are living in one of the regions in Oceania. Create a diary entry and write about how you or your ancestors have come to the region you live in, what you eat, and what you may do for fun. Include details about how you may feel about living in the Oceania region.

REVIEW

Maps and Geography of Oceania

You learned that topographic maps and political maps can tell stories about Oceania. Remember that a political map shows borders for countries, states, and counties, as well as locations of cities and capitals. A topographic map shows the elevations and shape of Earth's surface.

Oceania has a variety of different geographic features. The many islands provide coastal regions for people to enjoy. Australia has a dry, arid desert in the middle of the country, and the Great Barrier Reef is an amazing feature in the ocean. People settled in different regions to gain access to farming, a mild climate, fertile soil, and water.

Oceania is mostly composed of four types of islands: continental, volcanic, limestone, and coral. Each type was formed due to different landforms above and below the ocean. Continental islands are landmasses surrounded by water rising above a continental shelf. Volcanic islands are created when magma from deep in Earth escapes through holes in the Earth's crust. This magma turns to lava and cools, creating new rock.

Oceania or Australia?

Many people refer to the Oceania Continent as Australia. However, the continent of Oceania has so much more than just Australia. The region's defining feature is the Pacific Ocean, which holds or connects the region together. Australia is the largest landmass in the continent and the largest country. As you have learned, Oceania is much more than Australia! It includes all of the other regions, cultures, and histories of those places.

WRITE — Look at these maps of Australia. Write whether each map is a topographic map or a geopolitical map. Then write two to three sentences about what stories these maps tell.

REVIEW

Natural Resources in Oceania

Oceania has many types of natural resources, but they are not divided evenly throughout the region. Fish and trees are the most widespread resources, but some areas have developed ways to trade their goods to other countries outside Oceania, and others have not. Bananas, sugar, coconut, vanilla, wool, wheat, and cocoa are other natural resources from the region.

HUMAN MIGRATION

Polynesians first migrated to the Pacific Islands using voyaging canoes and their knowledge of the tides, stars, ocean currents, and nature. The chart shows the push and pull factors of migration.

PUSH FACTORS	PULL FACTORS
Lack of employment	Better climate
Lack of good schools, healthcare, or entertainment	Better economic conditions and political stability
Poverty: low standard of living	Better social environment
Discrimination	Better economic conditions
Violence, wars, or natural disasters	Better healthcare, education systems, and entertainment

TAKE A CLOSER LOOK

New Guinea

New Guinea is an island on two continents—Asia and Oceania. The west side is part of Asia, and the east side, Papua New Guinea, is part of Oceania.

PRACTICE

Three's a Crowd

Select which word out of each group that doesn't belong. In the space below each group, indicate why it doesn't belong.

1. erosion   solar farms   land clearing

   This word doesn't belong because _____.

2. Auckland   Melbourne   Sydney

   This word doesn't belong because _____.

3. volcanoes   limestone   desert

   This word doesn't belong because _____.

4. Melanesia   Micronesia   New Zealand

   This word doesn't belong because _____.

5. birds   forest products   fishing

   This word doesn't belong because _____.

6. bananas   eucalyptus   oranges

   This word doesn't belong because _____.

7. voyaging canoes   high winds   deserts

   This word doesn't belong because _____.

8. black box   cochlear implant   computer

   This word doesn't belong because _____.

9. volcanic   coral   desert

   This word doesn't belong because _____.

REVIEW

The continent of Oceania is divided into four regions; Micronesia, Melanesia, Polynesia, and Australia. The prefix micro means "small." This prefix can help you remember that Micronesia is the smallest of the four regions. What other words do you know that start with the prefix "micro?" Microwave, microorganism, and microscopic are some examples. How does the meaning of the prefix apply to these words?

The prefix poly means "many". The polynesia region has many, many, many islands. The prefix poly will help you remember this about that region. What other words start with "poly?" Polygon, polymer, and polygraph are some examples.

PRACTICE

Change in Oceania

In New Zealand, the Māori people reduced New Zealand's forest cover. Fill in the chart below by listing the positive and negative effects of the change made by the Māori people.

POSITIVE EFFECTS	NEGATIVE EFFECTS

REVIEW

Oceania's biggest and most populous city is Sydney. More than five million people live in the city. Sydney has the most diverse and multicultural population in Oceania. Over 250 languages are spoken there. However, it is not the capital. Many people assume that it is or mistake it for the capital city. The capital of Australia is Canberra. Canberra is located about halfway between Sydney and Melbourne.

PRACTICE

Oceania Board Game

Create a board game to practice what you learned about Oceania. Follow these steps:

1. Use a large piece of paper or poster board and divide the number of spaces into thirds.

2. Design around the spaces with features of Oceania, such as water, or the ring of fire.

3. Create your board game questions. Include the following chapter titles and information:

    A. The Stories in Maps

        i. the stories that different maps of Oceania can tell you

    B. Environment and Patterns of Human Settlements

        i. the geographic features and where people live

        ii. the physical geography of Oceania

        iii. responding to change in Oceania

        iv. the physical processes that created natural resources in Oceania

    C. Cultural Geography.

        i. the natural resources found in Oceania

        ii. the influence of cultural features in Oceania

        iii. the influence and lasting impact of cultural geography in Oceania

4. Play your game with your instructor or family and friends.

SHOW WHAT YOU KNOW

Think about what you've learned about in this chapter. Circle how you feel:

4 – I know this chapter really well. I could teach it to someone.

3 – I know this chapter pretty well.

2 – I am still learning this chapter. I am not sure about some things.

1 – I am confused. I have a lot of questions about what I've learned.

Talk to your instructor about your answers. When you're ready, ask your instructor for the Show What You Know activity for the chapter.